WHERE I FOUND CHRIST

Books by John A. O Brien

WHERE I FOUND CHRIST

THE ROAD TO DAMASCUS

TRUTHS MEN LIVE BY

THE FAITH OF MILLIONS

EVOLUTION AND RELIGION

THE PRIESTHOOD IN A CHANGING WORLD

PATHWAYS TO HAPPINESS

COURTSHIP AND MARRIAGE

WHAT'S THE TRUTH ABOUT CATHOLICS?

THUNDER FROM THE LEFT

DISCOVERING MEXICO

Where I Found Christ

The Intimate Personal Stories
of Fourteen Converts
to the
Catholic Faith

Edited by

JOHN A. O'BRIEN

✝

Doubleday & Company, Inc.

GARDEN CITY, N.Y.

1951

Nihil Obstat:
>> Rev. T. E. Dillon,
>>> Censor Librorum

Imprimatur:
>> ✠ John F. Noll, D.D.
>>> Bishop of Fort Wayne
> May 26, 1950

I am the light of the world: he that followeth me, walketh not in darkness, but shall have the light of life.   JOHN 8:12

Wir wandern von der Heimat weit hinaus;
Finden doch in der Fern' das Elternhaus.
                                   ANON.

CONTENTS

		PAGE
THE QUEST FOR GOD	John A. O'Brien	1
THE OUTSTRETCHED ARMS	Katherine Burton	10
THROUGH THE CHURCH TO GOD	Duane G. Hunt	28
HOUSE OF LIGHT	Lucile Hasley	47
COMING HOME	Avery Robert Dulles	63
FINDING CHRIST	Elizabeth Laura Adams	82
THE END OF A PILGRIMAGE	Edward O. Dodson	92
FROM COMMUNISM TO CHRIST	Dorothy Day	113
THE FLOWERING OF JUDAISM	David Goldstein	135
ON A FIRM FOUNDATION	Jocelyn M. C. Toynbee	152
THE PEARL OF GREAT PRICE	Daniel Sargent	158
INTO THE LIGHT	Dale Francis	174
THE MARITAINS FIND GOD	Raïssa Maritain	186
FINDING CHRIST'S CHURCH	Christopher Hollis	220
THE WHITE PEBBLE	Thomas Merton	233
THE OPEN DOOR	John A. O'Brien	251

WHERE I FOUND CHRIST

THE QUEST FOR GOD

John A. O'Brien

THE QUEST for the meaning of life and the destiny of the human soul is essentially a search for God. Without Him, life is a vast void, "full of sound and fury, signifying nothing." With Him, every moment of life is shot through with meaning and man's destiny is seen to be in union with God in perfect love.

God is the Alpha and the Omega, the beginning and the end of all things, particularly of the human soul, which stands as the climax of all the works of His hands. What the North Star is to the mariner tossed about on the tempestuous bosom of the mighty deep, God is to the earthly pilgrim peering through the mists of time for the harbor of eternity. God is the answer to man's groping cry for life, light, and love.

The search for the meaning of life, and consequently for God, is the most imperative, persistent, and universal of all the enterprises which press upon the conscience and the mind of man. He is driven by all the exigencies of his nature to find the Being who alone can appease the craving of the mind for truth, the hunger of the heart for love, and the thirsting of the soul for the spiritual and eternal realities hidden behind the façade of the material and the temporal.

As the branches of a tree, engulfed in a dense forest, reach up hungrily for the kiss of the life-giving sun, so man's arms stretch upward beyond the earthly horizon to clasp the hand of his Maker and his God. "Our hearts have been made for thee, O God," cried St. Augustine centuries ago, "and they shall never rest until they rest in thee." Such was substan-

[1]

tially the cry of the first-born out of the womb of time; such, too, will be the cry of the last of our progeny as our little planet passes off into the Stygian darkness of unending night.

Only when man is anesthetized by passion or blinded by intellectual pride is that feverish quest for God momentarily stilled. When the passions subside and pride slackens, the search continues with renewed vigor, heightened by a realization of the thoroughly unsatisfactory nature of the palliatives used to halt the soul's upward thrust.

Finding God and the deposit of divinely revealed truth in the institution established by Christ, the Son of God, to transmit those life-giving truths in their entirety to every generation is man's first duty and supreme responsibility. Volumes of philosophy and theology have been written to assist him in the fulfillment of that obligation. With no disparagement to the value of these two important branches of learning in aiding man in this matter, it can nevertheless be affirmed that the actual experiences of men and women in achieving these ends frequently afford a guidance and a practical help to the goal, which the busy man and woman of today often fail to find in abstract principles and theory.

"The way is long by precept," runs an old Latin proverb, "but short by example." Hence the great practical value of the stories of the men and women who tell in this book how they found God, Jesus Christ, and His Church, and thus answered the deepest questionings of their minds and hearts.

The stories of their spiritual quest are told with reverence, humility, and a sincere desire to be helpful to others. They are neither propaganda nor chapters of a sales talk. The writers have no axes to grind, no bread to butter, no premium to collect. They narrate their stories of a spiritual Odyssey with the sole thought that their disclosures may point out to other groping souls the paths that lead to Christ and His Church. If the pilgrims consulted merely their own feelings, they would have remained silent about their spiritual Aeneid; but they graciously yielded to the editor's suggestion that the disclosure of their experiences might serve as a torch to other groping feet and a channel of divine grace to souls grown weary searching for the truth. "It is good to hide the secret of a king," says Holy Writ, "but honorable to reveal and confess the works of God."[1]

For all the contributors, as well as for the editor, this is a labor of love with no compensation other than the joy which comes from lending a hand to others in the supremely important task of finding the truth. "You shall know the truth," said Christ, "and the truth shall make you free."

To secure the maximum help from this book in the quest for God and His truth, it is necessary to bring to its reading a spirit of humility, prayer, and moral sensitivity, plus a willingness to look with an open mind upon new facts and a readiness to follow the truth wherever it may lead you. The person who searches for God in a spirit of pride and hauteur is foredoomed to failure. Faith is a gift of God and is given only to the humble. "God resists the proud," warns the Apostle Peter, "but gives grace to the humble."[2]

Before the time of Christ, this truth was sounded by the author of the Book of Proverbs: "He shall scorn the scorners, and to the meek he will give grace."[3] Our Lord Himself stressed the necessity of childlike humility in coming to God, saying: "Amen I say to you, whosoever shall not receive the kingdom of God as a little child, shall not enter into it."[4]

No less essential than humility is the spirit of prayer. Christ teaches us to bring our petitions to our heavenly Father with trust and confidence. "Ask," He says, "and it shall be given you: seek, and you shall find: knock, and it shall be opened to you." The Divine Master taught us not merely by precept, but also by example. What reader of the Scriptures can forget that long period of prayer in Gethsemane, with which He prepared for the ordeal of the Cross? "All things whatsoever you shall ask in prayer, believing," He told His disciples, "you shall receive."[5]

[1]Tobias 12:7.   [2]Peter 5:5.   [3]Proverbs 3:34.
[4]Mark 10:15.   [5]Matthew 21:22.

[3]

When the father of the boy afflicted with an evil spirit besought Christ to cast out the devil, Jesus instructed him concerning the need for faith, for which prayer is the living expression. "And immediately the father of the boy crying out, with tears said: I do believe, Lord: help my unbelief." Such is the prayer which every seeker for Christ may well utter. No less generous will Christ be in granting such a request than He was in healing the afflicted son.

When Christ drew nigh to Jericho, a blind man called out: "Jesus, son of David, have mercy on me."

"What wilt thou," asked Jesus, "that I do to thee?"

"Lord," he replied, "that I may see."

"Receive thy sight," said Jesus, "thy faith hath made thee whole."[6]

There is the role which the seeker for the light of truth must play—a suppliant on his knees uttering with faith and confidence the humble prayer, "Lord, that I may see." Never does God fail to remove the scales from the eyes of such a supplicant and give him a vision of the truth.

The searcher for God must bring to his quest a clean mind and a pure heart. Vice dulls the sensitivity of moral nature, blinds the eyes of conscience, and deafens the inner ear to the delicate whisperings of divine grace.

When Ignatius, Bishop of Antioch, was being led to martyrdom, he was accosted by a Roman soldier:

"Tell us about this Christ of yours," he said leeringly.

Looking into his sensual countenance, the venerable bishop replied: "You will know Him when you are *worthy* of Him."

In that response there is emphasized that ethical sensitivity which must accompany the soul's search for God. The psychologist calls it "appropriate apperception mass" or "congruous linkage"; Newman calls it *pia credulitas,* a pious disposition which prepares the mind for the acceptance of spiritual truth. Suffice it to say here simply that a pure heart and a clean conscience are more essential in seeing God than a subtle intellect. Christ never maintained that those

[6]Luke 18:42.

[4]

of brilliant minds and of great learning would find God, but He did say that "the clean of heart" would see God.

This is the truth which two great prophets thundered repeatedly into the ears of the people of ancient Israel: the paths which lead to God are those of goodness and holiness. Speaking in the name of the Almighty, Jeremiah declared: "Thus saith the Lord: Stand ye on the ways, and see, and ask for the old paths, which is the good way, and walk ye in it: and you shall find refreshment for your souls."[7]

Pointing to the highway of holiness as the one that leads the wayfarer to God, Isaiah proclaimed: "An highway shall be there . . . and it shall be called The way of holiness . . . the wayfaring men, though fools, shall not err therein . . . the redeemed shall walk there: And the ransomed of the Lord shall return . . . they shall obtain joy and gladness, and sorrow and sighing shall flee away."[8]

The simple fact is that one can best find God when his heart is hungry for love, when his mind is thirsting for truth, and when his soul is hungering for holiness; for God is love, truth, and holiness. Only the ear that is attuned to the language of moral perfection can hearken to the gentle whisperings of divine guidance; for holiness is God's vernacular and it must be practiced to be understood. To the soul whose conscience is calloused and blunted with sin, whose inner ear has grown insensitive to the stirrings of divine grace, sanctity is an alien tongue.

The seeker for divine truth must bring to this volume an open mind and a willingness to look new facts in the face without blinking. Prejudice closes the doors of the mind to the entrance of truth; for, as its etymology indicates, it involves a prejudging of a case and the issuance of a verdict before all the facts are known. While this is true of investigations in all fields, it is particularly true of inquiries in the domain of religion. Here prejudice commonly sinks its deepest roots; emotions springing from family ties and childhood influences are most frequently involved.

Influences springing from environmental factors and

[7]Jeremiah 6:16.   [8]Isaiah 35:8–10.

[5]

family traditions frequently so condition the mind that only a positive effort of the will can open the intellect for the entrance of new facts. Truth often acts like a cinder in the eye: it irritates and disturbs and provokes a flow of tears to wash it out. Intellectual growth is achieved, however, only by uprooting the false to allow new truth to gain a foothold. Disillusionment is frequently the painful but necessary preparation for the reception of truth. Like the chambered nautilus, the mind must be ever at work for the building of more stately mansions as habitations for ever-expanding truth.

There should be no fear of the truth, no shying away from new facts under the misapprehension that they will cause any real injury. There may be brief periods of discomfort, necessitated by the making of new adjustments, but no permanent damage or loss. "The profoundest of all infidelities," observes Herbert Spencer, "is the fear that the truth will be bad." When that fear becomes chronic it habitually closes the gateway of the mind to new ideas, facts, and truth, and thus severs the spinal cord of human progress.

The men and women who here chronicle their discovery of Christ found their way by various routes into the Catholic Church. It is a temple with a hundred gates, and pilgrims enter from every angle. It has a long history, and its name can scarcely be mentioned without stirring emotions of love, loyalty, fear, or hatred. But what is needed most of all to understand this world-wide institution which binds the present with the ancient era of Christ and the Apostles is a calm, intellectual approach. Light, not heat, is needed to give those on the outside a true insight into the most unique and arresting fact in all of human history. Therein is found the distinctive value of the stories of these pilgrims, for they all approached the Church from the outside and worked their way through the distorting mists of preconceptions and prejudice before they came close enough to perceive its inner nature, its distinctive ethos, its divine foundation, and its divinely appointed mission.

If a reader refuses to look at that institution with open eyes, declines to gaze at its divine origin and its deposit of divine truth, and focuses his attention solely upon its frailest and weakest members, distortion will render this reading of little or no value.

"Of the Catholic Church, the greatest religious creation known to history," observes the eminent non-Catholic biblical scholar, Adolf Harnack, "students who leave our schools know absolutely nothing. They indulge in its regard wholly trivial, vague, and nonsensical notions." Even to understand the culture of our Western world it is necessary to gain a true insight into the Church which assimilated the best elements of the civilization of Greece and Rome, molded the thought and art of the Middle Ages, and has left her imprint upon a thousand aspects of modern life and thought.

This truth is set forth with a crisp brilliance by Evelyn Waugh. "From time to time," he says, "politicians have sought to impose an exploit of their own—the first French Republic, the Fascist March on Rome—as a more notable event from which to number the years. The old calendar came back for reasons of convenience rather than piety. But the Christian, when he dates his letters from the Year of Our Lord, is affirming his Faith. He is placing the Incarnation, where for him it must always stand, in the center of human history. Before that Year of Grace man lived in the mists, haunted by ancestral memories of a lost Eden, taught enigmatically by hints and portents, punished by awful dooms.

"The Incarnation," he continues, "restored order. In place of his bloody guilt offerings man was given a single, complete expiation; in place of his magic, the sacramental system, a regular service of communication with the supernatural; in place of his mystery cults, an open, divinely constituted human Society in which to live and multiply. All his history from then onwards seen through Christian eyes, all the migrations of peoples and the rise and fall of empires, comprise merely a succession of moods and phases in the life of that Society, the Church Christ founded."[9]

Lastly, intellectual honesty and courage are required to

follow wherever the truth may lead. Conviction which is not translated into action speedily withers and dies. The mere hearing of the truth is of little value if nothing is done about it. Against such a vacuous procedure the Apostle James utters a stern warning. "Be ye doers of the word," he says, "and not hearers only, deceiving your own selves. For if a man be a hearer of the word, and not a doer, he shall be compared to a man beholding his own countenance in a glass. For he beheld himself, and went his way, and presently forgot what manner of man he was. But he that hath looked into the perfect law of liberty, and hath continued therein, not becoming a forgetful hearer, but a doer of the work; this man shall be blessed in his deed."[10]

Our Lord likewise stresses the duty of making action square with one's belief and profession. "Not every one," He warns, "that saith to me, Lord, Lord, shall enter into the kingdom of heaven: but he that doth the will of my Father who is in heaven, he shall enter into the kingdom of heaven."[11]

Mere intellectual conviction does not issue in faith; that requires the grace of God and is best procured in humble prayer on one's knees. It is divine grace which incorporates one into the mystical body of Christ and enables him to share in the divine life. An electric bulb which does not make contact with the magic of electricity remains unilluminated and dull; but once that contact is effected, it glows with incandescent brilliance and beauty.

So the human soul which is not brought into union with the life-giving grace of God remains dull and lusterless; but once incorporated by faith in the living mystical body of Christ, the Church, it shines with new spiritual beauty and power. "My grace," said Christ to the Apostle Paul, "is sufficient for thee: for power is made perfect in infirmity."[12] It is through the divine grace of faith that the weakness of a believer is converted into a strength that mocks alike both swordsmen and gibbets. "In the darkness of my inner world," reports Avery Dulles, "the highest human instincts

[10]James 1:22–26.   [11]Matthew 7:21.   [12]2 Corinthians 12:9.

[8]

were confronted with a vacuum. Into that vacuum stepped the grace of God." Then the whole world took on a new face.

An open-minded reading of the experiences of the men and women who tell how they found Christ will afford the attentive reader many an insight into the mysterious workings of divine grace upon the human soul. Their gropings for the light, their struggle for the truth, and their final achievement will serve as beacon lights to the feet of many weary souls searching for the Light that shall not fail. Their disclosure of the drama of the soul's quest for God, revealing the path which led to the open door through which they passed to God and the Church, can scarcely fail to serve as a channel of divine grace to those with the proper dispositions of mind, heart, and soul.

In following Christ whithersoever He may lead them, they shall not be walking in darkness; for He said: "I am the light of the world: he that followeth me, walketh not in darkness, but shall have the light of life."[13] That all readers may walk in that light is the sole object of this joint labor of love.

[13]John 8:12.

THE OUTSTRETCHED ARMS

Katherine Burton

Prominent among the women writers of our day is Katherine Burton, editor, free-lance writer, and biographer. Born in Cleveland in 1884, the daughter of John and Louise Buttner Kurz, she graduated from Western Reserve University and immediately went into the teaching profession. In 1910 she married Harry Payne Burton, an editor, and to this union two sons and a daughter were born.

Her first book, *The Circus Lady,* a biography of Josephine DeMott, the seventy-year-old rider, was published in 1926. From 1928 to 1930, Mrs. Burton served as associate editor of *McCall's* magazine, and later in the same capacity on *Redbook;* she resigned in 1933 to do free-lance writing. Her articles were published in many of the leading magazines; and she conducts a woman's page, "Woman to Woman," in *The Sign.*

Busy with her magazine articles for a decade, she then turned her writing attention to the life of Rose Hawthorne, the youngest of Nathaniel Hawthorne's three children. Then, after embracing the Catholic faith, Rose became a Dominican nun and was instrumental in establishing a home for the cancerous poor. Mrs. Burton tells this story in her second book, *Sorrow Built a Bridge,* which has gone through ten editions.

Two years later she published *Paradise Hunters,* the story of the experiment of Emerson, Hawthorne, Thoreau, and other intellectuals at Brook Farm. In 1940 appeared *His Dear Persuasion,* in which she tells the story of Mother Seton. In *No Strange Land* she sketches the lives of some of the more outstanding American converts to the Catholic faith, chiefly during the nineteenth century, though a few belong to the twentieth.

Confident that she had found her métier in biography, she wrote in succession *Celestial Homespun,* the life of Isaac Hecker, founder of the Paulist Fathers, *Mother Butler of Marymount,* and *No Shadow of Turning*, the life of James Kent Stone, known in religious life as Father Fidelis of the Cross, a Passionist. In *His Mercy Endureth Forever* she sketches the history of the Apostolate of the Sisters of Mercy.

In *Brother André* she chronicles the life and deeds of that lay brother at St. Joseph's Oratory in Montreal who acquired the reputation of a miracle worker even during his lifetime.

The Next Thing is an autobiography, mirroring the happenings of a rich and full life, and abounding with interesting observations concerning people and movements, written in an engaging manner. Since her conversion to the Catholic faith in 1930, she has notably enriched the literature of the Church in America.

M Y JUMPING-OFF PLACE on the road to Rome was the Episcopal Church of St. Mary the Virgin. Set in the heart of New York City, this is truly a beautiful church. Its altars and chapels are lovely: the Sacred Heart altar; the Lady Chapel, a delicate gem where, I was told, is housed the Blessed Sacrament; St. Joseph's altar, with a fine mosaic of Our Lady's betrothal; and a black-and-white marble chapel for requiem masses.

In this church I learned many things I never knew before. Other churches had seemed cold compared to this place so alive with faith. St. Mary's has completely Catholic ceremonies and does not change their names, as so often happens in other churches. Benediction is benediction, not "devotions." Mass is called Mass, not "Holy Eucharist." I don't think I ever saw the *Book of Common Prayer* inside St. Mary's, for all the parishioners use books of private devotions. Although the Roman liturgy and many Roman prayers are used, it is always made clear that they are part of the "primitive Church" and that it is Rome which has brought in new things, while the Anglo-Catholics remain faithful to the original Church. When Bishop Manning came to confirm at St. Mary's, he wore a miter; the clergy there always wore birettas in the church, the curates black, the rectors black with a red tassel.

For months I rested contentedly in the church where I had

found a spiritual home. I was satisfied. But, perhaps because a Roman Catholic friend of mine kept asking me questions which I could not always answer easily, I felt that I ought not to be too thoughtless about my choice of a faith.

I began reading in order to answer her questions, and found that Sheila Kaye-Smith, an ardent Anglo-Catholic, had written convincing articles upholding the Anglo-Catholic viewpoint. And there were many others—Vernon Johnson, Arnold Lunn, and Bernard Iddings Bell—who were just as convincing. I was amazed at the interesting books I found. I had not realized there were so many on religion. After a while I began to wonder if people were writing about anything but religion. A visit to the Episcopal bookshop on Forty-fifth Street, owned by the publishing firm of Gorham, made me feel like my three-year-old son, who, after a summer spent at the seashore, looked out of a taxi caught in the traffic of Herald Square and remarked, "It's high tide!"

Patricia Jackson, who had started me studying the position of the Anglican Church in regard to Catholicism, kept right on needling me. The Anglican bishops, she said, had a very doubtful apostolic succession, and she spoke cynically of a certain Bishop Parker. She spoke of St. Peter's one and only successor, the Pope, and quoted verses from the Bible which she claimed established the fact beyond argument. She spoke of Henry VIII, who, she said, really founded my Church. She mentioned Newman, Hugh Benson, and others who had been made happy by going to Rome—"flopping," we Anglicans called it.

"There are two things fixed firmly in the Roman mind, it seems to me," I said to her one day sharply, "the Pope in heaven and Henry VIII in hell." But of course that was not a real answer to her arguments. So, in addition to reading, I also consulted Dr. Delany, the associate rector at St. Mary's. Then I began to come back with pamphlets which matched hers. She had given me one on papal infallibility by a Paulist Father, and I retorted with Gore's *Catholicism and Roman Catholicism,* marking the places where he said

St. Augustine had interpreted the Petrine text in three different ways. When she gave me *Advanced Anglican Assumptions*, I handed her Johnson's *Notes on the Catholic Religion*. When she found one for me called *Why Anglican Orders Are Not Valid*, I came across with Hughson's *Henry the Eighth and the Anglican Church*.

It was a merry bit of warfare. I began studying even more. I found out who Bishop Parker was. I spoke darkly, though somewhat confusedly, of "forged decretals," and finally, when she asked me why I didn't realize that the succession of the English Church had been cut off clean, I asked her what made her so sure that the Roman succession was all right. I had just been reading about the period when three popes claimed the tiara and the faithful were asking two of them to abdicate. "How," said I, "are you sure that the Pope with the proper succession eventually landed in the chair of Peter?"

But the more I read, the more argument began to tire me, for it was crowded out by something else—the beauty of the Catholic faith. I began very definitely to separate my faith from arguments about history. I thought of the man who said that every time he got his little candle of faith lighted, and was trying to go through the great dark forest of the world by its light, some theologian came along and blew it out. I made up my mind that would not happen to me.

It was at this time also that I began to admire the Roman Catholics whom I knew for their way of adhering to what they had been taught. I did not know many, but they all impressed me in the same way. There was Irene Sweeney, whom I knew in high school. There was Mrs. Robinson, the riding teacher in Garden City. And there was Patricia Jackson, a really well-read girl. Their minds and training differed, but they all knew the answers to questions about their faith and could defend it.

I also liked their way of being gay about their religion. Sometimes, in fact, when I heard them speak of the saints and Our Lady in very familiar terms, it made my Protestant soul nervous, for they spoke as if they were in the next room, as if they were part of a family.

For myself, past all the amusing bickering, past all the little arguments, there was one fact. The faith which I had learned to understand at St. Mary's, especially under Dr. Delany, had brought me peace. I loved its avenues of escape from the bitterness of life. It took care of many of my problems, and it seemed as old as the world and as modern as myself.

I loved it because of its sacraments and especially because I believed it stemmed from the Apostles. I remember reading that apostolic success was more important than apostolic succession, an argument of the "broad" Episcopalians. But, to me, that succession was like a long lifeline of hands touching hands, shoulders touching shoulders, a wonderful life-saving crew bringing in the worn, the troubled, from the deep waters of doubt and fear. I loved that sense of dependence on a church which went back, through dim days and fair, to Christ Himself. No loss, I was certain, would have been greater to me than to feel that I had lost contact with those who carried down to unimportant me the Body and Blood of Our Lord. Had I doubted apostolic succession in the church where I had settled, I knew I would have had no place there. But I was very certain that I would never have cause to question that fact.

One day I decided to brush up a bit on my Greek. I thought of going back to the essays of Plato or to the *Iliad*, which we had read in college; but Dr. Delany suggested that instead I get a New Testament in Greek. Much of it was already familiar to me in English, and one phrase would give me a whole paragraph's meaning and thus renew my vocabulary.

After some months I found I could translate with a good bit of ease, and then I became aware of differences here and there between the Greek and the English Bible with which I helped myself over hard passages. Some words did not seem to have the same meaning in translation as in the Greek; some things seemed actually left out altogether.

For instance, in Luke the Authorized Version read, "Hail, thou that art highly favored," and the Greek looked definitely like "Hail, full of grace." In Corinthians, I found a disturbing place which read in the Authorized, "Whosoever shall eat this bread *and* drink this cup"; my Greek Testament plainly said, "Eat this bread *or* drink this cup."

When I mentioned these things to Dr. Delany, he laughed. "You have a Protestant Bible," he said. "Get the Douay."

There was also, to trouble me, the matter of the rector of St. Mary's. Dr. Barry was in many ways the very opposite of his associate rector, though they had been friends since student days. He was not at all well and seldom preached at the services, but one day he announced that he would give three evening lectures on Rome during the following month. Dr. Delany suggested that I come to hear the talks, which might answer questions I had lately been asking him.

Dr. Barry seemed harsh to me the few times I met him. He wrote lovely meditations on Our Lady and the sacraments, but as soon as he got away from the subject of faith he grew bitter. In his talks on Rome he became sarcastic. He maintained that Rome was no good, up to no good, and never would be any good. The Anglo-Catholic Church was all that was left of the primitive Church. The Roman Church had adopted a lot of nonsense which the primitive Church had not practiced and, in fact, had never heard about.

But the attack was so bitter and so continuous that, in the end, I wanted to defend the Roman Catholic Church. I shared many of Dr. Barry's opinions, but it seemed impossible that any church could be that bad and survive for so many hundreds of years. I remembered, too, the Catholics I knew: the circus rider, the girl at high school, and the college woman who was still arguing with me. They were all good and sensible people. But of course I did agree that the rulers of their Church might be mistaken.

The Roman Catholics who had talked of their faith with me had one beginning and one end to every argument: the everlastingness of their Church. It was the first Church established by Our Lord, and there was no other and would

[15]

be no other. One day my New York Catholic friend showed me a list of the founders of the various Christian sects: Martin Luther, the Lutheran Church; Wesley, the Methodist; Henry VIII, the Anglican. There were others in the long list, but the last one of all was: Catholic Church— Founder, Jesus Christ.

The statement irritated me by its complacency, but the stark simplicity of it was impressive, too. My friend also showed me a letter of one of the popes on the subject of Anglican orders. I did not agree with it, but it was certainly not the work of a villain or a moron, as Dr. Barry hinted such statements might well be; just as he spoke of the fear that the Church inspired in its followers—fears upon fears, he said. But none of the people I knew seemed filled with fear. None of them ever talked to me about being afraid of their Church. They very evidently loved her.

Dr. Barry's discourses did not have the result I had hoped for. Instead of explaining in any way the Anglo-Catholic Church, he had, I felt, merely maligned the Roman, and by the end of the third talk he had roused in me quite an interest in the object of his attack. And then many other things followed.

I thought of Dr. Delany's story of his first parish. The members built a new church while he was there, and put a confessional in it. He trained them to use it. But after he went to another church they had the confessional taken out. They had built it merely to please him because they liked him.

Not long after the Barry talks I came across a historical article on benediction. The account stated that it was the invention of a Jesuit some three hundred years before. At St. Mary's we had benediction, yet three hundred years ago was obviously not far enough back for the primitive Church to have had anything to do with it. I discussed this puzzling matter with Dr. Delany, but for once he did not talk much. He did give me an Anglican book which discussed benediction, but that was all.

And then I forgot the whole argument. It was Lent, and

Lent at St. Mary's was a wonderful season. The evening Stations. The services of Holy Week. Holy Thursday, with its altar of repose in the Lady Chapel. The confessions that brought such peace and comfort. The three evenings of Tenebrae. The Good Friday Mass of the Presanctified. The climax of Easter Sunday, with Solemn High Mass celebrated on the beautiful high altar, the three priests in vestments of white and gold, the music swelling through the church. It was all so completely beautiful and so satisfying that I forgot the troubling doubts which seemed so small by comparison. Truth was beauty and beauty truth, I told myself. Keats was right: that was all I needed to know. I forgot my uneasy feelings.

My peace of mind did not continue for long. Soon after Easter, out of a clear sky, Dr. Delany told me that he was leaving the Episcopal Church to become a Roman Catholic. I stared at him in utter amazement, and only gradually, as he went on talking, did I even begin to believe it. He was telling only a few of his friends, he said; he would make a public announcement the next week.

I knew he had been at work on a book, but he had written others before and I had not asked about this one. Now he told me the title, *Why Rome?*, and gave me the manuscript to read. That is, he gave me all but the last chapter, which he said was not quite finished. But I think the truth was that he did not want to unsettle me with that last chapter, for it gave the reasons for his decision and no doubt he felt he ought not to trouble me or influence me unduly.

The New York papers printed the news at length on their front pages. After all, here was a man who had spent many years in the Episcopal Church, who was rumored close to a bishopric, who was well known in the city. Soon outcries arose against him from various quarters, and when it was learned that he was going to study for the priesthood, they grew louder. But much of the criticism was not directed at the Roman Church, as I had expected, but at the one he was leaving, at the special sort of religion practiced at St. Mary's. The definitely Protestant element was angriest, but there were High Church groups, too, who had different ideas and tenets, and they also attacked him.

I was really distressed: was this any sort of unity at all? Where was the love, the sense of agape about which Dr. Barry had been so eloquent? The primitive Church, yes. But where was the primitive love that was its basis?

It was on a day when I was pondering all these things that I came across the story of Athanasius, the ancient bishop who had held out for a single word, who had let himself be driven into exile from his see for the sake of that word, which he knew, with all his mind and his heart and his spirit, must be retained if the faith were not to suffer. Small as this last fact might seem as a reason to trouble a modern like myself, it was the one which affected me most and which eventually brought me to the door of the rectory of a Catholic church.

Dr. Delany made arrangements to sail for Italy to study for the priesthood at the Beda college in Rome. Because he was going to be out of the city for some weeks, Cardinal Hayes made arrangements with Msgr. Joseph McMahon, rector of the Church of Our Lady of Lourdes and for years the cardinal's associate at the cathedral, to receive Dr. Delany into the Church.

I attended the ceremony on June twenty-fourth, together with a group from St. Mary's. The service was simple and beautiful and entirely new to me.

I noted especially the white-haired priest who received Dr. Delany into the Church. He looked rather dour, I thought, but there was something in the way he went about the ceremony that caught me. It was businesslike; it was matter-of-fact; and it was also deeply devotional.

Dr. Delany's going to Rome left a void in my life. He had been my good friend and excellent adviser and the only confessor I had ever known. But it was more than that which was making me unhappy. At St. Mary's the irate Dr. Barry was delivering broadsides about his late colleague. Of course he was not the only one. Before he went away, Dr. Delany had come to my apartment one evening bringing with him a bag of letters received that week—mostly fan mail, he said a bit wryly. He and Elizabeth Boteler and I went through them, and it was a shattering and amazing experience. We sorted them, and three kinds of letters eventually emerged: the ones from parishioners who said they understood the high motives behind his act, even though they could not follow him; the ones from converts and born Catholics; and, from the third group, the painful ones.

Among the letters from his former parishioners were some frankly puzzling ones, including one from a woman who wrote that she thought "there must be some mistake." However, most of this set of letters expressed chiefly a sense of loss in his going from among them.

The convert letters were lovely. One of the best was from a nun who had once been superior of an Episcopalian convent. She wrote that she knew he would be happy, that even the splinter from the Cross no doubt now being pressed into him was, after all, a splinter from the Cross and so a happiness, because he shared the pain of Our Lord.

It was the letters from his fellow clerics that were, some of them, so unkind that they are still bitter in my memory. One wrote that he could not understand how Dr. Delany could leave his own beautiful church, and the cultured people there, "to sit in the company of the unwashed and no doubt pass the bottle with them, too." Other letters called him various names: renegade, traitor, poor Christian. So spoke the High Churchmen. The Low Churchmen were also virulent, but with a difference. They felt that he should have gone a long time ago, that he was now where he belonged and where it was hoped, all those who, like him, had aped Rome for years, would soon go.

One of the pleasantest letters came from Bishop Manning. It was gentle in phrasing, kindly and sympathetic. He said he understood, and he hoped that in his new life Dr. Delany would find a place to work for God as ably as he had hitherto done in the communion which had lost him.

I think it was the hate expressed by some of those of his

own communion that at last overwhelmed me: the realization that they did not honor a man who followed his conscience. The hate that came from those who disliked ritual was, if not Christian, at least understandable. But the hate which came from his own group I could not understand.

It was true that various things had bothered me even before this in regard to the Episcopal Church. But I had always told myself that Dr. Delany, who knew so much more about these matters than I did, was apparently undisturbed, and so I stayed. Now he was gone, and there was no one to consult.

I tried to continue at St. Mary's, but the security I had known there was gone and it would not return. I tried to go occasionally to St. Patrick's Cathedral, but I felt I did not belong there. I did not really belong anywhere. It was when I began to realize that only two roads lay before me, one pointing to agnosticism, that I decided to ask for advice from someone.

I wrote to Dr. Delany first to ask him what I should do. I was finding it very difficult, I said, to go back to St. Mary's, and besides, as he knew, I had had many uneasy moments there long before he decided to leave.

"It is not an easy question for me to answer," he wrote back. "I might say that you should not be influenced by what I have done, but what is life but being influenced by the various personalities God flings across the orbit of our progress through space? We have to choose which personalities we shall cling to. That is where we differ from the planets. But the choice must be our own, aided by divine grace. Do not try to escape from the Anglo-Catholic-Protestant-Episcopal Church unless you simply cannot stay where you are and practice your religion there any longer. And it must be an intelligent choice."

He suggested that I be patient about it, since the art of perfection consists in going slowly: "The slapdash methods which you use so skillfully in cooking and in magazine work will never enable you to master the science of the saints. 'The kingdom of heaven suffers violence and the violent take it by force'—but that doesn't mean that you can take it by epigram or a turn of the wrist."

That July, I had definitely made up my mind as to what I should do. Since none of my Catholic friends were in New York and I knew none of the clergy, I decided to call on Monsignor McMahon and get his opinion.

What I chiefly wished to ask him, I told Monsignor, was what I should do about going to church. Should I force myself back to St. Mary's for a while at least, or go to a Catholic church, or should I not go to any for the present?

"Don't stop going to church," he said instantly, "but go where you feel you want to go—either church. Do you read Newman?" he asked abruptly. Then he paused for my answer.

I admitted that my entire knowledge of Newman was what I had gained in an essay course at college where we had studied some pages of his writings, something about universities, as I recalled it.

He shrugged in annoyance, a gesture of head and hand with which I was to become very familiar in days to come. "The style, yes," he said scornfully. "They allow you to have a little of that. But the spirit, the reason back of the writing . . ." and he waved hand and head again.

He went upstairs and came down with *Difficulties of Anglicans*. Before I left he handed me the volume. "Go to church where you wish—but go—and keep on reading Newman. When you wish to, come and see me again."

I took *Difficulties of Anglicans* home with me and pored over it. It was not easy reading, but I kept at it; somehow Cardinal Newman was saying a great many things which I had felt but had not been able to put into words, or even into clear thought. When I had finished it, I borrowed a life of Newman from the library and read that. I paid shy, fugitive visits to St. Patrick's, usually to Mass before I went to the office. Dr. Delany's letters had encouraged me but were never urgent or insistent. In fact, he wrote mainly about his own life at the Beda in Rome.

The college, he told me, was made up of three groups of

men—converts, late vocations, and priests wishing to take advanced courses. From the first he liked this new life, so different from the old and, one would think, very difficult for a man nearing sixty years of age. The students followed a simple, almost strict regimen. They rose at five-thirty and went to bed at ten. They wore beaver hats and cassocks, even on the street. "I am getting used to walking in long skirts," he wrote. "And among our hardships are the most delicious red wine for dinner and white wine for supper. We never go out in the evenings. For years it has been my ambition to stay home evenings and get up early. Another dream realized."

He wrote about the students he met there: Vernon Johnson, a recent convert and formerly the popular rector of one of London's most fashionable East End churches; Algar Thorold, whose father was an Anglican bishop and who came to the Beda after years in the navy; Sir John O'Connor, an exceedingly brilliant man who had been a lawyer for years until, in his late sixties, he decided to be a priest; Peter Harris, formerly an Anglican Benedictine monk; Withnell, an ex-wine merchant of Liverpool; Brian Dillon, son of the famous Irish leader.

In November he met Cardinal Lepicier, who, upon hearing his name, said, "Oh, Father Delany of St. Mary the Virgin in New York. Of course I have heard of you." But Dr. Delany wrote me: "Don't tell this or it will be quoted by Anglicans as proof of the validity of their orders." He added that the fact was that all Beda men dressed as priests and were commonly addressed as "Father" all over Rome.

I did not go back to St. Mary's, but I heard from friends of mine what was going on there. Dr. Barry had by this time all but celebrated a funeral mass for his ex-friend, which was exactly how he referred to him. The Society of St. John the Evangelist, the American branch of the English Cowley Fathers, was moving in to take charge of the church. One woman with a rather crude sense of humor was referring to the departed rector as Dr. Delooney. Some of his feminine ex-parishioners were still greatly upset, and two

[22]

were busily reading up on Roman literature; one of them, in fact, was getting ready to make a trip to Rome—"planned for years," she told people.

Between Newman and Monsignor McMahon, and my own firm convictions, not many weeks passed before I announced to Monsignor that I was ready to be instructed.

He was mildly surprised to learn that I wanted to know nothing about indulgences. He thought they always bothered converts and were an obstacle in the path of many. They did not bother me, but I did have one difficulty, I told him, and that was the matter of hell.

"Hell? There is no difficulty about that," he said, puzzled. "Don't you believe there is a hell?"

It wasn't that. If the Church said there was a hell, then that was all right with me and I was perfectly willing to go along with her. It was only that I could not believe there were human beings in hell, although that, too, I was ready to assent to if the Church so defined it. I spoke of all the reasons why people became criminals: backgrounds, lack of good training in childhood, bad influences, many things which were not by any means entirely their fault. Surely, to go to hell, one must be invincibly and purposely and all-your-own-fault evil.

I looked anxiously at Monsignor to see how he was taking this bit of amateur theology. But he said it was all right with him, and he was certain it was so with the Church. If I thought there was no one in hell, I had a right to my opinion and I could still be a good Catholic. So, on the basis of a possibly empty hell, I made ready to enter the Catholic Church.

When I was ready to be baptized, Monsignor suggested I find myself a sponsor. I told him there was no Catholic whom I could ask. The few I knew were not in the city. Monsignor told me he would find me someone, and later called me up to tell me he had done so.

I spent the night before my reception into the Church at the Cenacle, for Mass was at eight and my reception was scheduled for seven. A few moments before that time I was told my sponsor was waiting in a cab to take me over to the church. Rather timidly I went down to meet, on this of all days, a stranger, and from the inside of the cab a warm, charming voice greeted me. When I got inside she introduced herself as Margaret Armstrong. She talked all the way to the church, telling me how Monsignor had called her up a few days before and asked her to be a sponsor for a convert—a special case.

It was only later, when Monsignor adressed her as Lady Armstrong, that I learned who she was. I had heard of her. Her husband was British consul in New York; she herself was an exceedingly busy woman, not only with the social duties connected with her husband's work but with her own far-flung charities. Yet she had taken time to come far uptown before seven in the morning to help a stranger into the Church. She would have been the first, I realized later when I grew to know her better, to insist that nothing could have been of greater importance.

It was September 8, 1930, the feast of Our Lady's Nativity, and I was going to take her name as mine. As I stood awaiting my reception, with the Monsignor and Lady Armstrong beside me, I was still wondering if I were taking a wrong step, still wondering if I ought not be back in the Church where I had been happy and where I knew so many people. I stood there in the house of God, and suddenly it was a strange house to me, and I felt nostalgic for that other Church and its shelter.

I was standing there beside a woman I had never seen before, and even Monsignor was like a complete stranger. I felt caught. The beautiful rite of reception passed over my head, rather than into it as did that of baptism—conditional, for my first may have been valid. I remember only that the thought came to me that the soul must be very important if all this trouble was taken for a single one.

It was not until later, when my godmother and I were kneeling in a front pew in that beautiful church, that I became aware of my surroundings and looked up at the paintings across the walls of the church, each depicting one of the great events in Our Lady's life. On the right, the Nativity, with Our Lord a wee aureoled baby; on the left, the Crucifixion, Our Lord a broken, pain-shadowed man; the panels between showed Our Lady alone—one as she listened to the angel's message, the other as she was taken up into heaven.

While I waited for Mass to begin I looked again at Our Lady, at the young girl accepting the gift of life from God, and at the woman accepting the gift of heaven itself. I thought how in that last picture she was ascending to God, who had given her the world's hope and was now giving her the world's fulfillment, and how I, too, had a small share in that now. I said small prayers to her, waiting there for Mass. And I looked at her with deep affection, for, in a way, she was my sponsor, too, since I had taken her name as my own.

Yet the feeling of being a stranger still lingered. And then Lady Armstrong put her hand on my arm and directed my eyes to the altar of the Sacred Heart, almost directly before us. I saw what she wanted me to see: the marble statue of Our Lord, His arms outstretched as if in welcome.

It was this that made me know I was at home. An uncertain guest, I had stood at the threshold, wondering whether I wanted to go in and whether I was really wanted inside. Now I saw that they had all been helping me to realize that this was my home—the rector, the nun in purple and black, the woman beside me. And here was the Owner of the House, standing at His own rooftree to welcome me.

From that moment I knew no doubts, and I have known none since. After all, if one is born in a certain house and there are witnesses to attest the matter, there can be no doubt of one's birthplace. And so with me, for in that House I was born.

That was some twenty years ago, and the adopted child has remained adopted and is almost forgetting she ever was adopted. Difficulties have beset my path, but never the difficulty of doubt. As a matter of fact, there is only one difference that separates the Catholic and everyone else as far as religious difficulties go. Here, too, as elsewhere, brothers quarrel and disagree. The lover of liturgical beauty and art is often bitter toward a tawdry art which others love; there are many who cannot understand why others prefer to sing commonplace hymns when there is so great a store of poetry to draw on; there are some who are too often conscious of their nationalities; there are some who see too much the side of the rich, and others who see too much the side of the poor. All such things are in every religious group. But in all Catholic disputes there is a unity of doctrine and belief. They are the only ones who have learned how vast and free is the world for him who is obedient to the law of the Church, which was Our Lord's gift to His people. They have kept as their keystone of Faith this gift which the others cast away.

Years ago there were three Catholic women with whom I argued, at various times, on religious questions. One was a riding teacher who had once been a famous circus rider; one was a woman of the world who later married a French title; and one was a girl I met at college, whose father was a Socialist and whose mother was a staunch Catholic. The one thing that had irritated me about all these three was the fact that they all had a very annoying habit in common. They were ready to talk on doctrine and religion, but at a certain point they all stopped and I could never get any of them to argue beyond that point. I thought it sheer bigotry then, and a sort of ignorant fear which their narrow religion had loaded them with. I know now that it was simply that there was no argument to prove or disprove. They had a Fact—an actuality. On that point there was nothing to argue about.

I have watched, during these later years of mine as a Catholic, those of my Anglican friends who still remain in that Church. They are happy because they have a "cause," and, after all, one can fight as joyously for a mistake as for a truth, if one's heart is in it. But there is a sadness to me about it when I realize they are "falling to a voice that is not calling."

[26]

Not all of them are entirely happy, either. More than once I have come across them kneeling in the Catholic cathedral, sometimes even before the shrine of the Sacred Heart, and I have wondered how it is that they, who obviously come because their own Church fails to give them something they find here, cannot come here completely and for all time. If once they could see that it is willfulness and not martyrdom which animates them, they would come to the Church not alone to pray there, but to live there. What I pray for them to see is what my godmother showed me twenty years ago on Our Lady's birthday: *the arms of her Son outstretched to welcome them home.*

THROUGH THE CHURCH TO GOD

Duane G. Hunt

It is a long way from a Methodist Sunday school to the Catholic bishopric of Salt Lake City, but that is the trail traveled by Duane G. Hunt. Scholar, editor, author, administrator, and radio speaker, Bishop Hunt ranks high among the pulpit orators of America. While his diocese embraces the whole of Utah, his constructive exposition of the Christian faith over a nation-wide radio network has brought his voice and message into millions of homes of people of every creed. He has been a speaker at numerous college and university commencement exercises and at civil and religious celebrations of a state and national character.

Born in 1884 of Methodist parents in Reynolds, Nebraska, Duane G. Hunt was educated in public elementary and high schools and graduated from Cornell College, Iowa, in 1907. After teaching for several years in the public high schools of Iowa, he entered the Law School at the state university in 1911 and later continued his law studies at the University of Chicago. His investigation of the Catholic religion led to his conversion and he was received into the Church in Chicago in 1913.

He taught public speaking at the University of Utah for several years and in 1916 entered St. Patrick's Seminary in Menlo Park, California, to study for the priesthood. During the summers of 1917 and 1918 he gave courses in public speaking at the University of California. He was ordained in 1920 for the diocese of Salt Lake City, where he served as chancellor, vicar-general, rector of the cathedral, and diocesan administrator. In 1924 he was appointed Papal Chamberlain, and in 1930 he was made a Domestic Prelate; he was appointed by the Holy See to the bishopric of Salt Lake City on August 6, 1937, and a few months later was consecrated a bishop.

In a state largely populated by members of the Church of Jesus Christ of Latter-day Saints, Bishop Hunt has won the respect and esteem of the general public and has been a leader in the civic as well as in the spiritual life of the commonwealth. For several years he was the editor of the *Intermountain Catholic;* he is a member of Phi Alpha Delta, Pi Kappa Alpha, Rotary, and is the author of *The People, the Clergy and the Church.*

For some years Bishop Duane G. Hunt was speaker over a radio network covering the intermountain states and later was featured on the Catholic Hour program broadcast over a nation-wide network. Because of his own background, he is able to understand and appreciate the religious conceptions and sensitivity of those outside the fold, and he has been singularly successful in revealing to them the historic Christian faith and in bringing help, light, and inspiration to vast numbers of them.

T HE FACILITY with which some converts have described the processes by which they found their way to the Catholic Church has always amazed me and aroused a certain feeling of envy. For my own part, it has invariably been a difficult assignment to sit down and attempt to detail the story of my approach to the Church. In the first place, and I say this without any illusion of false humility, it is not a particularly stirring or important story. In the second place, I confess to a certain distaste for advertising my personal adventure in grace. There, doubtless, emerges the irreducible puritan in my make-up. But if the narrative, for all it lacks of the spectacular, may serve as aid and comfort for those embarked on the same pilgrimage I made so many years ago, that is reason enough for embalming it in print. The editor assures me that such is the case, and I hereby bow to his judgment.

I was born in the very heart of American Protestantism, the Middle West, in the eighties of last century. It is hard for me to evaluate, much less to put in writing, the debt I owe my parents. They gave me a good home; they set before me a constant example of plain living and honest thinking. Devout Methodists, their faith was untinged with fanaticism, and they stood foursquare for all those principles of fundamental Christianity upon which the nation itself had been built and preserved through the ordeal of

[29]

the Civil War which was still a living memory to them.

With my hand in my mother's, I was introduced as a youngster to the mysteries of Sunday school. Vivid memories of those days survive, colored by the Bible stories, conned and repeated, and the prints and the chromos which were a part of this personal experience. As I advanced in years I was introduced to the regular church services, and at some date, in my early teens, I formally "joined the Church."

During this period of unclouded faith, what were my beliefs? As closely as I can clarify them now, they would seem to have been straightforwardly and typically Christian. There was certainly no question as to the existence and spirituality of God. With equal certitude I accepted the divinity of Jesus Christ, though it may well have been that an analysis of my belief would have revealed its imprecision and lack of any positive intellectual basis. As for the Bible, my respect for it was profound. It was the word of God, the source of divine instruction and guidance for the human race. Unhesitatingly I would have avowed my belief in its inspiration, though what I would have meant by that term is something that recollection fails to indicate. In a word, during my adolescent years I was an avowed and professing Protestant, a thorough conformist.

That there was such a thing as the Catholic Church, I was, of course, dimly aware. My childhood and youth were passed without any more contact with the actual Church than my sole acquaintance with only one Catholic family, though fortunately the example there was solidly edifying. By-passing this exception, however, I swallowed in its entirety the general verdict of my friends and associates that Catholics were people on a lower social level than our own, ignorant and inferior, held in durance vile by the evil machinations of their hierarchy. Someday, unquestionably, their emancipation would come (emancipation was still a word to conjure with) and they would all become good and enlightened Protestants.

With the sophomorism of youth, I condemned the Church as hopelessly out of date and obscurantist. Quite possibly the first centuries of Christianity were blameless, though my ignorance of the history of the early Church was appalling. Sometimes in later centuries, it is understood, the Church had yielded to corruption of the worst kind and had fallen into the hands of leaders who were tyrannical, cruel, and despotic. Hints of the Spanish Inquisition provided the lurid background, and there was always the convenient figure of Pope Alexander VI.

Against this nightmare of religious degradation, I reasoned, an enlightened Europe had at last revolted. Where the Church retained some semblance of her power, there the same old evils were continued. My contempt was particularly marked, good devotee of democracy that I was, for the monarchial powers of Catholic officialdom. It was the negation of the democratic ideal and the mainspring of the utter servility of Catholics everywhere. My analysis was devastating and made up with conviction what it lacked in originality.

It is interesting to recall now the strength of my dislike for the ceremonial of the Catholic Church, especially since at that time my acquaintance with that phase of the liturgy was entirely theoretical. But from what I had heard, it was easy to denounce it out of hand as a relic of empty formalism. Never having met or even seen a priest, my judgment bore heavily upon the reputed greed of all who wore the Roman collar, upon their alleged habit of charging for confessions, and upon the dubiousness of their morals generally. I should add that few of these prejudices were derived from my parents themselves. They did not like the Catholic Church, but they refrained from backstairs gossip.

With this as my religious frame of reference, I went to college: a sound Methodist institution in the heart of Iowa. It was the type of school that believed in fundamental education and instilled precepts of severe self-discipline. As I recall my freshman year, it was a period of quiescence; there was little that disturbed the even tenor of my theological prepossessions.

For myself, as for the majority of my fellow students,

there was the assurance that Protestantism was the only possible way of life, offering as it seemed the maximum of security in the relatively untroubled world of the early twentieth century. We would emerge, unquestionably, as the anointed leaders of our communities, the continental Pharisees. I cannot remember any particular religious fervor as a characteristic of my life during this phase, but simply a bland satisfaction with things as they were.

To the best of my recollection, it must have been somewhere along the course of my second year in college that the first rumblings of doubt began to make themselves heard in the recesses of my mind. The original source of the disturbance was the "Revival," which was then, and for many years thereafter, an accepted feature of Midwestern Protestantism. The recurrence of these periodic religious sessions began to arouse my distaste, and it was not long until they awakened an active repulsion. They began to impress me as crude and sensational, quite the opposite of anything I could conceive as a fitting expression of Christianity, and certainly as an unstable and highly emotional method of expressing religious convictions. If this were actually the substance of religion, I thought, and its effect on me was so adverse, perhaps there was something lacking in my approach. These musings, half formulated, continued to bother me, though I shared my disturbance with none of my companions in college.

As time went on, moreover, my difficulties became greater. Other features of the popular Protestantism of the day began to annoy me. There was, for example, the matter of extemporaneous prayers, and there was the exasperating practice of "giving testimony." Attendance at Sunday morning services and the weekly prayer meetings, punctuated with these usages, became increasingly obnoxious. Impromptu prayers, as I analyzed them, seemed to specialize in informing God about what was going on, information which surely He did not need; the testimonies, "see what God has done for me," impressed me as a macabre kind of boasting.

[32]

Neither struck me as reverent or properly humble. Even today, after the lapse of all the years, my dislike for them remains as strong as ever; my advice to Protestant leaders, if it were sought, would be to jettison them. They started me on my way out of Protestantism and they have had the same effect on many others. (If such advice seems inconsistent with my secure happiness in the Catholic Church, then I hasten to express my gratitude for these irritating features and urge their retention.)

The story of my religious discontent would not be complete without at least a brief reference to my reaction to the puritanism with which I was surrounded. There were the so-called "questionable amusements," for instance, such as card playing and dancing. I was brought up in the belief that to take part in them was wrong and unchristian. It was a matter of conscience. Even in college such was the current interpretation of Christianity. At first, as in all other departments of thinking and behavior, I was a strict conformist, and a sincere one.

It was only a matter of time, however, until the denunciation of "questionable amusements," following other and more important features of my religious environment, should come in for its share of criticism and challenge. It may well be that the puritanism of my locality was not fully in accord with Protestant theology; I didn't know about that. All I knew was that, practically speaking, the Christian religion was closely bound up and identified with prohibitions. It appeared as a composite of negations.

In the same category was my disapproval, once I started to disapprove, of the prevailing attitude toward even moderate indulgence in tobacco and liquor. This, too, was proscribed as unchristian. As an illustration of the extreme to which such thinking can be carried, I recall the insistence of some of my associates that the wine served at the marriage feast at Cana and the Last Supper was merely grape juice. To the reader of these lines it seems incredible that such an opinion could have been held in college circles. It was so held, however, and was passed on to me in all

[33]

seriousness. Need I add that disillusionment was inevitable?

As a college junior my dissatisfaction became so keen that I could no longer refrain from seeking counsel. The faculty members and ministers whom I approached were uniformly kind in their response, but their answers never satisfied me. Even so, my desire to remain within the bounds of conformity, my sense of loyalty to all that I considered my heritage, demanded that I make the best effort I could to accept the proffered solutions.

Some of my questions come to mind: What does it mean to say that "Jesus saves?" I hear my fellow students testify that they have been saved: How do they know? I hear them declare that they have chosen Jesus as their "personal Saviour." What can such a statement mean? Are "questionable amusements" sinful? If so, why? What is my status relative to the Church? Who has the authority to tell me that I am bound to attend church services? Who put the books of the Bible together? How do I know that they were inspired? How does it happen that the same Bible is the seedbed of so many contradictory doctrines? Why cannot religious truth be easily recognized?

Granted that these questions were clumsily stated and were far from boasting analytic maturity, still they embodied the doubts which tortured me. The Protestant critic of today might well say that my failure to find satisfaction in the solutions by my advisers reflected rather upon my judgment than upon the answers themselves. He might insinuate, with some degree of accuracy, that for a young man I was too introspective, that I did not expose my mind with sufficient candor. All I can say is that these doubts and difficulties were painfully real to me. They were no mere passing phase of restless youth. If my mentors in college did not grasp the depth of my disturbance, neither did I myself. I was floundering in what Bossuet has called the "variation" of Protestantism, and I could discover no anchor hold for my wavering faith.

This was a time of acute spiritual distress. I continued my attendance at the regular services, but my attitude was hardening into one of contemptuous tolerance. Probably the only thing that attracted me to church at all was my pleasure in singing. The sermons and testimonials I sat through with grim cynicism; the extemporaneous prayers I endured with ill-concealed ridicule and scorn. Christianity itself had ceased to evoke my reverence. Doubtless I was conceited and altogether too cocky, a very disagreeable young man going through a very disagreeable experience. However, I kept my thoughts to myself, unwilling to put them into words. They were too frightening. I sat back, detached, fretful, and worried.

A temporary interruption of my college course gave me an opportunity to recoup my finances by accepting a teaching position. This brought me to a small Iowa community where there was a Catholic church. Probably for no other reason than absorption in my own religious problem, I found myself reading some of the stock volumes of Catholic apologetics, obtained from newly found Catholic friends. Quite vividly do I recall my first reaction to Cardinal Gibbons's well-known *Faith of Our Fathers.* I read it, though it is doubtful if the book has ever had a more supercilious reader. Its conclusions I dismissed summarily; the Catholic Church was false and had to be false. The thought never crossed my mind that she might have something to offer me; she was the last place I would have considered as a source of truth. Nevertheless, I read on, and in some undefinable way was impressed.

As I look back on those days I remember thinking how utterly foolish it was for anyone to attempt any sort of defense of the Church on the basis of facts or logical deductions, and wondering how on earth this prelate, Cardinal Gibbons, could have the effrontery to try it. Still and all, the questions he posed were questions that had been disturbing me, and the answers he gave, as I reluctantly admitted, seemed to fill the bill. Because they were Catholic answers, they had to be wrong, but there they were, in black and white, and they held my attention.

The chain of Catholic reasoning annoyed me by its clever

[35]

linking of fact with fact, deduction with deduction. There was the divinity of Christ, the establishment of a Church by Him, and the conclusion that the Church so founded could never disappear and could not teach error. If the linking was genuine, then the Church must be Christ's Church, authorized to teach me. But of course, I stoutly maintained, there had to be a flaw somewhere. However inevitable the logic, the conclusion could not follow, because my first and last premise was that the Catholic Church was ruled out of court. Not even to myself would I admit that my reading had made a deep and lasting impression upon me. I scoffed at myself for bothering with the Catholic claims at all, but even as I scoffed the fascination grew upon me.

All the bigoted charges that I had ever heard against the Church came back to mind to reinforce my resistance. She was the Scarlet Woman, an impostor, corrupt, even diabolical. Far from being attracted to her, I knew I ought to resent, with all my power, her very existence as an insult to human nature. If, among her impostures, her logic intrigued me, then it was up to me to expose its basic fallacy.

I suppose it must have been at this time that I found myself, one day, actually reasoning in reverse. Since the Church, a priori, was false, and inasmuch as I was unable to disprove her foundation by Christ, then it followed that Christ Himself must have been a mere human being, and a misguided one, at that. He could not have been divine, otherwise the Church of His making could not have failed, as it obviously had. Such reverse reasoning pushed me to a denial of Our Lord's divinity. No longer a bumptious collegian, I could not be happy about this, for it brought a clean break with all Christianity, with the things for which I still retained an unconscious reverence.

If Christ were not God, why should I be interested in Christianity, a merely human religion? My mind turned momentarily to the religion of the Chosen People; was there anything there to hold me? The answer came quickly: If Christ and His transcendental claims were false, there was nothing in Judaism that could claim my allegiance. Similarly, the most cursory glance at the other religious systems of mankind sufficed to justify their abrupt dismissal. I felt myself drifting, drifting into skepticism if not into positive atheism. The very ground seemed insecure beneath my feet; my faith in everything seemed to totter. Yet all this while, and the experience continued through several years, I continued, quite inconsistently, though I hope not hypocritically, to attend Protestant church services. It was a way of trying to force myself to hold on, in the desperate hope that some salvation might be held out for me.

Sheer honesty compelled me, ultimately, to face squarely the root problem of Christ's divinity. As I review, in retrospect, the process of my study, with the limited and imperfect means I had at my disposal, the wonder is not that I reached the correct answer, but that I was able to reach any answer at all. It is quite clear to me now that the grace of God was guiding me through my intellectual inadequacy and the pitfalls of my imperfect theology to a definite conviction of the Godhead of Jesus Christ. This was, at any rate, the outcome of my study, the first and firm step along the road. For me, I concluded, Christ was indeed the Emmanuel, the Incarnate Word. He had come into the world to teach, to guide, and to save me, and I was bound to believe what He had taught, bound to obey whatsoever He had commanded, bound to worship Him according to His own terms.

There was no escaping the inevitability of the logic which, once more, brought me squarely up against the Catholic Church. I had to believe in Christ, but, with an emotion bordering on frenzy, I still sought to find a way not to believe in the Church He had founded. I was looking for a comfortable middle course, one that would be Christian but not Catholic.

My struggles to find that way continued for several years after graduation from college, during most of which time I was teaching in the public schools of Iowa. Here are some of the things I did in my anxiety to escape from the impasse in my thinking. On one occasion I remember browsing in a bookstore in a large city and, with a small-town youth's respect for the learning of the metropolis, asking the attendant for books on the Catholic Church. I was shown several typical works of apologetics, but I explained hastily that I wanted something against the Church—the strongest to be had. I purchased the books that were offered, hurried home, and read them eagerly. They left me completely cold.

On another occasion I called on the pastor of the Protestant church I was attending at the time. I asked him to let me sing in his choir and to keep me so busy with other activities that I would have no time to worry about the Catholic claims, hoping to discover eventually that they were only a passing illusion. He tried, and I believe I can honestly say that I tried, but it was of no use.

Again, I found myself at a summer encampment of the Y.M.C.A., at Lake Geneva, where prominent Protestant leaders were scheduled to speak and hold conferences. By appointment, I called on several of these men and presented my problem, with the distinct plea that they would show me how to "keep out of the Catholic Church." Their answers were varied. Some were patient with me and evidently concerned over my state of mind; others were casual and offhand; one of them ordered me from his presence. I left more discouraged than before.

Naturally enough, my friends were apprehensive. While I kept my questing to myself as much as possible, it was inevitable that some echoes of my struggle should reach them. In all good faith, I am sure, they did their best to head me off, supplying me with even more horrendous disclosures of the evils of Rome than the bookstore had furnished me. I do not recall now if they descended to Maria Monk, but Père Hyacinth was a fairly recent discovery in those days, along with Alfred Loisy and others of the current Modernist dissenting group. Alas, they were wasting their efforts so far as I was concerned. With ever-waning hope, I still consulted men I felt I could trust, ministers and former college professors; always the result was the same—a growing feeling of the inevitability of the step which I yet refused to take.

It was out of such processes of thinking that I was ultimately brought squarely up against a startling question: Is there nothing between the Catholic religion and atheism? If the former is rejected, does the latter become inevitable? Is there no middle ground? Is the Catholic faith the only way of saving me from the loss of all faith and the repudiation of all religion? Is it God's way of saving me and all other men from cynicism and despair? The answer was unescapable. With conclusive finality I admitted to myself that there was nothing between Christ and chaos, nothing between the Catholic faith and atheism.

The realization then struck me that I had been playing the part of a coward. Why should I be afraid of the Catholic Church? If facts and logic converged upon her, if reason demanded her as the answer to my problem, why should I allow my worn-out prejudices to stand in the way? I made up my mind to be fully honest with myself, to face the realities of the situation without flinching. The moment I made that resolution the doubts disappeared. As I was to learn later, I had begun to co-operate with the grace of God.

It was then, as I remember in clear detail, that I reviewed once more the whole process of my thinking. Starting all over again, I set down the premises which were undebatable. As though it was yesterday, I recall sketching my analysis: I believe in God; I need to be taught the truths which He wishes me to believe; since Christ is God and came on earth to teach me this truth, it is to Him I must look. But how does Christ teach me? There could be, I answered, only three ways: (1) by direct and personal revelation; (2) through a written record (the Sacred Scripture); (3) through the agency of men, that is, through an organization commissioned by Him for that purpose.

Did Christ, I asked, teach me by direct revelation? Not that I was aware. Furthermore, if, in spite of this insensitiveness on my part, He really had chosen this means, then He must teach all men in the same way. Honesty of intention and the sincere desire to hear His voice would be the only prerequisites. But how, then, could the fact be explained away that so many men of obvious and unquestionable good will held so many and such contradictory beliefs? With a gesture of finality, I discarded the first possibility.

Did He teach me through the Bible? Here was old ground, well-trodden, thoroughly mulled over. But how was I to know that it was the Bible, the inspired record of God's dealings with men? Perhaps it contained much spurious matter; perhaps its canon was uncertain—books left out which should have been retained, books incorporated which should be rejected. Again, how could I know the real meaning of the many disputed passages? There were, I reminded myself, over two hundred religious groups all claiming the Bible as their font and origin, all asserting their particular interpretations as correct. My common sense repeated, what I already knew, that Christ must have appointed some agent to compose the Sacred Scripture and to interpret its meaning for all men.

Why should I gag, then, at considering calmly and dispassionately the possibility of the third answer, even if it led directly to the Catholic Church? Who else could this appointed teacher be? What could she be but infallible? My right to certitude was as great as that of the fortunate few who heard the Master speak, who saw Him pass along the way. And if He was in truth divine, and if He had appointed His agents to teach and govern and sanctify in His name, He could not help but make them share His infallibility. I needed no biblical texts to bolster my assurance that His Church was founded upon a rock; it could not be otherwise. Her infallibility was as inevitable and as unescapable as His own. It was His own.

Perhaps this is the correct point in my narrative to indicate explicitly how I reacted to the stock argument against the Catholic Church. As my decision became apparent, it was unavoidable that I should be asked for explanations. Why was I attracted to the Church? Did I not know that she had ingloriously failed? How could I get around the facts of history? No doubt the reader is thoroughly informed about the oft-repeated premise that the Catholic Church had been untrue to her divine calling and had failed sometime during early centuries or Middle Ages. (There is no agreement among the critics about when the failure occurred.) The Church fell into evil ways, the argument continues; her ministers became selfish, dishonorable, and corrupt, even a few of the popes falling into public sins. According to the argument, the Church departed from the original Gospel of Christ and introduced spurious doctrines of faith. Therefore, the argument concludes, the Church lost the grace of God and the authority to speak as His agent. A reformation was necessary. The old Church had to be abandoned; a new organization (or organizations?) was needed to lead Christianity back to its pristine purity.

Over and over again I had heard and read this argument. As it failed to hold me back, my friends asked why. Was I ignoring it? Had I closed my mind to obvious facts? Let me say most emphatically that I had not ignored the argument. I had analyzed and studied it to the best of my ability. The result? The more I thought about it, the more illogical it seemed. How was it possible, I asked, for the Church to fail when the divine Lord had guaranteed that she would not fail? But then there were the evil deeds of the Church leaders. What about them? They could not be erased from the record. They were there for all to see and contemplate. Were they not conclusive? They seemed to be conclusive for others; why not for me?

Perhaps these facts were conclusive for me; but, if so, it was in the other direction. If they proved anything, it was that the Catholic Church is indestructible. She must be solid indeed, I reasoned, not to have been destroyed. The Church had lived through enough calamities to annihilate a mere human institution. The salient fact is that she had lived through them, a feat of survival which becomes more extraordinary the more the historical mistakes are played up. The sad experiences of the Church, to which my attention

[41]

had been called, only demonstrated her divine nature. Far from frightening me away from her, they helped open the door for me.

In this same connection there was the defensive claim of the Church that she had not written into her doctrines any effect of the misdeeds of her leaders. Was this true? Let me admit frankly that when this question first came to my mind the facts were hopelessly confused. Posing the question, however, set me in search of facts and pointed my thinking in what I now know to have been the right direction. I knew of other institutions that had accommodated themselves to the records and mistakes of their representatives. In fact, such was the usual experience. Was it true that the Catholic Church was different? Was she the one institution in human history that was foolproof, the one institution that could not be contaminated by the mistakes, no matter how great, of people and clergy?

What about the biblical proof that the Church had amended the gospel and introduced new doctrines? I had been told repeatedly that if I would only read the Bible with an open mind I would see for myself the falsity of Catholic doctrines. By the time in my conversion when this paragraph is pertinent, I had become very impatient with all efforts to disprove the Catholic Church from the Bible. How could the non-Catholic critic, I asked, interpret texts of Scripture more accurately than the Catholic Church? What possible advantage did he have? Could he read Greek manuscripts any better than Catholic scholars? Did he understand New Testament conditions and its Hebrew background any better? Was he in closer touch with Apostolic times? Did he have more complete knowledge of early Church history? The questions answered themselves. All the advantage was on the side of the Church. She had not broken with the past, as the critic had done. She had preserved an unbroken continuity through all generations back to the Apostles. Leaving aside the divine and supernatural protection against error, as promised by Our Lord, the Church had every human and natural advantage in defining the doctrines of faith.

As a matter of course, my attention was called to particular doctrines. How could I believe in praying for the dead? How could I believe in the infallibility of the Pope, in the Eucharist, in indulgences, in the veneration of saints, and in the resurrection of the body? How could I confess my sins to a priest? How could I harmonize the pageantry and elaborate ceremonial of the Church with the humble simplicity of early Christianity? These and other similar questions, which seemed to be particularly interesting to my contemporaries, were put to me. I answered them as best I could. If the truth must be told, however, I did not consider myself capable of running down all the evidence for or against particular doctrines and practices. Such a task would have been prodigious. My mind kept insisting that the way to find the doctrines of faith was to trace down to them from Our Lord and His Church rather than up to them from myself and my limited knowledge.

In fairness to myself, let me say by way of parenthesis that the more I considered and thought about particular doctrines, especially those that had been held before me in warning, the more reasonable they seemed. And yet, I continued to insist, they were true not because I happened to like them but because the Church taught them. As I tried to explain to those who cross-examined me, I had reached the point where I was compelled by force of logic to believe whatever the Church taught, whether I liked it or not and whether it seemed reasonable or not. My thought was centered in Christ and His Church. If He was divine and if He established a Church, neither of which facts I could no longer doubt, then it followed that I was bound to be a member of that Church and to believe what she taught. I must accept the doctrines of the Church precisely because they were doctrines of the Church.

So it was that, at last, I took the step toward which all my thinking had pointed through six years of troubled doubting and distress of soul. Finding myself in Chicago, in the autumn of 1912, enrolled in the law school of the University of Chicago, I sought out the nearest Catholic rectory, St. Thomas the Apostle. I introduced myself to the priest who met me in the parlor (Rev. Michael Shea) and asked for admission into the Catholic Church, expressing my eagerness to take all the instructions which were required. My time for reading was limited, but the fundamentals were already so fixed in my mind that all the rest followed with the ease of completing a picture puzzle once the key had been discovered. I am afraid I was a somewhat disappointing convert to my instructor. His battles were all over before I had rung his doorbell.

Here I must pause to relate one very unusual and pleasing incident. Shortly after I began my formal instructions in the catechism, a few good friends prevailed upon me to consult a certain prominent Protestant minister who lived near the university. They were disturbed about me and hoped that with his help they could turn me aside from my charted course. So it was that one evening, with these friends, I engaged in a long discussion about religion; it lasted half the night. In the debate, I was not only outnumbered, about four to one, I was outpointed. I was sure that I had made a poor showing of my reasons for becoming a Catholic. At the conclusion of the session, however, the minister made a most extraordinary statement, one that must have surprised my friends as completely as it did me: "My advice for you," he said, "is to go into the Catholic Church as soon as possible. Your mind is Catholic. You can be nothing else." If I could recall his name, I would publicize it now, in appreciation of his broad-mindedness.

My baptism (January 1913) was a private ceremony, witnessed by the priest and my sponsor only. My first Communion at an early Mass the next morning likewise was unnoticed, as I expected and wished. No one was interested in what I was doing. My coming into the Catholic Church was unannounced. It attracted no attention; it deserved none.

The rest of my story, being aside from the purpose of this

present writing, may be dismissed with a few words. Sometime in the spring of 1913, I signed up to teach at the University of Utah in Salt Lake City. When I went there in the fall of that same year I had not the slightest expectation that from then on my life would be set in Utah. The only plan I had, in so far as I can remember, was to teach there a year or two and then take more postgraduate work in my newly chosen department, that of Public Speaking, looking to some higher scholastic degrees.

It was soon apparent, however, that God and my own inclinations had charted an entirely different course for me. One day I was suddenly aware of a discovery: the only thing that I was really interested in was the Catholic religion. I thought about it; talked about it, whenever I could find a listener; I read about it; I consulted priests to learn more about it; I was deeply concerned about its welfare; I wished to be a factor in its progress. I found myself impatient with non-Catholics, amazed that they could resist the magnificent appeal and logical claims of the Church. Perhaps, I said to myself, if I could state clearly and correctly the position of the Church, perhaps someday I could win other converts to her fold. Here was a new challenge. Together with the realization that the Catholic Church meant more to me than anything and everything else in the world, it led me to the necessity of another decision.

This time I made no effort to resist the will of God. After a reasonable period of testing myself, necessary for certainty, I called on the Bishop of Salt Lake, the Most Reverend Joseph S. Glass, C.M., D.D., and asked to be adopted as a seminarian. Being accepted, I was sent to St. Patrick's Seminary, Menlo Park, California, where I studied under the Sulpician Fathers. I was ordained in June of 1920 for the Diocese of Salt Lake.

If certain of my former Protestant friends and acquaintances chance to read this story, I trust that they will find in it the answer to the question which at one time was in their minds. They wondered, some of them at least, if I would not be disappointed in the Church. Well do I remember the warning they held over me. I was attracted to the Church, they insisted, only because I did not know her as she really was. Someday, if I should enter the Church, which God forbid, I would be sadly disillusioned. Then, when it was too late, the real character of the Church would be exposed, with the mask of virtue torn off. What a pity for me to choose a course which could have but one end: heartaches and bitter regrets!

On the other hand, there were one or two close friends who were most helpful to me, a help which I wish I could acknowledge to them directly. They gave me the opportunity, through repeated discussions and arguments, to clarify my thinking. They understood the problem I was trying to solve and, although they did not approve of the step I was contemplating, they expected me to be honest and to follow my conscience. They would be genuinely sorry if the Catholic faith had not proved to be the answer to my quest.

If any reassurance is needed for them, let it be seen in my life as a priest. As to whether or not my priesthood has been and is useful, only God can judge. But at least it gives me the opportunity to save my own soul. Certainly it is a thrilling adventure. It demands the best that I have, indeed far more than I or any other man has to give; but its rewards are superlative.

I close with this further comment. The more I know about the Church the more do I regret that I lost so much time coming within her fold. Without intending the slightest reflection on my parents, I have wished many times that I had had the good fortune to be born and reared a Catholic. Perhaps my point of view is sufficiently expressed in the motto I chose to mark my episcopacy: "Through the Church to God."

HOUSE OF LIGHT

Lucile Hasley

Lucile Hasley combines the duties of a wife and mother with those of a popular writer of short stories, articles, and essays. Born in 1909 in South Bend, she has spent most of her life there. She was educated at Milwaukee-Downer College, and at the University of Wisconsin, where she majored in art. In 1935 she married Louis Hasley, a writer, a professor of English, and assistant dean of the College of Arts and Letters at the University of Notre Dame. The Hasleys have three children: Susan, Janet, and Danny.

It was a long illness that started Mrs. Hasley on her literary career. The products of her gifted pen have appeared in *Sign*, *Extension*, *Catholic Digest*, *Woman's Day*, and *Mademoiselle*. While she has written serious short stories, which have been reproduced in various anthologies, Mrs. Hasley is more widely known for her light personal essays written in a sprightly and entertaining style.

In 1948 she won the first prize in the Catholic Press Association short-story contest, which brought in thirty-one hundred entries, with her "The Little Girls."

"If I have any literary standard at all," remarks Lucile modestly, "it is this. I consider it a mortal sin to bore people. Somehow I seem to goad people into leaping to their typewriters, and my mailbox is liable to yield most anything. Nothing surprises me any more. I get threats, boos, jeers, from those who would like to excommunicate me; I get lavish bouquets (strangely enough) from the clergy; I receive gifts, advice, and prayers from the solicitous. . . . I think the two extremes have been fan letters from Una O'Connor, the Hollywood character actress, and a request from the Holy City for an article on the missions in Nigeria."

Mrs. Hasley was one of the organizers of the Blessed Martin

Study Club, composed equally of white and Negro women, who meet biweekly in the homes of one another for the study and discussion of various aspects of Catholic thought and life.

Recognizing the wide following which her writings had won for her, Sheed and Ward brought out in 1948 a volume of her articles, *Reproachfully Yours*, which is further enhancing her reputation as a literary artist with a distinctive style—sprightly, vivacious, and always interesting.

A "WHY I BECAME" conversion story is generally the first project on a convert's agenda, but I, in my writing, have always skated neatly around the subject. It was *my* story: personal to a degree, important only to myself, and almost embarrassing in its simplicity. Alongside the soul-wrestling, truth-ferreting, pillar-to-post epics of other converts, it would sound like *Little Red Ridinghood* compared to Tolstoy's *War and Peace*.

Yet this is not to imply, heaven forbid, that I didn't *like* my own story. To me, it was a fascinating demonstration of the inscrutable ways of God: suddenly thrusting the gift of faith into the surprised hands of a *most* unlikely candidate. It was just that I saw no need (nor did I have the heart) to expose my own witless role in the whole proceedings.

In now doing so (thanks to the inscrutable ways of editors), I can only hope that my non-intellectual approach to the Church will have, if nothing else, a certain air of novelty about it. Maybe the reading public doesn't even *know* that conversions like mine take place?

In other words, I am outside the pale of that intellectually respectable league of converts who can say, "It was Augustine who led the way," or "Aristotle left me strangely dissatisfied," or "The shackles fell from my eyes when I first read the *Summa* in the original," or "After twenty years as a Communist I one day chanced to read the Pope's Encyclical on Labor," or "My years of intensive biblical research finally led me to question private interpretation," et cetera, et cetera.

My sole intellectual approach to the Church consisted in lifting a finger and pushing the buzzer at a Catholic rectory. True, I wasn't trying to sell Fuller brushes, but I can't say that I had anything much heavier on my mind. I pushed that buzzer guided by little more than my woman's intuition (a valuable faculty that philosophers refuse to recognize) that here, perhaps, was the place to fulfill my part of a childish bargain.

Thus, in a very literal sense, I can say in the words of Bloy: "For my part, I declare that I never sought or found anything unless one wishes to describe as a discovery the fact of tripping blindly over a threshold and being thrown flat on one's stomach into the House of Light."

Six weeks later I, a twenty-one-year-old Presbyterian, was baptized a Catholic. In retrospect, I would be tempted to say—if it were not for my profound respect for the doctrine of Divine Providence—that it was all a matter of sheer fool's luck and nothing else.

All convert stories, in the telling, seem to fall into sharp divisions: the "man pursues God" versus the "God pursues man" plot. Yet something tells me that *all* converts—even the most "self-made" ones—will, in the lucid light of Eternity, see their little plots as a clear-cut case of God pursuing *them*.

I am perfectly aware that this is an attitude that frequently irritates, even scandalizes, the more "humble" citizens. "You mean," they say, "that God was paying all that attention to *you?*" To which, as far as I can figure out, there is only one truly humble answer: "Yes." And I think that this open-faced acknowledgment—with its "You have not chosen Me, I have chosen you" implication—is one of the most stirring aspects of conversion.

I bring this up for the benefit of brand-new converts or those outsiders who are making a first tentative move toward the Church. I think they sense this drawing power— this thrilling and personal feeling that God has, so to speak,

[49]

put His finger on them—but are almost afraid to think it out loud. Presumption! Enough to make the high priests rend their garments! Yet, how they'd like to believe it.

To those timid souls I say: "Go on. Believe it." Not only is it the truth, based on straight doctrine, but it begets a deeper gratitude and a deeper gratitude, in turn, begets a deeper love of God.

Therefore, when I say that I—entirely under my own steam—pushed that rectory buzzer, don't get me wrong. I have no illusions whatsoever that I, despite my splendid steam, engineered the whole project by myself. All *I* really did (as will be explained later) was to keep my part of a bargain and . . . God was not to be outdone in generosity.

There is also the possibility that Catholicism, like a hidden virus, was already in my blood stream. As I later discovered, I *should* have been a Catholic all along. My mother had been baptized a Catholic, but *her* heritage, while she was still a small child, and through no one's fault, had also been lost by the wayside. Then along came her marriage to a staunch Presbyterian who couldn't abide Catholics, and that was that.

So, with my father a Presbyterian deacon and my mother a "fallen-away" Catholic, my three brothers and I automatically became little Presbyterians. Very bored and automatic ones, too. God (a vague character, He) belonged strictly in Sunday school—and Sunday school, with just its Moses in the Bulrushes stories, was pretty deadly. Any resemblance between those stories and a personal vital religion was purely coincidental.

With great relief would I loudly and busily help fold up the collapsible chairs at the close of each session. True, there still remained the grown-up sermon, in the regular church pews, to squirm through, but the halfway mark—the folding-up-chairs stage—at least represented a cheering note of time marching on.

I cannot claim to have closely examined, in my youth, the Presbyterian tenets of belief and found them wanting. But if I *had* wanted to examine them, I'm sure it would have taken considerable research first to find them. For instance, the only "doctrinal quiz"—in order to graduate into the Intermediate Department—was to memorize St. Paul's "Now I see as through a glass darkly" epistle to the Corinthians. Nothing could have been more appropriate.

In the Senior Department my glass grew even darker. I remember, in particular, how darkly irritating were the "Thought for the Week" bulletins that were posted in the front churchyard. The most irritating one was "God Is Love."

I remember thinking they had the verb wrong. Did they mean "God is lovable" or "God represents love" or "God wants love" or "God loves us" or what? "God *Is* Love" was certainly a senseless tidbit to throw at a person.

Since becoming a Catholic, I have discovered (especially through Thomas Merton) that "God Is Love" is one of the most bona fide, most metaphysical, most "heart of the matter" statements in all theology. But my Presbyterian teachers never attempted (and with very good reason, probably) to explain it. God, *in himself,* was never discussed. Perhaps they felt that St. Paul, with his dark mirror, meant you shouldn't even *try* to investigate God?

What you *could* do, though, was investigate and weigh and examine the current minister. (Did he smoke? Chew? Drink? Play cards? Vote the Democratic ticket? On the positive side, did he have a firm handshake? Resonant voice? A way with the kiddies?) The current minister, not God, was the one to keep your eye on.

It is more than possible, of course, that I was an extremely religion-resistant child, but the point remains that I scorned every inch of that church. I can still see the big gilt organ pipes and the minister's platform with its wooden pulpit, flanked by the American flag at one end and a potted palm at the other. Empty, empty boredom.

Stage properties, naturally, have nothing to do with religion per se, but I have since been in incredibly ugly and garish Catholic churches and still found what was needed. A sense of prayer and a sense of mystery. One need not even

[51]

know about the Blessed Sacrament to catch the general idea that *here* is a place to kneel, not just sit and be talked *to*.

Or prayed *at*. Prayer in my Presbyterian church consisted in slightly lowering your chin while the minister, raising his chin, did your praying for you. There was never so much as even three minutes' quiet during the entire service to "freewheel" on your own. And yet they talk about that personal and direct Protestant approach to God!

May all good Protestant readers forgive me my vehemence. *It is, by no means, a blanket indictment.* It's just a personal recording of what *I* found in my own Presbyterian church. (Or, rather, *didn't* find. Neither, apparently, did my three brothers find anything. Today two of them have no religion, while the third one attends, in desultory fashion, a church that currently has an eloquent minister and an outstanding drama department.)

When I went off to Milwaukee-Downer College ("An institution of higher learning for cultured and refined young ladies"), I was happy indeed to leave my "religion" behind me. But what did I find awaiting me? Not only daily nonsectarian chapel (with the same pulpit, American flag, and potted palm), but the ruling that we *had* to attend some Milwaukee church every Sunday. It wasn't even done on the honor system; there were monitors to flush you out of your room at ten-thirty. So, to relieve the tedium, I went—with a beautiful impartiality—to a different Protestant church each week, and when I had run the gamut I quit.

Thereafter I cheated. When it came time for church I hid in my clothes closet, sitting cross-legged on the floor, and spent the time reading by flashlight. I preferred sitting there, amid laundry bags and tennis shoes and with my dresses batting me about the ears, to a church of any kind.

Two years later I switched to the University of Wisconsin, the so-called "Playground of the Middle West." Here, certainly, there was no need to hide in any closets. All the while I was at Madison, I darkened no church door and, naturally, wouldn't have been caught dead saying any private prayers.

Now, at long last, I was "free." Life, for me, came to mean only clothes, dancing, men, and the number of prom bids and fraternity pins one could collect in a season. As far as anything spiritual went, I was just waltzing along . . . not searching, not interested, not even aware that anything was missing.

There was just one little thing, at Wisconsin, that might have indicated that Divine Providence was closing in on me. In my Gamma Phi Beta sorority there were only a few Catholics, and I, Lucile, had to draw one for a roommate: a McCarthy!

When I discovered, in quick order, that I had drawn not only a Catholic but a naïve little Bernadette, I felt that I was putting up with a great deal. Perhaps we would be in the thick of one of those bull sessions (What is the meaning of Life-Sex-Art?) out on the smoking porch. Suddenly I'd look around. Where was the roommate? It would irk me that she would slip quietly away, sincerely not interested in our final judicious verdicts. She would also slip quietly away in the middle of a risqué story.

Then, too, she embarrassed me not only by actually kneeling down to say her night prayers, glass rosary in hand, but in going about it as earnestly as if she were calling God, or one of his saints, on the telephone. She never paraded or explained her religion (and I let well enough alone), but every once in a while she'd say things, weird little things. If I were upset over something, she'd say casually, "Don't worry. I offered up my Communion for you this morning." Or "I'll remember to ask the Little Flower to help you out." I never said much more than "Umm" to any of this, and she never expected more. But (believe me!) I would have said more than "Umm" if she had ever said outright: "I am praying for your soul." (Perhaps the most enraging remark in the English language.)

The *pièce de résistance,* however, was the way she—a bright, pretty, popular, and apparently normal girl—would get up in the morning and tiptoe off to Mass, rain or shine. Sunday was all right . . . Catholics were *forced* to go on

[53]

Sundays . . . but this was during the week, for Pete's sake. Ah well, it took all kinds to make a world. . . .

Only it was odd the way I began to regard one of my English instructors with growing distaste. His was a class in Renaissance Satire, and some of these little classics of Erasmus and Rabelais were crawling with innuendoes (to put it mildly!) against my roommate's religion.

Well, no one loves a nice vicious satire more than I, but for some odd reason I began to feel a little huffy and defensive. I felt defensive on behalf of defenseless McCarthy in much the same way as I would blindly defend an underdog. McCarthy was an underdog because she was saddled, from birth, with a religion that could only mean a hard life for a female.

Poor McCarthy! Never any reasonable divorce, never any reasonable birth control. I could only picure the worst: poor McCarthy chained for life to some drunken brute who beat her every Saturday night; drearily bearing an unwanted child every year because the Church demanded it.

Since this caricature was the sum total of my knowledge of Catholicism, small wonder I felt sorry for McCarthy. At the same time, as I say, I began to resent that professor's witty and mocking remarks in class. Catholicism might be a hard and backward religion, but it didn't strike me as one to be treated as a joke. Something also told me (that valuable faculty that philosophers refuse to recognize?) that Erasmus and Rabelais were not presenting the whole of Catholicism. I could see for myself that my roommate seemed to be living another version.

Finally one day I let loose on a term paper. I did a beautiful job of abusing the Church (later receiving an "A" for my efforts) and then, at the bottom of the paper, I wrote belligerently: "Okay. Here's your paper, but someday *I'm* going to be one of these Catholics."

Why I wrote that, I'll never know. Naturally I intended no such thing. Perhaps I just wanted to show that "laughing boy" of a professor that I wasn't swallowing everything hook, line, and sinker.

[54]

I was completely happy, having a wonderful time on the shores of Lake Mendota, wearing a Protestant's fraternity pin, and God (that vague character, He) was the least of my worries. One's broken-down old age was time a-plenty for looking into the "life is real and life is earnest" stuff.

Nevertheless, just four months after writing that thoughtless and belligerent threat on my term paper, I *was* baptized a Catholic. This, I feel, calls for a little explanation.

In my last semester I suddenly became mysteriously ill and was sent home from college. Not only was I alarmed and frightened by the illness, but I was upset at the possibility of not getting back with my graduating class. The doctors only shrugged their shoulders as I entered the clinic for treatments, and so, alone and frightened, I had but one alternative. I wrote McCarthy not only to send home my trunk but send *up* some of her prayers.

I also decided to pray for myself (what did I have to lose?), but I found out it wasn't so easy. God had, by now, become a mere will-o'-the-wisp, and I felt very awkward and foolish and *alone* in my approach. I wavered uneasily between the notion that there must be some sort of a God and the feeling that I was addressing thin air. I felt very much as Emily Dickinson had expressed it:

> Of course I prayed
>   And did God care?
> He cared as much as if a tiny bird
> Had stamped his foot upon the air
> And cried "Give me!"

Moreover, I had just enough Emily Post in me to be socially embarrassed about the "Give me!" situation. How have the nerve to beg help from someone you'd never paid any attention to? Someone, in fact, who had bored you to distraction all your life?

So, to save face, I struck a bargain. "God," said I, "whoever and wherever you are, *if* you'll deliver me from this unknown plague, I promise, on my word of honor, to investigate you."

Thank God I kept that promise. By April I was cured, and as soon as the last bandages were removed I hied myself to a priest. Not only had I never talked to one before, but I *still* don't know why I thought a Roman Catholic priest was the logical person to explain God to me. Certainly my Renaissance Satire class hadn't extolled the Roman clergy!

Moreover, I still wasn't particularly interested in God or too profoundly grateful for my recovery. I was just, uneasily, keeping my part of a solemn bargain.

One session with that priest and God became the most exciting and absorbing topic in the world. My attitude was not so much *"Prove* God exists, priest!" as "Can you make God seem real, priest?"

He could. Not in the sense that he *reduced* God's mystery, but that he *increased* my conception of the staggering "Before Abraham was, I am" reality of the mystery. There was, I found, a vast difference between "fuzziness" and "mystery."

Naturally I had no penetrating theological questions on tap to disconcert and floor that priest. I couldn't even think (my mind was so barren) of any particular problems I wanted solved. So the Church, ever solicitous, *presented* me with problems. One of the first questions in the Catechism was a honey: "Why was I born?"

After letting me flounder around for a while ("To do good? To develop one's personality? To seek Beauty, whatever that might be?"), the Church gave me the answer in one sentence: "To know God, to love Him, to serve Him in this world and be happy with Him forever in the next." Then the Church, ever solicitous, started turning on the floodlights. . . .

Never was there any apology or hedging or timidity or compromising behind those floodlights. There was no "It is generally conceded" or "We feel perhaps that this doctrine is the more reasonable of the two" preamble to anything. The Church was *positive* it had the right answers and the Divine right to guard those right answers.

After nineteen years, it is difficult to remember just what it was in Catholic apologetics—that firm, logical, relentless, brick-upon-brick, apologetical "stacking-up"—that impressed me most. One doesn't stand at the foot of Pikes Peak and say: "Ah, isn't that sixth crag from the top impressive?" For me, it was the impressive *whole*.

What I most vividly remember is that, after only a few sessions, I was positive I *wanted* to become a Catholic. I wanted to become a Catholic so badly that I became frightened lest—any minute!—I was going to hit a doctrine I couldn't accept. Even after I became convinced of the infallibility of the Church, I was still afraid. I might grant that the Church *had* to be right—and I, therefore, wrong—but I just might prefer to *be* wrong.

When we arrived at the doctrine of Transubstantiation, a cold chill ran down my backbone. This was it! This finished me off! I arose from that session—very quiet, very subdued —and went home and read, as per instructions, the sixth chapter of St. John over again. After several readings I could only agree with the Jews that it was a hard saying, and I didn't blame them for turning away. I, too, must turn sadly away, but still I would go back for one more session.

On that next session the priest happened to take me into the Log Chapel at Notre Dame. (I'd lived in South Bend all my life but had never been anywhere on the campus except in the football stadium.) He was giving me the tourist's tour—pointing out the burial place of the first priest ordained in the United States, the Indian murals on the walls, the ancient altars—when I (only half listening to him) suddenly burst out with what was really on my mind. It was that old time-honored Protestant question: "If Catholics really believe that God is really and truly present on their altars, why don't they *crawl* into church on their hands and knees?"

And suddenly I knew, with a shock, that what I was really thinking was: "Why aren't *we* on our hands and knees, right this minute, instead of standing here like tourists?"

It is impossible for me to explain this sudden turn-about-face. All I know is that the Blessed Sacrament, all these past nineteen years, has been the strongest point in my faith.

After the Transubstantiation crisis, I felt only a great urgency to be baptized immediately.

One might well think that the swiftness and impulsiveness of my conversion boded no good. This could never last! All I can say, lamely, is: "Well, but it *did*." Moreover, I resent those people who always quote: "First fervor is always false fervor." If that be an infallible rule, then practically all of the New Testament conversions were mighty shallow affairs. Too, those New Testament conversions were very *speedy* affairs. Christ's apologetics were often just two words: "Follow me," and his listeners fell over their own feet to do so.

But back to my own story. That June, instead of receiving my diploma as an art student, I received the seven gifts of the Holy Ghost. Who is to say I didn't get the best of the bargain? Moreover, one year later my mother took instructions and—after forty-seven years—returned to the fold. One year later I met and married a very solid "born Catholic," Louis Hasley, an English instructor at Notre Dame.

Two children arrived in quick succession, and the following years were more involved with pursuing *them* than in pursuing higher theology. All went smoothly as far as the Catholicism was concerned, with never a doubt or a problem on the horizon. As I now look back, it was just *too* smooth. I now look back on this period as The Great Lull.

I had enough Catholicism to operate on but not enough to "grow on." The straight apologetics were now fairly well under control (I'd belonged to a Catholic study club for six years), but apologetics, as I now see it, are only a necessary prelude. After digging the cellar, you should go ahead and build your spiritual house.

Six years ago, into this Great Lull there suddenly came another one of those neatly camouflaged blessings. I suddenly found myself flat on my back with a heart condition that the specialists cheerfully assured me was permanent. From now on I would be a heart cripple and a semi-invalid.

There is nothing, I maintain, like staring at the ceiling for four weary months, thinking that Life has ended up a blind alley, to make one's disposition become either very submissive or completely rebellious. I was the rebellious sort. This was a fine trick for God to play on a friend who was just minding her own business and not hurting anyone.

I now concede it *was* a fine trick. It was lying there in bed, reading everything and anything I could get my paws on, that I stumbled across a veritable gold mine: *good* Catholic writing. Bernanos, Péguy, Mauriac, Bloy, Sigrid Undset, Chesterton, Caryll Houselander, and others. These gifted writers could, in one flashing metaphor, illuminate certain truths that the theologians and philosophers—with their dry, measured approach—simply deadened for me.

Even more important, from my standpoint, were the saint writers who could tell you how to build spiritual houses: St. Teresa of Avila, Francis De Sales, St. John of the Cross, Elizabeth of the Trinity, Catherine of Siena. Doors started opening on doors. . . .

At this point the practical reader may ask: "With a born Catholic husband, teaching English in a big Catholic university, *why* this belated discovery of the Catholic classics?"

I, too, ask "Why?" For years I had been dusting some of those very books I was now so enraptured over. Why hadn't my husband told me to quit my infernal dusting and read them? Why hadn't the priest who converted me left me with a spiritual reading list? Why hadn't *anyone* told me these things?

Lying there in bed, I began to get a little bit annoyed at all born Catholics. A selfish, selfish crew. Finally I could contain myself no longer and, calling for pencil and pad, I furiously composed my first Catholic essay. If no one would share the hidden wealth with converts, *I* would look after them.

That first essay of mine would have made the scholarly Newman turn over in his grave. It was very much like writing a book on Mexico after spending only a week end across the Rio Grande border.

When I showed it to the priest who came over to the house to bring me Holy Communion, he practically collapsed with uncouth mirth. "No Catholic editor in his right

mind," said he, "would print this but . . . well, you might
try. It's . . . uh . . . rather refreshing."

Lo! To my great amazement, this housewife suddenly
found herself a so-called Catholic writer overnight. Personal
essays started sliding off my bedspread with an alarming
rapidity, and no one, to date, has managed to stem the tide.

But let us not leave me in bed. After four months of this
feverish one-man Catholic revival (hardly recommended
for heart ailments), I arose from my pallet and went to the
Ann Arbor Clinic to see how many more months I had left to
live.

Although I was so weak I could hardly walk, I gathered—
from their reports—that they had seldom seen a finer speci-
men of rugged American womanhood. My heart was not
only in splendid condition—splendid!—but they didn't think
anything had been wrong in the first place.

My first reaction was nothing short of murderous. Sticking
a busy housewife and mother in bed for four months for no
good reason! My second reaction, as the blood pressure sub-
sided, was a little more mellow. That session in bed had
amounted to a "second conversion," and, like missing my
diploma years before, I had come out ahead in the bargain.
I had discovered, among other things, the existence of
Ascetical and Mystical Theology: meaning that precise,
well-documented, well-illustrated study of the spiritual life.
"Why was I born?" The saints thought it was in order to
start becoming a saint and were only too eager to point the
way.

I had, in particular, discovered gentle Francis De Sales,
and De Sales had urged: "If thou wouldst walk in earnest
toward devotion, find some good man to conduct and guide
thee." That is, a personal spiritual director.

I'd never heard of such a thing before, but it seemed like
a sound idea. Since you can't see yourself as you really are,
better ask a professional to take a look. The result might be
(and in truth proved to be!) quite startling: like turning a
flashlight on a dark cobwebby corner and watching the

spiders run for cover. Self-love, pride, impatience, intolerance . . .

But if I thought that a spiritual director would immediately put me on a very interesting monastic schedule of some sort, and that I would become lean, holy, and ascetical in three easy lessons, I was to be disillusioned. My monastic schedule—with the exception of frequent weekday Mass and Communion, *if* it didn't interfere—proved to be a firm turning back to the kitchen sink. However, I learned that I was to return to my accustomed state of life with a new Catholic awareness and set of values, thus shifting gears from the purely natural to the supernatural.

One day I happened to hear Ann Harrigan, then director of the Chicago Friendship House, give a talk on the Mystical Body, with special reference to race prejudice. Once again I found myself profoundly jarred. I had been busily polishing my own little soul (or, rather, starting to sand off the sharper edges) but not paying any attention to anyone else. Was I, as a Catholic, being the salt of the earth, my brother's keeper, a Christ-bearer into the market place? Not so you could notice.

This first introduction to the Lay Apostolate, along with my subsequent close friendship and work with Ann Harrigan, proved another turn in the road. I was now—at long last!—getting God, self, and neighbor into the proper Catholic focus, but new converts to the Church today needn't take as long as I to do it. Since the war there has been a great stirring of the waters: a new awareness, along all fronts, of the urgent need to restore all things in Christ. It is not the time for an ivory-tower Catholicism. Catholics are called to spread Christ's fire upon the earth; not just hug their wonderful gift of faith to themselves.

Only in a very limited sense can one say at Baptism: "Here's the finale. Peace, it's wonderful." The Church offers peace, yes, but if it's just a rocking-chair sort of peace you're after, I would recommend some nice quiet sanitarium in the hills of New Hampshire rather than the Roman Catholic Church.

Baptism is only the beginning: the orchestra tuning up; the curtain rising on the most important and absorbing drama in the world, man's relationship with God. As Chesterton says: "Have you ever known what it is to walk along a road in such a frame of mind that you thought you might meet God at any turn of the path? For this a man must be ready, against this he must never shut the door." A perpetual receptiveness; not a placid "Peace, it's wonderful" closing of the door.

It is precisely this wonderful, endless exploration *along the right road* that I, personally, would hold out to people interested in Catholicism. "Peace" is perhaps the last word to come to my mind. I can think only in terms of the adventure, the aliveness, the challenge, the diversity, and—*yes!*—the joyousness of the Catholic way of life.

COMING HOME

Avery Robert Dulles

Avery Robert Dulles, the youthful author of *A Testimonial to Grace,* was born at Auburn, New York, in 1918. Upon the completion of grammar school in New York City, he attended preparatory schools in Switzerland and New England and, in 1936, entered Harvard College. While in boarding school and college, his summer home was on Long Island, New York, but he spent large parts of his summers traveling in Europe or cruising by sail on the Great Lakes and in the Gulf of St. Lawrence.

After graduation from college, he entered Harvard Law School in the autumn of 1940 and, in November of that year, was received into the Catholic Church. Upon the entrance of the United States into the war in December 1941, he interrupted his law course to join the navy. He spent much of the war period on submarine chasers in the Caribbean and, later, in staff and liaison work in the Mediterranean theater.

Immediately upon being released from active duty in August 1946, Mr. Dulles entered the Society of Jesus at St. Andrew-on-Hudson, Poughkeepsie, New York. He has completed a two-year novitiate and, at present writing, is in the course of his philosophy studies at Woodstock College, Woodstock, Maryland, preparing for the priesthood.

While at sea in the Mediterranean, during some weeks of relative leisure following the invasion of southern France in the summer of 1944, Avery wrote a short account of his conversion. Entitled *A Testimonial to Grace,* and published by Sheed and Ward in 1946, it attracted widespread attention and brought forth high praise from the general public as well as from literary critics.

Reviewing it in the *Tidings,* that discerning critic, Father John S. Kennedy, observed: "Others have written in greater detail of their journey home, but none that I know of has been so pellucid as to essentials and so exact in analyzing and articulating the

[63]

constituent elements of a conversion. The book is particularly interesting because it shows the way, step by step, out of the morass of modern doubt and delusion to the lighted uplands." It is a little masterpiece, *multum in parvo.*

He has likewise written a monograph on the Italian Renaissance philosopher, Pico della Mirandola, published in 1941 by the Harvard University Press under the title *Princeps Concordiae;* his study of "Religious Pragmatism" was published by the *Journal of Religious Instruction.* His full-time job for some years ahead is the study of philosophy and theology and the mastering of the most fascinating science in the world—the science of saints. When the goal of the priesthood has been reached, we may be sure that his pen will find further opportunity to carry to more of the churchless people of our country a knowledge of divine revelation in its fullness and beauty.

W HO'S AFRAID of ghosts, anyway?" exclaimed my ten-year-old sister as she and I were playing croquet on the lawn of our summer cottage in Connecticut. "When people die they are put in a grave and they *can't* walk around the way ghosts are supposed to."

"When I die"—I glanced proudly about the sun-drenched lawn as I answered my older sister—"I'm going to become the *Holy* Ghost."

"Sh! Why, Avery, you can't say that. Joking that way is a sin. And Jesus said that if you sin against the Holy Ghost you can't ever get to heaven."

"What? Not get to heaven! I didn't mean anything wrong. I was just kidding."

I went into the house and up to my room. A few minutes later I walked into my sister's room, my eyes streaming with tears.

"What's the matter with you, Avery?" she asked. "What are you crying for?"

"My sins. I'm so sorry to have hurt God by all my sins. I have been bad so many times."

"Don't worry, Avery; and stop crying. God will forgive you if you love Him."

In some such dialogue as this, I received, at the age of six, the earliest lesson in theology that I can remember. My sister's correction, which made up in love for whatever it may have lacked in discretion, is but one of many recollections which make me appreciate with what strong religious influences I was surrounded in my childhood. As the son of Presbyterian parents, and the grandson of a minister, I received, a few days after being born, the priceless gift of Baptism. As a little child I was not tucked into bed without my mother having knelt at my bedside with me to recite the Our Father.

Hardly had I learned to read when, on an evening that I still remember vividly, my sister introduced me to the Sermon on the Mount. " 'Consider the lilies of the field,' " she read from the book while my eyes followed. " 'They toil not, neither do they spin. Yet Solomon in all his glory was not arrayed as one of these.' Isn't that beautiful?" Yes, I was thinking, and how true! No king was ever so splendidly clad as the flowers in springtime, and they don't do anything but let God take care of them. So why should we get all worried about things like that? . . . My sister handed me the copy of St. Matthew's Gospel from which she had been reading, a little book bound in red paper, and told me to keep it for myself. I put it in my night table and used to read a little of it nearly every night, my heart brimful of the love of God.

From this rather promising start I became, in the course of ten years of schooling, a very different sort of young man from what might have been expected. The change for the worse began to appear in my grammar-school days in New York City. Every Sunday, during this phase of my life, I used to be taken to a Presbyterian church on Park Avenue. I rather enjoyed the walk there, as a member of the family group led by my father in top hat and morning coat, but during the services that followed my mind would be woolgathering somewhere on another planet. As for Sunday school, after several miserable experiments, I simply refused to be sent there again.

I did continue to read the Bible—particularly the colorful

stories of the prophets and kings of the Old Testament—but not under very religious circumstances. Generally this reading was done at night, when I was supposed to be asleep, by means of a lamp buried under my covers.

During these years I occasionally prayed, and even offered God little sacrifices (I could not understand why one time, when I wanted to give God a bright new dime which I had received, He refused to make it vanish into thin air!). In moments of loneliness at school, I would think how different Jesus was from my classmates who were always teasing and bullying.

I was vaguely aware of the Catholic Church as that which our servants used to attend. While I never suspected that Catholicism might be meant for me, I was not consciously prejudiced against it. In fact, I can remember that one Christmas, when I wanted to show kindness to two of our Irish maids, I went to the ten-cent store and bought them some brightly colored pictures of the Madonna and Child. At my gift they were amused, surprised, and, I think, somewhat moved. Is it possible that they said a prayer, since granted, that I might one day come to love the Mother of God and have a picture of her for myself?

During the second decade of my life, while receiving an excellent schooling, I gradually lost my love of God and even, though it is painful to write the words, my belief in His existence. At the age of eleven I left grammar school with my memory amply stocked with English poems and my mind well drilled in parsing and Latin declensions. I was then sent to school in Switzerland. During my two years there I traveled considerably on the continent, and from these travels, particularly a six-week Easter holiday in Italy, gained a lasting love for Renaissance painting. I was fascinated by color and design, perspective and foreshortening, but for some reason untouched by the religious themes celebrated by the old masters. I enjoyed visiting churches, but looked upon them as just a species of museum. I never adverted to the spirit of faith which had moved men to build

such magnificent cathedrals and abbeys, cloisters and bap-
tistries, for the glory of God. I do not remember even being
aware that there were persons praying to a God sacra-
mentally present on the altars which we so admired for their
workmanship.

We arrived in Rome about ten days before Easter. Many
of the finest statues and murals in the churches were veiled
in purple.

"That's because it is Passiontide, dear," my mother explained. "In memory of Christ's sufferings, the Church goes
into mourning at this season every year."

In my impatience to see the works of art, I am afraid that
I only half understood. Some years were to pass before, as a
Catholic, I entered for the first time into the spirit of Pas-
siontide.

At school my best friend was an Austrian Catholic who
wore a medal of Our Blessed Lady about his neck. Perhaps
he could have taught me something of the Church, but I
casually assumed that his religion was to him no more than
mine was now to me. And mine at this stage involved no
clear beliefs or, on weekdays, any distinctive practices. On
Sundays the Protestant students in the school would be sent
to the village church. There we would spend an hour of restless fidgeting while the minister preached in a foreign language about matters of small interest to children like ourselves.

From Switzerland, I returned as a lad of thirteen for four
more years of boarding school in New England. The only
courses for which I did much work there were those in English literature, a subject taught by able and inspiring teachers. I read rather widely and solidly for my age, but rather
too far above my head. As a result, a year or two before
graduation I began to think, and even, in my immature way,
to philosophize.

The more I thought, or imagined that I was thinking, the
more I became entangled in the errors of present-day materialism. My basic ideas, although not yet molded into any
system, were already quite consistent. I considered that

nothing was fully real unless it had bodily existence, and that such apparently immaterial things as human thoughts were real only because rooted in physical changes in the brain. With our materialistic outlook, I and most of the companions of my philosophical discussions would have had no quarrel with definitions such as these:

The universe: A whirring mass of electrical charges acting mechanically upon one another without plan or purpose. Man, as a tiny eddy in this huge maelstrom, had no right to expect the whole universe to be explicable to his puny mind. Humanly speaking, then, there was no "reason" for the existence of the world. It simply was, always had been, and probably always would be.

The earth: A ball of cooling fire which had been accidentally cast off by the sun millions of years ago. Through a chance arrangement of molecules, living matter had coalesced on the earth.

Man: A species of hairless ape who for the time being enjoyed supremacy in the animal kingdom. Although capable of more elaborate mental processes than his simian ancestors, he was not an essentially different kind of being.

Man's highest good: To live intensely; to experience such keen awareness of reality as was immortalized in the great masterpieces of art and literature.

Morality: Obedience to a set of conventions which the group had approved as being in its own interests.

God: An imaginary person invented to explain facts not traceable to any known physical laws. As men found out more about the universe and got away from the primitive tendency to personalize all natural forces, it was becoming less necessary to make reference to the supernatural.

Christ: One of a number of great religious and ethical teachers, regarded as divine by his simple-minded followers.

Miracles: Unusual events which the ignorant or the superstitious attributed to supernatural intervention.

My character and conduct were shaped by this general philosophy of life. By the time I graduated from school, at the age of seventeen, I think I would have appeared, to a critic unbiased by friendship, as a disobedient, pleasure-seeking, and antisocial intellectual snob.

The chapel services which were held daily at school ought perhaps to have prevented me from accepting the unwarranted and even blasphemous opinions which I have listed. But, so far as I can remember, we did not get much Christian doctrine in chapel. Christ was often mentioned in sermons, but principally as the starting point for an edifying lecture on how to be a helpful member of society, or how to find success and happiness in one's own life. In the absence of solid doctrine, mere sentiment tended to govern all devotional practices, including prayer. Like many young Americans, I felt ill at ease praying to a Christ who might not be risen from the grave, or to a God who perhaps never intervened in the affairs of men, for blessings of a supernatural order which one might or might not believe in. I became shy of church services and announced that I did not intend to be confirmed.

My family wanted me to go to Princeton, but I insisted on going to Harvard for my college course, partly because my best friends were going there, but principally because I felt that there I would have access to the most learned instruction of our day. Such names as Whitehead, Kittredge, Lowes, and Conant cast a spell over my eagerness. I did not suspect that I would find light at Harvard, not from these gentlemen, but from quite another quarter.

The years from 1936 to 1940, during which I was an undergraduate at Harvard, might be labeled the years of my conversion. Each one marked a definite stage in my progress toward Catholicism.

The first year was mainly negative in its discoveries. I experienced the futility of a life governed by no higher law than the search for private enjoyment. The thrills of sleepless nights and hard liquor soon lost their luster. Man could not be really happy, I noted, unless he sought something higher than his own happiness; he could not be really wise unless he respected the wisdom of others. Gradually, then, I wearied of the worship of liberty and grew suspicious of

[69]

the dogmas of individualism. I began to seek for some objective law by which to rule my actions and some authority by which to guide my beliefs. But where were these to be found?

In my second year I began to get intimations of the answer. From history courses in the Middle Ages and the Renaissance, I learned that there were other outlooks on life than that of twentieth-century materialism. In the past, great numbers of men had attempted to order their actions to the service of Christ, seeking not so much the pleasures of this life as the blessedness of eternity. In the Middle Ages the predominance of this ideal had produced a culture of great richness and beauty. When, in the Renaissance, men focused their interest more on the things of this world, disorder and decay crept into Western civilization. Italian art lost its aura of mystery and budded into gross sensuality. Poetry forsook its lofty themes and became a vehicle for private emotion. Rulers grew cynical about right and wrong and waged wars for sordid gain. The world was launched on a series of struggles that could not be settled on principle, but only repressed by force.

In my studies of the Protestant Reformation, I felt attracted by the strong religious convictions of Luther and Calvin. But I noted that what appealed to me in their creed they shared with their Catholic adversaries, and what the Church had condemned in their writings was unacceptable to me also. Neither I nor the Protestants of my acquaintance believed with Luther that man was saved by faith alone to the exclusion of good works. Neither I nor they could adore a harsh despot like Calvin's God, who condemned vast multitudes to eternal perdition without allowing them any opportunity to save their souls.

If the Renaissance and the Reformation were blunders, should one not admit that the Church which had opposed them had been right? Perhaps, I thought; but, after all, one could not restore the Middle Ages to life! However right the Church had once been, certainly it was no longer right today. It was now a rotting hulk on the shores of time, left stranded by the advance of science and the recession of religious faith.

My views might have crystallized according to this pattern if I had studied nothing besides history; but from history I fortunately branched out into philosophy. For I found it impossible to understand the Renaissance thinkers without delving into medieval philosophy, and to understand anything of this I was forced to go back to Plato and Aristotle. These two great schoolmasters of the Western world effected a "Copernican revolution" in my outlook on the universe.

Plato, whom I read fairly extensively during the summer of my sophomore year, dispelled from my mind the illusion that morality was nothing but a tissue of artificial conventions. He proved conclusively that man is able to discern, in a sure intuition of objective reality, the excellence of virtues such as wisdom, justice, courage, and temperance. He then went on to demonstrate that these virtues are always and everywhere better than their opposites, that the good has a claim on our obedience, that evil is on no account to be done, and that those who do it are liable to punishments in a future life. Plato convinced me that man is not fully a man unless he subjects his passions to his will and his will to the dictates of right reason. My own experience confirmed this lesson. It took this kind of self-mastery, I noticed, to study on an evening which could have been more pleasantly spent in a barroom or a "bull session." And such self-mastery was nobler and more satisfying than merely following the path of sensual self-indulgence.

The next autumn, with the opening of my junior year, I took a semester course in Aristotle. He, even more than his great master, Plato, taught me that law and purpose, rather than chance and brute force, were the key to the operations of nature. He enabled me also to see that a thing can be real, most real, and yet not material. Material things, subject to change and decay, appeared in his system as the lowest and frailest of beings. Organic matter was higher in the scale of being than inorganic because endowed with an invisible principle of unity which enabled it to conserve and perfect its being in a manner adapted to the circumstances of the moment. Schooled in these truths, I began to see how the highest reality might be, as Aristotle said, Pure Act, unchanging and undimensioned, hidden from the senses but accessible to the spiritual intellect.

This study of Plato and Aristotle was something more to me than a means of gaining a few college credits. I had found the materialistic philosophy of selfish pleasure too shallow to be livable. I was seeking to order my life by more rational and human norms. Thanks to the Greek philosophers, I was able to reverse my precollegiate position on nearly every fundamental question. I knew now that reality was more than a mere aggregation of material particles, that life was instinct with progress and could not be fully explained in terms of mere chemical formulae; that man, whatever his origin might be, was bound to pursue the good which his reason could discern; and that God, far from being a vague abstraction, was the highest reality, necessary and eternal.

At a certain point, however, both Plato and Aristotle left me unsatisfied. The supreme reality in Plato's system, the Idea of the Good, was a thing and not a person, and thus failed to appease man's instinct to serve and to adore. Aristotle's Pure Act, although indeed personal, was a cold and self-absorbed being, and not the God of love for whom the human heart was made.

When I turned, then, in the second half of my junior year, to a more careful study of medieval philosophy, discoveries of great moment were in store for me. To my surprise I found that the thinkers of that age, enlightened by the truths of Christian Revelation, were able to reason more accurately about philosophic problems than any before or since. Plato and Aristotle, for all their wisdom, gave the impression of men groping for the secrets of the universe. St. Augustine and St. Thomas spoke with the finality of men in sure possession of the answers. The modern philosophers, in comparison, proved but poor guides. I could not see how anyone of common sense could be consistently a skeptic like Hume, an idealist like Hegel, a materialist like Marx, a positivist like Comte, or a pragmatist like James. Rejecting the seasoned wisdom of Christianity, these theorists seemed to have fallen back into the same fallacies which Plato and Aristotle had refuted.

What I had found lacking in Plato and Aristotle, then, the medieval philosophers supplied, not merely on faith, but by a more perfect use of rational arguments. The Greeks, for example, had correctly reasoned to the existence of a Prime Mover to account for motion in the world; but they had left unsolved the problem of being. The Christian philosophers showed that in like manner the existence of finite beings must be explained in terms of the activity of Infinite Being. Thus the Christian dogma of Creation was more philosophical than Greek necessitarianism. The Greeks, again, had noted that there was purpose in the order of nature. St. Augustine, in his *City of God,* elevated and rationalized this intuition by applying the Christian concept of Providence. And St. Thomas Aquinas, with the simplicity of genius, demonstrated by rigorous syllogisms that Aristotle's Pure Act must be unique, infinite, wise, loving, and free—that, rightly conceived, He could be none other than the God whom Christian faith adores. The ultimate answers to the problems of philosophy were the supreme dogmas of Christian orthodoxy.

Under the floodlight of these realizations, the whole universe glowed with new beauty. I saw it as issuing from the hand of Loving Omnipotence, unfolding under the guidance of Almighty Wisdom, and swept back—in a movement not of self-annihilation but of indescribable self-enrichment —to union with Omniscient Love. Every least stone and blade of grass, the lofty stars and the wild hail and wind, all proclaimed themselves to be works of God, mirrors of God, ladders to God. The very beasts obeyed God's will by following the law of nature. And was not I myself, I reflected, an instrument in this vast hymn of glory? How could I presume to devise standards of conduct according to my personal convenience? Only by conformity with God's law could I be true to the principle of my own being, and thus find both myself and Him. I glimpsed, as it were for the first time, the malice and deformity of sin as a deliberate violation of God's holy decree. I felt the need of calling upon Him for mercy, light, and strength. For the first time in years, I prayed.

The God to whom I thus found myself praying one spring evening of my junior year in college was no pagan deity. He was unmistakably the God of Christianity. He was our loving Creator and provident Benefactor; His adorable Will was the path of our sanctification; He was powerful to forgive the insults which our sins had heaped upon His majesty. As I knelt before Him, I perceived that the words of the Our Father, with which I addressed Him, expressed His relationship to us, and ours to Him, more intimately and exactly than the highest reasonings of the philosophers. Reciting these words, I was stricken with love for the Eternal Lord of all things and longed to know His Will.

To learn more of Christ, the teacher of the philosophers and the author of my prayer, I adopted the practice, which I recommend to all, of reading every day at least one chapter of the New Testament. In studying the history of Christ, I felt increasingly attracted to Him as a Person. Who, so marvelously as He, had united grandeur with simplicity, firmness with tact, insistence with compassion? Who had ever spoken with comparable assurance of the things of God or manifested a like power over the created order?

The Gospels were sufficient evidence of their own substantial accuracy, for no human imagination could have invented this Person whose every word and act was a revelation of the deep things of God. And if the Gospels had but the accuracy of ordinary human documents, nothing was more obvious than that this Christ had worked miracles, risen from the dead, claimed to be the Son of God, and demanded our complete faith and trust. How could I give Him less? He was a teacher without rival, but far more than a teacher. He was also a model in whom shone forth all meekness and majesty, a spotless victim slain for our sins, a victor who could lead us to eternal life. Every reason for loving any creature was, I sensed, even more cogently a reason for loving Him—our Creator and Preserver, our Teacher and Model, our Physician and Deliverer, most beautiful, most wise, most strong. And He was our Lover, who had loved us even to death, that we might have life in closest union with Him, on earth through grace, through glory in the life to come.

My response, I saw, must be one of loving faith. The evidences for Christ's Godhead, as I studied them during my last year in college, were unanswerable. And the urgency of God's grace sweetly inclined me to cry out with the converted Thomas, "My Lord and my God!"

Looking upon Christ as the source of true life, I desired with all my heart to approach Him more closely. He must, I knew, have established some bridge by which we could come to Him across the gap of two millennia to hear His authentic teaching and receive His ministrations. It would argue a contradiction in God if He had revealed the truth through Christ and then suffered that Revelation to be mutilated. It would violate the logic of the Incarnation for Christ to have left no visible Sacraments to serve as channels of His grace. And in fact, as the Gospels themselves clearly testified, Christ had instituted a Church to keep His doctrine incorrupt and to carry on His work of sanctifying souls. To the Apostles He had given a share in His own infallibility, so that to despise their words was to despise the words of Christ. He had endowed them with power to baptize, to forgive sins, and to celebrate the mysteries of His Body and Blood. Thus He enabled us not only to approach Him with our minds but to unite our very being to His by the partaking of His Body. To reason, this might seem a "hard saying," but love, believing all things, was impatient to receive Christ's Sacrament of Love.

In my thirst to be thus incorporated in the living Christ, I turned to the churches. But not, at first, to Catholicism. My

Protestant traditions were too strong; the Mass too strange a ritual. So I attended various Protestant churches, Sunday after Sunday, often twice in the morning and even a third time in the evening, singing hymns and listening to sermons. Yet I received no satisfaction. In none of these churches did I find a clear insistence on the unique authority of Christ's revealed word. Instead I found the same indefinite moralizing which had failed to attract me in preparatory school. Personal opinion, rather than implicit faith, was the byword. Not infrequently individual tastes were made paramount over objective facts. One preacher, for example, distressed me by his emphasis on subjective considerations in his defense of the Anglican *via media*. Anglicanism, he maintained, ideally combined the advantages of Catholicism with those of evangelical Protestantism. Yet there were some persons, he added, whose temperament called for a more authoritative religion, and these might do well, like Newman, to become Roman Catholics. This approach seemed to ignore what to me was the critical question—whether or not the Pope was Christ's vicar on earth. If he was, obviously all men, irrespective of temperament, should submit to his authority.

Gradually I turned more and more to Catholicism. I began to become aware that the Catholic Church was not a fossil of the Middle Ages, but a very living force in the world today. As I read the works of living Catholics—men like Maritain, Martindale, Knox, Watkin, Lunn, and others —I discovered that they had clear and convincing answers to the objections to faith supposedly founded on modern science. I became familiar with the Papal Encyclicals and found that they prescribed masterly remedies for the economic, political, and ideological diseases of our day. I heard a few sermons of Monsignor Sheen, and recognized that his oratorical powers were rooted in a wisdom and a charity not of this world.

I became conscious, too, that there were large numbers of persons about me—if not among my friends at Harvard, at least in Cambridge—who adhered to Catholicism out of something more than inheritance and routine. One weekday morning before daylight I chanced to pass St. Paul's Church. From the door of the lower church there streamed a crowd of men of every station in life who were attending the annual mission. It was obvious that only a vital faith could have drawn them there at that hour against every natural inclination.

I myself began to visit St. Paul's rather frequently during the day, and felt the sweetness and warmth that seemed to radiate from the silent tabernacle. At night I would walk over to St. Paul's again (it was only a block from my dormitory) and, standing beneath the stone crucifix on the outer wall, implore the dying Christ to draw me closer to Himself.

Though He owed me nothing, God did not refuse my petition. "If you, being evil, know how to give good gifts to your children, how much more will your Father from heaven give the good Spirit to them that ask Him?"[1] To find the truth about God, it may be helpful to read and to ponder, but it is indispensable to pray. For faith is a blessing which it is not in our power to lay hold of, nor in the power of any man to bestow, but a free gift which must be asked of God.

To read, to ponder, and to pray. . . . Such, in brief, was my program throughout my last year in college. I bought myself a Catholic catechism and read as much as I could of medieval Catholic literature from the *Confessions of St. Augustine* to the *Divine Comedy* of Dante. All this was in line with my college course and helped me to grasp the inner logic of the faith. Soon, on my solitary voyage of adventure, I hove in sight of the port.

A solitary voyage it was, but not a lonely one, for Christ was my constant companion. At times I made timid efforts to take my friends into my confidence and prepare them for the conversion which I saw in the offing.

"You know," I said to my friend Spencer one day when he came to my room to discuss some points in the course in Nationalism which he and I were taking together, "I am convinced that much of the insanity and suicide in the

[1] Luke 11:13.

United States today is due to the fact that people don't know why they are alive. Hitler and Mussolini, with their nationalism, have at least given their people something to live for."

"Yes," he replied, "but that nationalistic creed is so false and dangerous that it would be better to have none at all."

"It is an evil creed," I concurred, "and, moreover, a poor substitute for religious faith. For a man to mobilize all his resources, he must feel that he is working for God."

"That is just what Baldwin was saying the other day. The hardest worker in his chemistry class is a priest doing graduate studies. And we would all work hard if we had the motives that that priest has."

"In other words"—I felt that I was making real progress—"there is a vacuum in the hearts of our generation due to the atmosphere of doubt and debunking in which we have grown up. Into that gap some faith, rational or irrational, must enter. What an opportunity for the Catholic Church!"

"The Catholic Church?" he echoed incredulously. "You might as well say for voodooism!"

Voodooism! I groaned inaudibly. I was still quite far from getting Spencer to see my position.

The autumn following my graduation from college, when I returned to Harvard to enroll in law school, it was evident that the moment for action had come. I had passed my twenty-second birthday and was entering professional school. To keep up my program of reading and reflection about the Church might prove impossible and, in any case, could hardly continue to be fruitful. I was familiar with all the principal arguments for the faith and had found them fully persuasive. There were, to be sure—and always would be so long as I was in mortal flesh—details which I did not fully understand. But the essential had been amply demonstrated. Two paths, then, lay open before me. I might do nothing, and remain an impartial admirer of Catholicism, adopting religion as a sort of intellectual hobby. Or I might amaze, and perhaps antagonize, those closest to me by an overt acceptance of the Catholic faith.

[78]

The second course of action was obviously called for. I knew that I could not be at rest until I had given God the obedience of my mind in Faith. What could be so reasonable, so noble, or so loving as to submit without question to all that He had revealed, accepting it as the most sure rule of my own judgment? God had given me the grace to see, without room for reasonable doubt, that the Catholic Church was the true Church of Christ. That persuasion carried with it an obligation to act affirmatively. If I should reject the present grace, with what right could I expect like graces in the future? "Now is the acceptable time," God seemed to declare. "Now is the day of salvation."

Not knowing any priests, I went to a Catholic bookstore and asked the lady in charge if she would make an appointment for me to meet one. A day or two later the priest she had selected came, at my request, to my apartment. I opened the interview by proposing difficulties about several minor texts from Scripture, half hoping to spend months in this sort of purely academic discussion. But he saw quickly what I already knew in my heart—that I had sufficient information about the Church and was faced with the need of coming to a practical decision. He therefore asked me whether I intended to become a Catholic.

For several days after this interview I went through an inner struggle for the outcome of which I feel indebted to the prayers of others. Each morning I would wake up in the frame of mind of a godless materialist. All this business about Catholicism, a voice would seem to be telling me, is a senseless dream. The real world is the world which you can touch and see, and the rest mere fantasy. So, as I dressed, I would begin from first principles, questioning myself and answering, in the manner of a Socratic dialogue:

"Do you believe," the inquisitor within me would ask, "that there are realities of a moral and spiritual order, or that nothing is real except material bodies?"

"The former," my reason would testify, "I have often seen it proved."

[79]

"And do you believe in God as the highest being and the source of all morality?"

"I do," I would confess. "Nothing is possible unless it comes from Him."

"And do you further acknowledge in Christ the great teacher from whom man has learned of God?"

"No one else has spoken of God with a like clarity and certitude."

And thus I would go on until I had exacted from myself a profession of faith in the Divinity of Christ, the existence of a visible Church founded by Him, and the identity of that Church with the Roman Catholic Communion of today. Once I had completed this process of self-catechizing, I felt my former impatience to be received into the true fold of Christ.

Not many weeks later, on a November evening of 1940, I was at the baptismal font in the lower church of St. Paul's, kneeling before a priest in the midst of four or five witnesses, with my right hand on the Gospels. Peace and freedom flowed almost sensibly into my soul as my lips pronounced the formula for the reception of converts: "I now, with sorrow and contrition for my past errors, profess that I believe the Holy, Catholic, Apostolic Roman Church to be the only and true Church established on earth by Jesus Christ, to which I submit myself with my whole soul. I believe all the articles of Faith that she proposes to my belief, and I reject and condemn all that she rejects and condemns, and I am ready to observe all that she commands me. And I make the following profession of Faith . . ."

Peace and freedom . . . These very words are used by almost every convert to describe his experience. But what wonder? For are they not the words of our Divine Lord who said, "My peace I give you" and "The truth shall make you free"?

In comparison with Faith, there is nothing sure or lasting in the world. The opinions of men are rooted in appearances and change from day to day, but the words of God do not pass away. Through Faith, the human spirit, assisted by the Spirit of God, goes beyond the doubtfulness of worldly appearances and the fickleness of the human heart and enters, though darkly, into the wisdom and rest of God. The certainty that is born of Faith—so effortless, so calm—is bound to be mistaken by the world for its human counterfeits, hypocrisy, and fanaticism. Yet the world is confounded, for those who have eyes to see, by the sincerity and balance which Faith implants in the believing soul.

As I look about from within the Catholic Church, I find it sad to see that so few men return thanks to God for all that they daily receive from His hands, that so few believe the message of hope sealed by the blood of His dying Son, that so few approach the Sacraments, those rivers of life which flow from Christ's five wounds. Independence and enjoyment! Such was the cry of the Prodigal Son in the Gospel tale; such, not many years ago, was the cry by which I lived; such, for several centuries, has been the cry of Western man. Servitude and want! Such was the harvest reaped by the Prodigal Son, such the harvest that I reaped. Such, too, is the harvest that the world is reaping amid the tyrannies and wars of our time. "I will return to my Father's house!" Such was the resolution taken by the Prodigal Son, and such the resolution that I took. And I would that all the world might share with me the joy of coming home.

FINDING CHRIST

Elizabeth Laura Adams

Miss Elizabeth Laura Adams, a Negro author of distinction, was born in 1909 in Santa Barbara, California, and has lived in that state all her life. Her mother, Lula J. Adams, was the only colored student in the School of Art and Design in Los Angeles; she became a teacher of art and won awards for landscapes and flower paintings in oils and water colors. From her father, Daniel Henderson Adams, she inherited a marked talent for music.

After graduating from Santa Monica High School, Elizabeth continued her studies at Von Stein's Academy of Music at Los Angeles and at the Ross Studio in Santa Barbara. Supplementing her advanced work in music, she studied dramatic art at the Beattie Dramatic School at Santa Monica and with Mr. Ralph Freud, Director of Drama at the University of California at Los Angeles. After a search for religious truth, covering almost eleven years, she embraced the Catholic faith in 1929.

Miss Adams's talents have found expression in music, drama, poetry, and prose. She has contributed poetry and prose to *Westward* and to *Torch,* while *Poetry,* a national magazine of verse, has featured a number of her poems which have been highly acclaimed. Her book *Dark Symphony,* published by Sheed and Ward in 1942, stamps her as a writer of originality and power. Miss Adams is a member of the Third Order of St. Francis, of the Gallery of Living Catholic Authors, and plans to specialize in writing plays on Negro life. Her literary and dramatic talents have already won for her wide recognition and they presage a still more brilliant future.

DIVINE GUIDANCE led me through various disheartening experiences into the Catholic Church where I found God. My search was long, covering a period of almost eleven years. It was wearisome. There were times when I lacked courage. All efforts to reach my goal seemed in vain. Determination waned. Hope faltered, but I believed *"there must be a God . . . somewhere."*

For the benefit of one soul or countless souls trying to find the "peace that passeth all understanding," the story of my conversion is related with the hope that it will inspire all seeking the Redeemer.

I was born in Santa Barbara, California. God had encased my soul in a dark body and I belonged to the American Negro race. My paternal grandmother, having come from Madagascar to this country, abandoned certain tribal beliefs and customs of the dark people to marry a Christian American Negro. My mother was a Methodist.

Mother, who was always very devout, firmly believed in church attendance. Father attended services occasionally to please her. He had his own philosophy of life. He despised the theological wranglings caused by denominational differences over biblical interpretations and maintained that a high percentage of the world's suffering resulted from the intolerance of bigoted and contentious Christians. Often I heard him say: "I see some of the white Christians turning hungry black men from their doors, and black Christians so filled with hatred that they refuse needy white men bread. You go to church, my dear wife, and pray for Baby and for me."

And so, when Sunday came, Mother took me to church. But it seemed that I inherited my father's dislike for religious service. Mother usually spent Saturday giving me religious instruction which invariably slipped my memory by Sunday morning.

I was the chief dunce in Sunday school. The only two outstanding memories I have retained of this period are: first, the joy of receiving holy pictures (especially the ones wherein Jesus was pictured blessing little children and healing the sick); second, my admiration for my first Sunday-school teacher. Bitter were the tears I shed the day promotion elevated me to the ranks of the first-grade religious class. The requirements demanded that I learn Bible verses. In my childish opinion, this was more punishment than honor. I knew four verses:

(1) "The Lord is my Shepherd, I shall not want."
(2) "Suffer little children to come unto Me and forbid them not, for of such is the kingdom of heaven."
(3) "Jesus wept."
(4) "God is love."

Generally a race took place between boys and girls to inform the teacher that "Jesus wept" and "God is love." But I detested church attendance—except for the music.

Music always aroused me from lethargy to spiritual alertness. When deep tones resounded and a robed choir sang, I sat up and took notice of what was happening. Now and then bass voices would proclaim the unseen Creator "King of Kings" and the sopranos added "Lord of Lords." Then, suddenly, the trend of service would change. Choir members seated themselves. The minister stood silently before his congregation. His eyes were closed. The congregation became motionless. The silence filled one with awe and reverence. The hush that fell over the vast number of Negroes was almost indescribable. Now, as I recall its effect, I know it was like the pause following a prelude—those moments of profound quietude during which a music master sits with upraised hands over a piano keyboard before continuing to play a great composition; the silence of evening awaiting the approach of night; the silence of the desert awaiting the sunrise. Then someone in the congregation (usually an elderly, white-haired, member) began to hum the first notes of an old-fashioned hymn or spiritual. Slowly, other voices joined in.

Negro voices! If you have never heard hundreds of Negro voices singing, you have missed a great concert. In my memory, I can hear the sweet mellow voices of my people. Sometimes the tones were almost inaudible—seemingly afar off like the distant murmuring of the sea. The soft tapping of their shoes made accompaniment not unlike the beating of drums. Dark bodies swayed slightly to the rhythm. Sometimes the sacred song depicted the saints marching up the "stairs of glory," or Daniel walking about the lions' den unharmed because God's protecting power overshadowed him. I admired Daniel's faith, but continued to be afraid of lions and other wild animals when present at a circus. It took me a long time to realize the symbolical significance of God's protecting love in the midst of temptations. Shouting frightened me. It became the principal orgy of churchgoing. I feared conversion the moment a Sunday-school teacher informed me that the "Holy Ghost would descend" some-day and prompt me to "shout for joy."

I thought of God as the Divine Creator. His home, I believed, was somewhere "way up" in the sky. He made the earth, set out the brown hills and green valleys, streams and rivers—erected the purple mountains and placed the sun, moon, and stars in the blue sky. He had a great golden throne, glittering with jewels and beautiful angels with golden trumpets surrounding it, always faithfully carrying out His Commands. God was far, far away. How impossible it was to imagine Him interested in a little girl! My mother was shocked when I told her that I loved her much more than I loved God. Horrified, she hastened to explain that parents were supposed to watch over their children, but they should always love God first and adore Him.

I remained unconvinced. I believed it was proper to love God, but when a door closed on my finger it was "Mamma dear" who kissed the pain away and made the finger "all well again." My own "Mamma dear" tucked me into bed and told me stories while Papa was at work. God? God had many things to do. He had to light up the moon and the silver stars. He had to keep the waves of the ocean rolling. The sun had to be reminded to shine the following day. Millions, billions and trillions of sick people had to be healed. Why, then, should God be concerned about me?

Many times, when I was in church, I saw children of my

[85]

own age testifying: "Jesus walks and talks with me." I listened to them, but I had an analytical mind. Knowing that these same youngsters played many pranks and told me confidentially that they never intended telling their parents of their misdeeds, I wondered why Jesus favored them and slighted me. I knew that I was not a perfect child; but I tried to remember to obey my parents. So I concluded that Jesus selected certain people to "walk and talk" with but had excluded me because I feared the descent of the Holy Ghost. And so—my biggest childhood problem was secretly to evade the Holy Ghost. I told no one of my plans. Strange though it may seem, I hesitated to speak to my beloved mother about religion. But I was afraid she would become ashamed of me because I could not boast of "walking and talking with Jesus." Thus it was that my first "Steps to Glory" were marshaled by religious workers in a Methodist church.

Then came the Good Friday when friends drove us in their car to religious service at the historic Santa Barbara Mission. We entered the Mission, and I, an eleven-year-old colored girl, looked about with wonder like that of Alice in Wonderland. Members of the congregation were prayerfully kneeling. I noticed that those nearest me were not distracted by my impolite staring. Some were reading small books with black covers; others fingered strings of beads. I did not know, at that time, that the small books were prayer books and the beads rosaries. I beheld the altars. I listened to the voices of the priests. I heard the words "Ave Maria"—not knowing the meaning was *Hail Mary*. This was a new world. While sitting there I thought to myself: "If this is church—why have I disliked it so much?"

Conversion is defined in Webster's dictionary as "a change from one state, or from one religion, to another." Chocarne, speaking of it, says: "Conversion, that phenomenon of light to the intellect and persuasion to the heart, is not ordinarily produced in the way of sudden illumination, like a flash of lightning in a dark night, but rather under the form of growing daylight, like that which precedes the sunrise."

In my case the Great God knew that I, a little colored girl, feared conversion because of a Sunday-school teacher's prophetic description of the descent of the Holy Ghost. The Great God knew also that deep down within the soul of this same colored girl was a simple wish that the Son of God would "walk and talk" with her as the colored Methodist children described Him "walkin' an' talkin' " with them. And so conversion came to me quickly and quietly. I experienced no emotional reaction other than the desire to attend service at the Santa Barbara Mission forever.

My father objected to my becoming a Roman Catholic. He was a member of the Masonic Order, my mother affiliated with the women's auxiliary, known as the Eastern Star.

Although the permission I sought was not granted by my father, I want to make it clear that it was not denied because of slanderous or derogatory gossip circulated in the world to prejudice people against the Church. My parents were too fair-minded to be swayed in opinion by evil gossip.

I had been taught to obey my parents. Therefore my father's decision left me no alternative. I dismissed the idea of becoming a Catholic—but I knew that I would never forget that Good Friday service and the small books from which some of the congregation read; the beads and the altars, and the voices of the priests and the words "Ave Maria." As a mirror reflects images, so the memory of the old Santa Barbara Mission and its ancient form of worship was always to be reflected in the mirror of my soul.

Life brought about many tragic changes. The sudden death of my father. A prolonged illness that made my mother a shut-in for a time. Grammar-school days ended. Then came joy over entering high school. It was in high school that I met an Italian girl, a Catholic who taught me much about the faith. There are many paths that lead to God. Sorrow and disappointment are paths well trodden. While trying to find God and yet be loyal to a dead parent's wishes, I joined a church and was later asked by the pastor not to return because "white parishioners" objected to kneeling at the altar with colored people. I never set foot in the church again. I passed by, though, a couple of Sunday mornings and heard the congregation singing—singing hymns of praise to the Almighty.

For a long time I tried to avoid thinking of religion or mentioning it. Since the majority of colored ministers were Methodist or Baptist, I did not think they could be of help in solving my problem of trying to find the church of my choice. And then—I began the great pilgrimage to find out for myself whether or not God really loved the colored race. I made up my mind to find out everything I could about the Creator if it took me the rest of my life. I was dissatisfied with the opinion I had formed of God. I certainly considered Him a God for the white race after being turned from a church. I decided that unless I could be convinced that His Son's death for the redemption of all people included the colored, I could put my time to better use than praying to One who heard only the fair of skin. If God was just and loved the colored—then, I reasoned, by not trying to solve the problem of how to serve Him, I would miss the benefit of His help.

In preference to wasting time listening to people broadcast scandals about Protestant clergymen or evangelists and Catholic priests or nuns, I selected the companionship of good books and walked in the company of the valiant. I read the life of Rose Hawthorne Lathrop, younger daughter of the great writer, Nathaniel Hawthorne, a convert to the Catholic faith who, inspired by Christ, opened an impromptu hospital for cancer patients too ill and destitute to support themselves; who later forsook the world, became a religious, and was known as Mother Alphonsa, foundress of the refuge for the cancer poor, Rosary Hill Home. I read the life of the Anglican nurse, Florence Nightingale, who had followed the Son of God "forth to war," and in thought walked beside her at the Crimea and at Scutari. And a spark from the bright flame burning in her lamp of dauntless courage kindled the smoldering coals of hope struggling within my own soul.

In spirit, I twice sailed on a vessel to the dreaded isle of Molokai where crippled, mutilated, and sore-infected lepers were isolated. On the first trip I saw a young follower of Christ taking census of eight hundred of the outcasts—he who had exiled himself to work among them as priest, physician, and teacher—Father Damien DeVeuster. And on the second trip, in spirit, I saw him, years hence, a weary soul, beginning a sermon to the outcasts with the words: "We lepers"—knowing that he would die in the service of Christ, a victim of the loathsome disease. And so I found consolation and gained courage, as all do who walk in the company of the valiant. And then I realized that if a soul wanted to find God and was earnest about it, that soul would not falter when confronted by obstacles.

Hoping to find out how the Negro was regarded in the Catholic Church, I obtained a copy of a Negro magazine that listed all the religious denominations which had exhibited racial prejudice. My heart sank when I read: "The Roman Catholic Church of America owes the American Negro an apology." That meant that somewhere, at some time, my people had suffered humiliation because of segregation. I asked myself: "If some members of the Church that claims to be the One True Church treated Negroes unkindly —why belong to it?"

Then I read the book *Wonder Works of Lourdes*. Who can read this book and doubt the presence of Christ in the Blessed Sacrament?

It described the thousands of pilgrims who prayed annually at the famous shrine. All were not Catholic, all were not white. Here the blind waited for The Light. The crippled and diseased hoped to be cured. Priests chanted prayers: "Hosanna to the Son of David! Blessed is He that cometh in the Name of the Lord." A procession of the Blessed Sacrament wended its way through the crowds. *All were not healed in body—some only in spirit. But faith was a living thing at Lourdes!* I had read both—the Negro magazine and the *Wonder Works of Lourdes*. I made the final decision: I would continue the quest.

Disappointments? Yes—there were many. Obstacles? Yes— there were many. But I met a nun in the public library and she invited me to the Holy Name Convent. She took me to the chapel and told me that Our Divine Lord would always be waiting for me in the Tabernacle; and the Blessed Mother of God would always be my Heavenly Mother.

And then I found a confessional, having decided that I would begin making confessions and receiving spiritual help. I selected the confessional because the priest could not see me—and I would not be turned away because my skin was dark. I would hear his voice . . . he would hear mine asking how to find God. I was making a brave effort to find a church home. Determined to find a spiritual guide, I overcame discouragement after being told that I should join a convert class as the priest *could not give me absolution* until I became a Catholic. But when I learned a priest could give a non-Catholic a blessing—I asked for the blessing.

One day I met the priest whose voice had guided me—a highly intelligent person, deeply spiritual and eminently kind. On learning that I had sought the confessional as a refuge from race prejudice, his interest in my spiritual progress increased. His inspiring talks helped to shatter the fear of prejudice and instilled assurance. He gave me books—prayer books, meditations, church history, and others—to help me toward the goal of becoming a writer. His implicit faith in me and in my determination to reach a high goal was to me like lamplight on a dark path. He it was who convinced me that God was no respecter of persons—that His graces were not limited to the fair of skin. And in time I came to realize that this priest had a white soul and so fine a spirit that his aspirations and ideals soared above the standards of the prejudiced of his race. And I promised him that I would strive to follow Christ though stoned by persecution; that I would try to serve God faithfully.

And so—I became a Catholic. The words of my spiritual director were a blessing: "Remember, child, though the world may segregate you to a hilltop, God can lift you to mountain heights. When every door is shut in your face, go to the Blessed Mother Mary and she will wrap you within the sheltering folds of her mantle and shield your soul from harm."

The road is often beset with stumbling blocks for the Negro. But I keep in mind the lines written by one of my people, James David Corrothers, who wrote *The Negro Singer*, for he has said:

> But I shall dig me deeper to the gold,
> Fetch water, dripping, over desert miles,
> From clear Nyansas and mysterious Niles
> Of love; and sing, nor one kind act withhold.
> So shall men know me, and remember long,
> Nor my dark face dishonor any song.

I found the Nazarene Whom I sought . . . how long and winding the road is before me I do not know. Of this one thing I am sure: I have more valleys to walk through, hills and mountains to climb. I would have no one say that I had or have an exceptional gift of faith. "Seek and ye shall find . . . knock and the door shall be opened unto you."

I have told my story.

May my prayer to Mary, the Mother of God, become the prayer of every child of God . . . every seeker for the Kingdom of God . . . the words of a poet:

> Ave Maria . . . let earth's last sunrise break on me
> Still reaching arms and heart to thee.

THE END OF A PILGRIMAGE

Edward O. Dodson

Edward O. Dodson is a young scientist whose accomplishments give promise of a brilliant future. He was born of Protestant parents in 1916 in Fargo, North Dakota, and in the family on his father's side were several ministers of the Disciples of Christ denomination; the mother, as a young girl, was reared in the Presbyterian faith.

Edward was educated in the public schools of Minneapolis and Illinois, and later attended Carleton College at Northfield, Minnesota. While in high school, he had become a member of the Congregational Church, but events occurred during his college course which caused him to investigate the Catholic religion. He was received into the Church in 1938 by Father James Ward in Northfield.

While at Carleton, he won many scholastic honors, including the Elliott Prize in Greek, was elected to Phi Beta Kappa and also to associate membership in the Society of the Sigma Xi, honorary scientific society. He was graduated in 1939 *magna cum laude,* with honors in Greek and zoology.

He was awarded a graduate assistantship in zoology at the University of California, where he received his Ph.D. degree in 1946. While at the university, he won first prize in the Newman Hall Essay Contest with his essay on "The Eucharist and Life." He held a lectureship in zoology at the University of California at Los Angeles and came to the University of Notre Dame as a member of the Department of Biology in 1947.

His doctoral investigation, entitled "A Morphological and Biochemical Study of the Lampbrush Chromosomes of Vertebrates," was brought out by the University of California Publications in Zoology; his study, "Some Evidence for the Specificity of the Feulgen Reaction," was published in *Stain Technology.* Another scientific study, entitled "An Additional Available Passenger

Pigeon Skeleton," was published in *The Condor;* his "Lateral Loop Chromosomes and the Theory of the Gene" was published in the *Proceedings of the Indiana Academy of Science,* and his "Surface Areas of Chromosomes in Relation to Their Activity" was published in *Anatomical Record.* He has likewise contributed articles to the *American Midland Naturalist.*

In the summer of 1940, Edward married Mary Katherine Street, to whom he had become engaged while at Carleton. The Dodsons have four children. Dr. Dodson's favorite diversion, when not engrossed with his scientific work or busy with his growing family, is cabinetmaking, in which he has acquired great skill.

I WAS RAISED in the Congregational Church and, within the limits of definitions given, I held an orthodox doctrine and I loved the Church whose ministrations I received.

There was very little doctrinal instruction, either in Sunday school, which I attended regularly from an early age until I went away to college, or in church proper. In the early years in Sunday school we read simplified Bible stories, sang hymns, and were given short talks on devotional subjects. Later we discussed present-day social problems in the light of Christian teaching. In church the service centered around the sermon, which was usually concerned with one aspect or another of social or international problems. Biblical texts were always chosen to "keynote" the sermons, and statements which implied doctrine were often made; but doctrine as such was rarely, if ever, stated.

I think that my old Congregational pastor, for whom I have great respect and admiration, was himself a man of excellent faith, but I don't believe that many of his parishioners were. He certainly made no direct effort to instruct them, apparently not regarding doctrinal faith as essential to their salvation, or else making the assumption that, in some mysterious way, quite apart from the overt function of the Church, they would be infused with the same faith which he himself had.

We sang, "Holy, holy, holy, Lord God of Hosts . . .

Blessed Trinity," and it never occurred to me to doubt the fact of the existence of the Trinity, yet reference to the Trinity in any more explicit way was so slight that I had not the remotest idea of what the term actually implied. Questioning by a person who really knew what he believed and why he believed it revealed that I had never thought of Our Lord as anything more than a very wonderful man. His godhood simply hadn't occurred to me.

I did consciously believe that God had created heaven and earth out of nothing; but I'm sure that the majority of my fellow Congregationalists, when they thought of the origin of the physical universe at all, thought of it in purely mechanistic terms.

The virgin birth was referred to in my early Sunday-school years, and I never doubted it as a fact. It was never referred to in church beyond a reading in biblical texts, and I'm sure that very few members of the congregation shared my belief. As to the Virgin herself, all but the most casual and clearly secular mention was taboo, as was reference to all the other saints, except the Apostles.

None of us doubted in the least the fact of the crucifixion, but it means little without the resurrection; and the majority of us thought of the resurrection, as of all biblical miracles, as purely symbolical, having no historic validity whatever. After a recent lecture on the Christmas stories of the Bible at Yale Divinity School, in which Dr. Kraeling had developed in some detail the objections of the so-called rationalists, he was asked, "Do you mean that these stories are fiction?" "They belong," he answered, "to a generation and kind of thinking which does not ask. They hover between fiction and fact in that they create value judgment which is in appreciation of fact. But actually they do this by fiction." I think that this is an excellent statement of the attitude of most of the so-called "modern" Protestants toward the miraculous aspects of Christian religion, and it was certainly the predominant attitude in the congregation in which I was raised.

If asked for a definite answer as to whether they believed

in life after death, I think that most in that congregation would have said that they were uncertain or that they had no such belief. They were almost unanimous, however, in their disbelief in hell: they couldn't believe that a merciful God would subject His creatures to anything of that sort.

The idea of sin was rarely given any thought. It was more or less assumed that churchgoing people lived reasonably decent lives, and that was enough. The concept of sin was considered as a heavy gloom which had been cast off with the Dark Ages. Besides, most of us did not think of our God as a personal god who could see into our inmost thoughts, although our pastor prayed to "Almighty God, to Whom all thoughts are known and all hearts are open." Without a personal god, there can be no personal judgment, and so, though most of us expressly believed that it was our duty as Christians to lead upright, moral lives, the idea of being held to account for our thoughts and deeds before the tribunal of an all-just and omniscient God was completely out of the question.

Most of us had a true religious faith in our Church. Many of us had never heard of the apostolic succession, and probably would not have been particularly impressed if we had. We didn't think of the Church as founded by Christ, but we did believe that it was founded on the principles of Christ. We believed that the Church was holy because it taught the principles of Christ (but I think I have made it clear that we really didn't take the teaching function very seriously), but more especially because it was an institution dedicated to the communal practice of the Christian way of life. We believed that God was, somehow, especially associated with the Church. As to unity, catholicity, and apostolicity, we simply never gave a thought to such things. We thought of all churches as being equally valid, or, rather, we simply didn't question any church as to its validity. But while we thought of one church as being much as good as another, we considered the Catholic Church as being definitely wrong and outmoded; a few others we damned as fanatical.

Of the sacraments, only baptism and Holy Communion were recognized, although I'm sure that their sacramental nature as channels of the grace of God through the Holy Ghost was not at all understood or appreciated by more than a very few. Baptism of infants was customary and was done by sprinkling. It was generally thought of as a naming ceremony, and as a promise on the part of the parents to raise the child in the Church. The ceremony was ordinarily performed only once or twice a year, and was done at a regular Sunday service in the presence of the whole congregation, a custom which I think is excellent.

Holy Communion was celebrated only three or four times in the course of the year. Very few, if any, believed in transubstantiation, but considered the bread and wine (grape juice) as simply memorials of Jesus. There was no personal preparation for the sacrament, but only the public preparation, which consisted of prayer, hymns, and Bible readings, most of which were not too closely related to the subject; prayers or hymns to the Blessed Sacrament as such were unheard of. First the bread and then the grape juice were distributed by the ushers, the grape juice being contained in small glasses on a convenient rack. Both were received sitting: no one ever knelt at any time.

Children were not regarded as members of the Church, even though they had been baptized, so it was customary for children of high-school age to "join the Church" at a ceremony which was not regarded as sacramental in any sense. Nonetheless, it might be regarded as somewhat analogous to confirmation, since they promised to take Christ as their example in life and were then blessed with a laying on of hands by the pastor. This ceremony was usually held once a year at the same time as baptism, usually in the Eastertide. That day was called "Children's Day."

Ordination of ministers and marriage were performed, but neither was regarded as a sacrament, or even sacramental, for sacramentals were never used, and those of the Catholic Church were regarded as superstitions smacking of idolatry. There was nothing in any way comparable to penance or extreme unction.

During the high-school years, Sunday school was largely given over to the discussion of current social problems and how we should face them in the light of Christian teaching. Although I had always attended Sunday school regularly and had tried conscientiously to get the most out of what was offered, I felt that I had no real idea at all of what these Christian teachings were. I felt reasonably sure that none of the others did either, unless a very few might have been instructed in their homes, which I doubted.

And so I suggested to a church leader whom I liked and admired very much, as I still do, that it might be a good thing if we would pause for a while and study these Christian principles in the light of which we were asked to judge important current events and formulate our basic politico-social attitudes. He rebuked me very sharply: "That isn't the Congregational way. We believe in practicing, not preaching."

This is all well and good as far as it goes. I felt as strongly as he that religion became important only as one practiced its tenets in his daily life, but I couldn't see that it was at all inconsistent with practice simply to learn one's principles. I objected that one would never reach his destination if he didn't study his road maps occasionally. He missed my point completely, and I deeply resented his attitude on the matter.

In the course of one of our Sunday-school discussions, there came up the matter of nonessentials in Christian religion acting as sources of interdenominational strife and as stumbling blocks to the practice of essentials. The standard example of such nonessentials—the virgin birth— was immediately brought up and disparaged. I protested that I personally believed in the virgin birth and that, if it were a fact, I saw no excuse for regretting that it had ever been preached or for regarding it as a nonessential. The assistant pastor of the church, who was leading the discussion, asked me to see him after class. He then tried to show me why

[97]

Christian morality and ethics (which, apparently, he regarded as the whole of "essential" Christianity) were independent of the virgin birth and other miracles. When he saw that the virgin birth did not constitute a difficulty for me, he dropped the discussion. I, however, considered it significant that an ordained minister would assume that a doctrine which had been taught from the very beginning must constitute a difficulty to anyone who held it.

Then I went to a summer youth conference conducted by the Congregational churches of Illinois. On the whole, I found this a very stimulating and heartening experience, yet there were some things even there which tended to weaken my faith in my Church as a sound and unified organization, worthy of my full support, and of which I could be proud to be a member.

Along with several others, I took a course entitled "What Can I Believe?" We had a right to expect a fairly comprehensive survey of fundamental Christian doctrines. We rather expected a rationalistic approach, but we weren't too sure. But we got something quite different: the minister who taught the class spent the whole time explaining in some detail why he thought the doctrine of hell should form an integral part of Christian belief. I was disappointed because so many really important things had been left completely untouched, and I could not but wonder that his belief on the one point he did discuss was so strikingly different from that of most Congregationalists, ministers too, whom I knew.

Then I took a course on "The Life of Christ." The minister who taught it was one of the most prominent in the city of Chicago, but I was greatly disappointed in him. Two things stand out among my impressions of his course. First, he thought that Jesus's happy and wholesome home life as a child accounted for the fact that he referred to God as "Father." He didn't recognize at all the possibility that a true parent-child relationship between God and Jesus might be a factor in Jesus's choice of the word Father in speaking of God. Second, he greatly admired Socialist loyalty and party solidarity. He said that if the more conservative parties could not go further than they had toward solving our social problems that he would be strongly inclined to join the Socialist party.

While we were at the conference, a communion service was held for us. The minister who officiated gave a sermon in which he expounded his views on the sacrament. He was very reverent, he spoke eloquently, and I'm sure that many of us received the sacrament with greater reverence than ever before because of his sermon. Yet, as one meditated upon his remarks, it became clear that he regarded the bread and wine not as the true body and blood of Our Lord, but simply as a memorial to Him.

Dancing was not allowed at this conference. The reason? Some of the churches represented did not approve of it. I thought, as did most of the others present, that this was narrow-minded. Organizations in most of our churches commonly gave dances as a means of raising money. Yet they were condemned as immoral by other churches of the same denomination!

I have mentioned above that one of our leaders had a strong socialistic tendency. Back home again, I found an unmistakable socialistic tendency in the Sunday-school leadership and in the leadership of the high-school students' club. Now I myself have a good deal of sympathy for a great many socialistic principles, yet I saw in this growing minority in the church a threat to a principle which I held very important: that people of all political creeds should be able to find a common meeting ground in the Church, united on principles which are above political and social distinctions.

I greatly enjoyed the discussions which we had in Sunday school, but I never did give much assent to the church service proper. It centered around the sermon, and I never could see that it had much to do with the worship of God, especially since the majority of the sermons were on very definitely secular subjects, international affairs more commonly than any other. The service was made up usually of a processional hymn sung by the choir, a call to worship composed anew each week by the minister, a number of hymns sung by the congregation, an anthem, or perhaps two, sung by the choir, a long "pastoral prayer" composed anew each week by the minister, followed by a congregational recitation of the Lord's Prayer, then a scripture reading and a sermon by the minister, a closing hymn or two sung by the congregation and, finally, benediction by the minister and a recessional hymn by the choir.

I found little beauty in it. Most of the music wasn't really too good. The best of it seemed planned more to show off the choir than to worship God. One of the members of the choir was a very well-known singer, and there was a noticeably larger attendance on the Sundays on which it was announced that he would be there.

There was no continuity in the service, proceeding to a definite climax. There was seldom any logical connection between the successive parts or hymns, except that the scriptural passage read served as a text for the sermon, but even here the connection was often far fetched. The various other parts did not point toward the sermon, which was the principal part and which should have been built up to as a climax.

But had the other parts of the service led up to the sermon in a climactic fashion, I fear that there would commonly have been an anticlimax. Not, however, in the church where I was raised: our pastor was a brilliant man, an excellent speaker, and his sermons were almost always stimulating and inspiring. But as I visited churches in other communities and heard visiting ministers conduct the service in our own church, I gradually came to realize that in the Congregational Church the man in the pulpit means everything and the Church itself nothing, so far as doctrine taught and effectiveness of public worship are concerned. Where there were first-class ministers this was not an important thing, but the average minister, like the average man in any calling involving large numbers of people, must be a mediocre man. We boasted that our prayers, with the exception of the Lord's Prayer, were personal, spontaneous prayers. But to whom were they personal and spontaneous? To the minister who composed them. This worked out well when skillful, talented men did the composing, but commonly they were very uninspired prayers, varying little from week to week, either in thought, which was usually vague, or in wording, which bore the stamp of forced artistry instead of a personal, spontaneous communion with God. These were greeted with indifference by the congregations, which seldom listened attentively.

Now, there are many excellent ministers in small parishes of poor financial standing, yet I think it is undeniable that the better ministers are, taken by and large, soon called to the wealthy parishes and the middle-class or poor parishes must accept mediocre or poor ministers.

My own church was a very wealthy one. In spite of all the talk of Christian brotherhood, I knew that there were many people in our community who, because of religious affinities, would have liked to attend that church but did not because they were made to feel that social and monetary "class" lines barred them. Not that there were not many members who were of very ordinary financial standing and who never received any notice on the society pages of the local newspapers; there were many such. But, nonetheless, that aspect was unmistakably a strong factor in determining the membership of the church, and I know at least one member who stopped attending during the depression because he felt that it was humiliating to go. And it was just then that he most needed the ministrations of the Church!

And yet our chief boast, our *raison d'être* as a separate denomination, was that we represented the highest development of ecclesiastical democracy—congregational government of each church, and each church independent of all others!

I went to a college which had been founded by the Congregational Church, and although the Church had never had any official control over it, the college had many ministers

[101]

on its board of trustees and faculty, the president of the college himself being an ordained Congregational minister. Religion was never touched upon in classes, except in my Greek class, where once a week we read the Greek New Testament. The college, however, conducted two chapel services during the week and a vesper service Sunday evening, all of which were compulsory. The chapel services were conducted by faculty members, with occasional ministers invited from the outside. They were rarely religious in nature, and the college did not intend them to be. They were simply college convocations.

The vesper services, on the other hand, the college regarded as divine worship, on a par with any church service. The outstanding Protestant ministers of the state and of the nation were invited to conduct these services. Yet my impression was not at all favorable, and many shared my view. Very few of these men—and they were selected as ministers of Christ—spoke on religious subjects. Sometimes they did: some of the finest, most reverent, most truly religious sermons I have ever heard have been preached in that chapel. But the overwhelming majority had purely secular messages, and we students commonly felt that they really carried no meaning whatever.

When I went home after my freshman year I told our assistant pastor that I was seriously considering entering the ministry. He advised me against it, on the grounds that the Church was a luxury in society today and that ministers, especially young ones, would find it very difficult during these times of economic depression to earn a living, as did all those engaged in "luxury" businesses. But the Church was not a luxury to me: it was a vital necessity. I felt strongly the need of a vigorous religious faith and of companionship in worship.

The president of our students' association invited the president of the college to address the student body. He used the occasion to expound his views on religion. Rhetorically, it was an excellent speech. Religiously, it was anything but what one would expect from an ordained minister. His God was an impersonal one: a sort of summation of the vital forces of the universe; a creator only in a very passive sense, and not existing apart from the created. As to the actual Godhood of Christ, the virgin birth, the resurrection, and other things which differentiate Christianity from other religions which teach a good morality, he said, "Rather than anything else in the world would I have you get rid of these ideas." Christianity was, to him, nothing more than what he liked to refer to as "the simple teachings of Jesus," by which he meant the moral and ethical implications of the Gospels.

Once I found in the library a rather old book which purported to be a comprehensive survey of the Congregational Church, its principles and practice. I read parts of it and found a passage according to which the Wesminster Catechism had been approved as the authoritative summary of Congregational doctrine. So I looked up the Westminster Catechism. I found a very systematic and complete treatment of Christian doctrine, although there were parts to which I objected, such as the doctrine of predestination. I showed the catechism to the son of a prominent Congregational minister. He told me that if I would talk to Congregational ministers about it, I would find that most of them thought that that stuff was a lot of bunk.

We were quite proud of basing our church on the Bible, and of having given the Bible, as we thought, to the laity. Yet there was really very little Bible reading in church. Usually only one passage was read at a service, and it was sometimes—quite often, in fact—so short that it could not be considered in relation to its context. As to private Bible reading, I never felt that I was at all strongly encouraged to do it, and although I did do some, I certainly did not do enough to boast about it, and I know that very few of my friends were much given to Bible reading.

And so it was that, through a multitude of influences, I gradually came to feel that the Congregational Church was inadequate.

There was no definite time at which I decided that it was so and that I must look for a Church that could serve my needs. Dissatisfaction developed slowly, and as it increased, my interest in religion and religious institutions increased commensurately. I read widely on the subject, a fact which probably contributed to my dissatisfaction, so that by the time my problem had become sufficiently clear for me to be really aware of it, I had already gone far in my quest for a solution.

As I read the contemporary literature of Congregationalism and of other Protestant churches, it gradually became clear to me that the faults which I had found in my own Church were, taken by and large, not its own peculiarities but were inherent in the nature of Protestantism.

If I were to pick any one fault which, more than any other, seems to pervade and vitiate Protestantism as a whole, I should say that it is one-sidedness. Each church seems to be a distinct unit because it emphasizes disproportionately some one aspect of Christianity at the expense of many other equally important aspects. This is signalized by the very names of many sects: they are Baptists, Congregationalists, Presbyterians, Episcopalians, or Seventh-Day Adventists.

While I was not raised in an anti-Catholic home, I was raised in a very definitely non-Catholic home, so I gratuitously assumed from the beginning that whatever the merits of any other Church might be, the Catholic Church was wrong, narrow-minded, and had a history of oppression and of opposition to progress.

Several things happened, however, which made me wonder if it might not be worth while to investigate the Church to which I had never given any serious thought whatever and which I had so lightly dismissed as certainly wrong and outmoded. My Greek professor, whom I liked and admired more than any of my other teachers, once remarked that "the Catholic Church is the strongest force for good in the world today."

Again, as I read the current literature of Protestantism, I found unmistakably that the leaders of present-day Protestantism were still pleading the justification of the Reformation. It seemed to me that after four hundred years they would assume the justification an accomplished fact, unless they themselves were in doubt as to whether the events which led to the formation of their respective churches were actually justified. Furthermore, it became clear that the things of which they were proudest and to which they clung with the greatest tenacity were things which might be called their Catholic heritage, although they did not often acknowledge the source openly: they referred to such things as a return to Primitive Christianity, the New Testament practices, or the heroism of the Martyrs. Such things are the sacraments, especially baptism and Holy Communion, though various churches recognize some others; the idea of ordination through the authority of Christ as represented through apostolic successors; some of the very old prayers, hymns, and ejaculations, such as "In the name of the Father, and of the Son, and of the Holy Ghost," the Gloria in Excelsis, and the creeds, especially the Apostles' Creed.

I read an excellent book on art and worship in Protestant churches which pointed at every step to the Catholic Church as the model to which Protestant churches should look, being careful, of course, not to contaminate themselves with the outmoded and undemocratic doctrines of Rome.

Reading about the Catholic Church through Protestant sources, I found that there was in it no trace of the apparently universal tendency of Protestant churches to weaken in faith from one generation to the next. I strongly disagreed with some of the tenets of the Catholic Church, outstanding among which was the infallibility of the popes, but I was greatly impressed, nonetheless, by its stability, so strikingly in contrast with the crumbling faith in the Protestant churches. I clearly saw that there was great variation among the Protestant churches in this as in all other respects, yet even in the most steadfast of them the germ of dissolution seemed to me to be present.

Gradually, then, I came to believe that my case against Congregationalism was a case against Protestantism generally, and concurrently I became interested in the Catholic Church. But it seemed inevitable, as I turned toward Rome, that I should linger for a time at Canterbury, both because High Church Episcopalianism does represent an ideological halfway point between the rest of Protestantism and Catholicism and because most of my best friends were High Church Episcopalians, my Greek professor being an ordained minister—he regarded himself as a true, sacrificing priest.

It was my Episcopalian friends who gave me my first real understanding of what is meant by apostolic succession and what is the significance of validity in a church. They defended well many of the things which I had formerly associated only with Catholicism, such as liturgical worship, veneration of the saints, the use of sacramentals such as the rosary, the true nature of the sacraments as channels of grace, together with the Real Presence and auricular confession.

I was greatly impressed. But as I studied the Episcopal Church carefully, it became evident that the same faults which had forced me to break with the Congregational Church were here also, masked though they were in many respects.

My Episcopalian friends claimed unity throughout their communion of forty million souls on the grounds that they all received the same sacraments. But what a tremendously different nature various groups of Episcopalians ascribed to the sacraments! They claim that their bishops are divinely appointed guardians of faith, yet there is obviously great difference of opinion among them on many doctrinal points, and they certainly are not able to exercise any considerable authority in restraint of doctrinal abuse. No, there is no unity in the Episcopal Church. There is perhaps as much variation within the Episcopal Church as there is in all the rest of Protestantism.

No doctrine is really worth much if one cannot put it to use in his spiritual life and worship, and the Episcopal Church is crippled in this regard so far as many of its tenets are concerned. They claim that they offer sacramental confession to their people, but it is only in theory. The fact is that they are not equipped to hear confessions. With rare exceptions, there are no confessional booths in Episcopal churches. There are no regular times at which confessions are heard. If anyone really wants to make a confession, he must make an appointment. All possibility of anonymity is completely lost, and, with it, the possibility of a complete and holy confession on the part of a penitent whose need is really great. Perhaps even more important is the fact that it simply isn't done: a person trying to live a Catholic life in an Episcopal church could not have the strength that comes from the knowledge that one's associates are struggling beside him toward the same goal.

Most of all, my Episcopalian friends claimed the apostolic succession, their insistence upon which had given their church its name. They strongly resented the fact that the Catholic Church had declared their orders invalid. Their argument always assumed that the Catholic Church had declared Anglican orders invalid on the grounds of the divorce of Henry VIII and the subsequent oath of supremacy of the English Crown over the Church in England which English bishops were forced to take. The same bishops remained in power, they said, so why didn't their orders have the same standing as Greek orders? Yet the Catholic Church has never maintained that either the divorce or the oath of supremacy vitiated Anglican orders, but rather that Anglican orders were descended from a Bishop Matthew Parker, who was consecrated a bishop by a Bishop Barlow, who had previously been degraded because of his refusal to give up heretical doctrines. But this was long after Henry VIII had died.

This indicates a rather important thing which I found commonly characterizing Protestant writings on Catholic subjects. Protestants do not usually represent the Catholic argument as at all the same thing that Catholics do. Yet I found that Catholic writers do represent Protestant arguments as Protestants do. I presume that this is caused by an assumption on the part of the Protestants that they know the Catholic case without studying it. One Protestant friend of mine told me that he didn't think that any study was necessary to understand Catholicism, and he is a college graduate, too. But I don't believe that ignorance is always the cause. Last spring I heard the dean of one of the greatest of the Protestant theological schools deliver a Phi Beta Kappa oration in which he said that the Wycliffe Bible was the first English Bible, and he implied that the King James Bible preceded the Douay Bible. A man in his position cannot plead ignorance, and one has a right to assume that a Phi Beta Kappa oration does not contain careless errors.

My Episcopalian friends also claimed catholicity. I could not find their claim justified. My finding that their claim to the apostolic succession was false made it impossible for me to concede to them catholicity—universality—in time, for it dated their origin at a time more than fifteen hundred years after the death of Our Lord. That the Episcopal Church is not catholic in doctrine is strongly indicated by the split into High and Low Church factions with a multitude of degrees within each of these sharply contrasting theological groups, and by the fact that both groups now generally disregard the famous Thirty-Nine Articles upon which they were founded.

But, most of all, the Episcopal Church is not catholic because it is the Church of England, or of the descendants of English colonists and their conquered subjects. How much this statement is open to criticism I well realize. I am cognizant of the extensive missionary work which has been carried on by the Episcopal Church. I know that the American Episcopal Church does not recognize the supremacy of the British Crown, or of the Archbishop of Canterbury. I know that the Book of Common Prayer has been translated into the languages of the missionary districts. But, for all of these admittedly significant things, I think that it must be clear to everyone who considers it advisedly that the Episcopal Church throughout the world is, essentially, a national church: the Church of England.

This characteristic of nationalism, or of limited group appeal of some other sort, I found to be a rather general characteristic of Protestantism. The various Lutheran sects are fundamentally German or Scandinavian. The Presbyterian Church is Scotch. The Church of the Nazarene and the Salvation Army appeal almost exclusively to the economically downtrodden. The Unitarian Church draws its membership principally from intellectuals who for the most part substitute ethical culture for religion. But none seems to have universal appeal for all peoples and all classes.

And so it came about that I turned my interest more fully to the Church whose days I had once thought to be numbered.

The Mass did not mean much to me the first time I heard it. The choir was one of remarkable beauty, and the altar, with its candlelight, and the vestments, too, were beautiful. But I went alone. There were no missals in the pews. I had never read or heard a word about the real nature of the Mass. I had no idea of what prayers were being said or what part the congregation had in them. So, in spite of that degree of beauty which must be evident to any stranger hearing a High Mass well sung, I left with the feeling that I had very little to show for the time I had spent.

It was the better part of a year before I again heard Mass. In the meantime I had read and discussed a great deal about the Catholic Church and her central act of worship. As far as my Protestant conception of sacraments would allow, I knew what to expect, and went prepared to enter into the worship. It was Solemn High Mass on Christmas morning. Everything associated with it was marvelously beautiful. My understanding of the ceremonies scarcely extended beyond the knowledge that Catholics believed it to be the sacrifice of the body and blood of Our Lord, yet I felt greatly rewarded for having attended this time.

I had long since become convinced that the Congregational Church, with the greater part of Protestantism, was inadequate. I was still strongly interested in the high Episcopal Church. But I heard Mass fairly frequently from then on, and so, as I saw the Episcopal Church more and more clearly to be simply a Protestant church with all of the weaknesses which I had found in Protestantism inherent in its structure, I was becoming familiar with the Catholic Church in her public functions as I had long been coming to know her in literature and discussion.

I will never forget that moment in which I decided to present myself for instructions! I had attended an evening Lenten service at which the rosary was said and the Benediction of the Blessed Sacrament given. As I arose to leave, I questioned whether I should go to the priest and ask for instructions. What a storm of emotions, desires, prejudices, and longings surged through my breast in that brief moment when I had to decide upon action which might change my life completely, and that of those closest to me, or upon delay which might become an eternity lost! As I stood there before the altar, I could feel my heart beating with hard, rapid blows against my ribs. I could hear ringing in my ears the protests and pleading of past generations of my own flesh and blood, men and women who had firmly believed that the Catholic Church was the instrument of the devil and who had suffered to lay the foundations of that very Church which I was now on the verge of forsaking in favor of their enemy! Yet I felt that I must make a decision to find that truth which I was no longer able to believe that their sacrifice had won for me, and so, after an infinite moment of violent conflict, I stepped up to a nun and asked if I could see the priest.

She sent me back into the sacristy. I told the priest that I wanted to receive instructions, and so together we began a thorough, systematic study of Catholic doctrine and practice. Fortunately, the priest to whom I presented myself was a skillful catechist. He met all of my objections with understanding and with flawless reasoning. More than that, he gave me excellent references relating to points on which I was not fully satisfied or upon which he himself was not immediately informed. Of the many points on which I was already in accord with Catholic doctrine we touched only lightly, but we treated in exhaustive detail those doctrines and practices with which I was not in agreement. Before we had finished I was completely satisfied, intellectually, on all points of difficulty, including the papacy, the veneration of the saints, especially of Mary, the celibacy of the priesthood, and many other things.

Here I found a Church of strong faith, constant through all ages and in all places, which realized the tremendous importance of thoroughly teaching all her children.

From the pulpit, I heard only religious themes, whether from the priests of the parish where I was receiving instructions or visiting priests, whether in a different parish or diocese entirely. The Church preaches Christ and his religion: the pulpit is not turned to political and other secular uses. There are exceptions, of course, but they are rare.

Catholic priests must inevitably vary in abilities just as do Protestant ministers, but I found that the effectiveness of divine worship was not vitiated by mediocre priests. Their sermons, to be sure, vary with their abilities. However, the sermon is not the principal part or the climax of the service, but only an incidental, nonessential part of it which can be left out completely, as it often is, without at all affecting the completeness of the service. The Mass is always beautiful, holy, and inspiring, regardless of the abilities of the priest who celebrates.

I found that the Catholic Church actually is catholic. It is catholic in point of time, because its corporate existence has been uninterrupted since its founding by Christ. It is catholic in doctrine because it has always taught the same orthodox doctrine in all places. It is catholic in teaching because it has always taught the whole faith and has not yielded to the tendency of Protestant churches to develop pet doctrines at the expense of others. It is catholic in appeal because in all nations people of all classes kneel at its altar, and social lines do not determine which Catholic church in a given community one shall attend: for white and black, merchant and laborer, rich and poor all kneel at the same altar, side by side.

The Catholic Church cannot be considered as a social luxury. For every Catholic it is the first among his necessities. The tremendous number of priests and nuns who give their lives—not simply their professional services—to the Church must certainly be a cogent indication, to anyone who will consider it, of how vital and important a factor the Church must be to Catholics.

I have said that I was intellectually satisfied on all points of Catholic doctrine and practice during my instructions. But conversion is not only of the mind but also of the heart. I needed the nourishment of the Blessed Sacrament before I could ever grow in emotional and spiritual appreciation of the Church. During the last weeks of my instructions I went often to Low Mass, and saw the faithful going up to the altar rail and receiving the body of Our Lord. How I longed to be among them! How I thrilled on hearing the words of blessing pronounced by the priest as he gave the Host to each one!

At last my day came, and I received my first Communion. Brilliant as is the aura which surrounds every first experience of beauty and sublimity, I have felt that the reception of the Blessed Sacrament has meant far more to me since than it did then. For, nourished on the Sacrament, I have grown in the emotional appreciation of a fact of which I had principally an intellectual appreciation on that day when, for the first time, I knelt at the altar rail and received the body of Our Lord: the Real Presence.

In my own life the reception of the Eucharist has been the climax of a spiritual pilgrimage which commanded my interests and energies, both intellectual and emotional, for a period of about eight years. Now that pilgrimage is over: I have come home, and I have found rest in the house of my Holy Mother.

FROM COMMUNISM TO CHRIST

Dorothy Day

It is a long road from active membership in various Communist organizations to the leadership of the Catholic Worker Movement and other forms of Catholic action. Yet such was the road traveled by Dorothy Day, lecturer, editor, author, and apostle of charity. Born in Brooklyn, New York, in 1897, she went as a small child with her family to California, where they remained until the earthquake of 1906. They then settled in Chicago, where Dorothy attended the public grade and high schools.

From 1914 to 1916 she attended the University of Illinois and then came to New York and began reporting for the New York *Call.* She joined the Socialist party and later became a member of the Industrial Workers of the World and of various Communist organizations. Though she did not sign up as a member of the Communist party, she championed its objectives by her writings in radical publications. After leaving the *Call,* she was successively associated with the *Masses,* the *Liberator,* and the *New Masses;* she likewise reported for dailies in Chicago, New York, and New Orleans.

Though Miss Day gave up religion, she retained her belief in God. After her conversion to the Catholic faith in 1927, she devoted herself to writing for periodicals and reporting in New York, California, Florida, and Mexico. Returning to New York in 1933, she launched, with the aid of Peter Maurin, the Catholic Worker Movement. The monthly paper, the *Catholic Worker,* was founded in May 1933, and in 1946 it reached a circulation of sixty thousand. It champions the principles of social justice and the sanctity of labor.

In an effort to translate the principles of the Catholic Worker Movement into action, a chain of houses was established, providing lodging and free meals for those temporarily unemployed. No questions are asked and thousands benefit by this charity. The homes are known as Houses of Hospitality, and a number of the members of the Catholic Worker Movement live in such establishments and share the simple fare of their guests. In New York City six hundred are fed daily, and in 1943 there were thirty-two Houses of Hospitality in several states. In addition, farms for such jobless people are operated near Easton, Pennsylvania; Upton, Massachusetts; Cleveland, Ohio, and Detroit, Michigan.

Having no personal means, Miss Day relies on charity and prayer for the necessary funds to carry on her far-reaching apostolate of charity and, with her co-workers, practices voluntary poverty, sharing with those in need. Her clients are the poor, the underprivileged, the victims of discrimination; and, like a modern Francis of Assisi, Dorothy Day has given her talents, energy, and devotion without stint to win for them the economic and social decencies of life in a civilization calling itself Christian.

Her struggle for social justice for the laboring classes constitutes the most effective answer to Communism, because it seeks to remove the conditions which breed advocates of class strife and revolution. Her pioneering and courageous work have won for Dorothy Day a unique place among the apostles of charity of our day. She is a Benedictine Oblate and, though wearing the garb of a laywoman, she is doing the work of a religious in the market place. Her two books, *From Union Square to Rome* and *House of Hospitality*, tell the story of her life and work.

AFTER my conversion, many of my relatives and friends who are Communists kept asking with dismay: "How could you become a Catholic? After all, you did believe with us that religion is the opium of the people." The circumstances that led to my conversion are strange—so strange that even now, after many years in the Church, there are those who do not believe that I am a Catholic, but rather an enemy boring from within.

This story is a dipping back into the past to the time when I believed what many Communists profess to believe today. The story is not always pleasant or easy to tell, and it ends with my conversion, when my real work began.

While it is true that horror for one's sins often turns one to God, what I want to bring out in this sketch is the succession of events that led me to His feet, glimpses of Him that I received through many years which made me feel a vital need of Him and of religion. I will try to trace for you the steps by which I came to accept the faith that I believe was always in my heart.

I write in the very beginning of finding the Bible and the impression it made on me. I must have read it a great deal, for many passages remained with me through my earlier years to return and haunt me. The Psalms were what I read most when I was in jail in Occoquan. I read with a sense of coming back to something that I had lost. There was an echoing in my heart. And how can anyone who has known human sorrow and human joy fail to respond to these words of the Psalmist: "Out of the depths I have cried to thee, O Lord"?

The *Imitation of Christ* is a book that followed me through my days. Again and again I came across copies of it, and reading it brought me comfort. I felt in the background of my life a waiting force that would lift me up eventually.

I later became acquainted with the poem of Francis Thompson, *The Hound of Heaven*, and was moved by its power. Eugene O'Neill recited it first to me in the back room of a saloon on Sixth Avenue where the Provincetown players and playwrights used to gather after their performances.

I fled Him, down the nights and down the days;
   I fled Him, down the arches of the years;
I fled Him, down the labyrinthine ways
   Of my own mind; and in the mist of tears
I hid from Him . . .

Through all my daily life, in those I came in contact with, in the things I read and heard, I felt that sense of being followed, of being desired; a sense of hope and expectation.

Through those years I read all of Dostoevski's novels, and it was, as Berdyaev says, a profound spiritual experience. The scene in *Crime and Punishment* where the young prosti-

tute reads from the New Testament to Raskolnikoff, sensing
the sin which weighed upon him more profound than her
own; that story, *The Honest Thief;* those passages in *The
Brothers Karamazov;* the sayings of Father Zossima, Mitya's
conversion in jail, the very legend of the Grand Inquisitor—
all these helped to lead me on. The characters Alyosha and
the Idiot testified to Christ in us. I was moved to the depths
of my being by the reading of these books during my early
twenties, when I, too, was tasting the bitterness and the
dregs of life and shuddered at its harshness and cruelty.

Do you remember that little story that Grushenka told in
The Brothers Karamazov? "Once upon a time there was a
peasant woman and a very wicked woman she was. And she
died and did not leave a single good deed behind. The
devils caught her and plunged her into a lake of fire. So her
guardian angel stood and wondered what good deed of hers
he could remember to tell God. 'She once pulled up an
onion in her garden,' said he, 'and gave it to a beggar
woman.' And God answered: 'You take that onion then,
hold it out to her in the lake, and let her take hold and be
pulled out. And if you pull her out of the lake, let her come to
Paradise, but if the onion breaks, then the woman must stay
where she is.' The angel ran to the woman and held out the
onion to her. 'Come,' said he, 'catch hold, and I'll pull you
out.' And he began cautiously pulling her out. He had just
pulled her out, when the other sinners in the lake, seeing
how she was being drawn out, began catching hold of her
so as to be pulled out with her. But she was a very wicked
woman and she began kicking them. 'I'm to be pulled out,
not you. It's my onion, not yours.' As soon as she said that,
the onion broke. And the woman fell into the lake and she is
burning there to this day. So the angel wept and went away."

Sometimes, in thinking and wondering at God's goodness
to me, I have thought that it was because I gave away an
onion. Because I sincerely loved His poor, He taught me to
know Him. And when I think of the little I ever did, I am
filled with hope and love for all those others devoted to the
cause of social justice.

[116]

"What glorious hope!" Mauriac writes. "There are all those who will discover that their neighbor is Jesus himself, although they belong to the mass of those who do not know Christ or who have forgotten Him. And nevertheless they will find themselves well loved. It is impossible for any one of those who has real charity in his heart not to serve Christ. Even some of those who think they hate Him have consecrated their lives to Him; for Jesus is disguised and masked in the midst of men, hidden among the poor, among the sick, among prisoners, among strangers. Many who serve Him officially have never know who He was, and many who do not even know His name will hear on the last day the words that open to them the gates of joy: 'Those children were I, and I those working men. I wept on the hospital bed. I was that murderer in his cell whom you consoled.'"

But always the glimpses of God came most when I was alone. Objectors cannot say that it was fear of loneliness and solitude and pain that made me turn to Him. It was in those few years when I was alone and most happy that I found Him. I found Him at last through joy and thanksgiving, not through sorrow.

Yet how can I say that either? Better let it be said that I found Him through His poor, and in a moment of joy I turned to Him. I have said, sometimes flippantly, that the mass of bourgeois smug Christians who denied Christ in His poor made me turn to Communism, and that it was the Communists and working with them that made me turn to God.

Communism, says our Holy Father, can be likened to a heresy, and a heresy is a distortion of the truth. Many Christians have lost sight, to a great extent, of the communal aspect of Christianity, so the collective ideal is the result. They have failed to learn a philosophy of labor, have failed to see Christ in the worker. So in Russia the worker, instead of Christ, has been exalted. They have the dictatorship of the proletariat maintained by one man, also a dictator. The proletariat as a class had come to be considered the Messiah, the deliverer.

[117]

A mystic may be called a man in love with God. Not one who loves God, but who is *in love with God*. And this mystical love, which is an exalted emotion, leads one to love the things of Christ. His footsteps are sacred. The steps of His passion and death are retraced down through the ages. Almost every time you step into a church you see people making the Stations of the Cross. They meditate on the mysteries of His life, death, and resurrection, and by this they are retracing with love those early scenes and identifying themselves with the actors in those scenes.

When we suffer, we are told we suffer with Christ. We are "completing the sufferings of Christ." We suffer His loneliness and fear in the garden when His friends slept. We are bowed down with Him under the weight of not only our own sins but the sins of each other, of the whole world. We are those who are sinned against and those who are sinning. We are identified with Him, one with Him. We are members of His Mystical Body.

Often there is a mystical element in the love of a radical worker for his brother, for his fellow worker. It extends to the scene of his sufferings, and those spots where he has suffered and died are hallowed. The names of places like Everett, Ludlow, Bisbee, South Chicago, Imperial Valley, Elaine, Arkansas, and all those other places where workers have suffered and died for their cause, have become sacred to the worker. Whenever men have laid down their lives for their fellows, they are doing it in a measure for Him. This I still firmly believe, even though you and others may not realize it.

"Inasmuch as ye have done it unto one of the least of these brethren, you have done it unto me." Feeling this as strongly as I did, is it any wonder that I was led finally to the feet of Christ?

I do not mean at all that I went around in a state of exaltation or that any radical does. Love is a matter of the will. During a long strike, the spirit falters and it is hard for the leaders to keep up the morale of the men and to keep the fire of hope burning within them. They have a hard time

[118]

sustaining this hope themselves. St. Teresa says that there are three attributes of the soul: memory, understanding, and will. These very leaders, by their understanding of the struggle, how victory is gained very often through defeat, how every little gain benefits the workers all over the country, through their memory of past struggles, are enabled to strengthen their wills to go on. It is only by exerting these faculties of the soul that one is enabled to love one's fellow. And this strength comes from God. There can be no brotherhood without the Fatherhood of God.

"It is impossible," says Mauriac, "for any one of those who has charity in his heart not to serve Christ. Even those who think they hate Him have consecrated their lives to Him." It was from men such as these that I became convinced, little by little, of the necessity for religion and for God in my everyday life. I know now that the Catholic Church is the church of the poor, no matter what you say about the wealth of her priests and bishops. I met few Catholics before my conversion, but daily I saw people coming from Mass.

Never did I set foot in a Catholic church but that I saw people there at home with Him. First Fridays, novenas, and missions brought the masses thronging in and out of the Catholic churches. They were of all nationalities, of all classes, but most of all they were the poor. The very attacks made against the Church proved her Divinity to me. Nothing but a Divine institution could have survived the betrayal of Judas, the denial of Peter, the sins of many of those who professed her Faith and who were supposed to minister to her poor.

Christ is God or He is the world's greatest liar and impostor. How can Communists who claim to revere Him as a working-class leader fail to see this? And if Christ established His Church on earth with Peter as its rock, that faulty one who denied him three times, who fled from Him when he was in trouble, then I, too, wanted a share in that tender, compassionate love that is so great. Christ can forgive all sins and yearn over us no matter how far we fall.

A conversion is a lonely experience. We do not know what

is going on in the depths of the heart and soul of another. We scarcely know ourselves. How did it all come about, this turning toward religion? I have to go back to the beginning, to my first memories of God.

My search for God began out in California, where my family had moved from New York a year before. We were living in Berkeley in a furnished house, waiting for our furniture to come around the Horn. It was Sunday afternoon in the attic. I remember the day was very chilly, though there were rose, violets, and calla lilies blooming in the garden. My sister and I had been making dolls of the calla lilies, putting rosebuds for heads at the top of the long, graceful blossoms. Then we made perfume, crushing flowers into a bottle with a little water in it. Even now I can remember the peculiar, delicious, pungent smell.

And then I remember we were in the attic. I was sitting behind a table, pretending I was the teacher, reading aloud from a Bible that I had found. Slowly, as I read, a new personality impressed itself on me. I was being introduced to someone, and I knew almost immediately that I was discovering God.

I knew that I had just really discovered Him because it excited me tremendously. It was as though life were fuller, richer, more exciting in every way. Here was someone that I had never really known about before and yet felt to be One whom I would never forget, that I would never get away from. The game might grow stale, it might assume new meanings, new aspects, but life would never again be the same. I had made a great discovery.

Of course I had heard of Him previous to this. Before we moved to California my older brothers and I had gone to school in Bath Beach, and there, every morning, the teacher read something from the Bible and we bowed our heads on the desk and recited the Lord's Prayer. I had forgotten that until this moment of writing. It did not impress me then, and I remember now simply raising my head after the prayers to watch my breath fade upon the varnished desk.

In my family the name of God was never mentioned.

Mother and Father never went to church, none of us children had been baptized, and to speak of the soul was to speak immodestly, uncovering what might better remain hidden.

In all the first years I remember nothing about God except that routine chapter and prayer in school which I did not feel. It was that Sunday afternoon up in the dim attic, and the rich, deep feeling of having a book which would be with me through life, which stands out in my mind now.

I had been reading books for a long time—since I was four, in fact. I can remember some I read: children's stories, and the fascinating *Arabian Nights*, which I enjoyed when I was six. But this was the first Bible I had ever seen. It came with the furnished house, and I wanted even then to keep it always.

When I was eight we moved to Chicago, and there I met my first Catholic. It was Mrs. Barrett who gave me my first impulse toward Catholicism. It was about ten o'clock in the morning that I went up to Kathryn's to call for her to come out and play. There was no one on the porch or in the kitchen. The breakfast dishes had all been washed. They were long railroad apartments, those flats, and thinking the children must be in the front room, I burst in and ran through the bedrooms.

In the front bedroom Mrs. Barrett was on her knees, saying her prayers. She turned to tell me that Kathryn and the children had all gone to the store and went on with her praying. And I felt a warm burst of love toward Mrs. Barrett that I have never forgotten, a feeling of gratitude and happiness that still warms my heart when I remember her. She had God, and there was beauty and joy in her life.

All through my life, what she was doing remained with me. And though I became oppressed with the problems of poverty and injustice, though I groaned at the hideous sordidness of man's lot, though there were years when I clung to the philosophy of economic determinism as an explanation of man's fate, still there were moments when, in the midst of misery and class strife, life was shot through with glory. Mrs. Barrett, in her sordid little tenement flat, finished her breakfast dishes at ten o'clock in the morning and got down on her knees and prayed to God.

When I was twelve years old an Episcopal minister, canvassing the neighborhood for his parishioners, came to the house and, discovering that my mother had been brought up in that Church, persuaded her to send me to the confirmation class that was being started. I had not yet been baptized, so I learned the catechism; I was preparing at the same time for confirmation. I cannot remember being particularly affected by these formalities. I went willingly every Monday afternoon because my fourteen-year-old playmate went also.

The godparents who were chosen for me were two parishioners, mother and son, whom I had never known before and whose names I do not recall now. I remember being much embarrassed at being baptized, tall, gawky girl that I was, and the fact that I was one of many being confirmed did not make me feel any easier. Going to the communion rail was an agony. Fortunately, one did not have to do that more than a few times a year. What I did love were the Psalms and anthems, the rubrics of the church. When the choir sang the *Te Deum* or the *Benedicite*, my heart melted within me. They expressed pure truth and beauty to me, and for a year or so I never missed Sunday service.

While still a student in high school, I left the Episcopal Church quite definitely. Mother had taken up Christian Science to help herself, perhaps, and because I was suffering from bad headaches at the time, she had treatments for me too. There was a practitioner living across the street, and I read *Science and Health* and some of the pamphlets, and this new revelation seemed as convincing to me as the tenets of the Episcopal Church.

The pastor of the church where I had been baptized two years before came to struggle for my soul and remained talking to me all one afternoon, but I was obdurate in my refusal to return to church. I was in a "free" mood, and my reading at the time made me skeptical. My belief in God remained firm and I continued to read the New Testament regularly, but I felt it was no longer necessary to go to church. I distrusted all churches after reading the books of London and Sinclair. So, from that time on, I ceased going, much to the relief of my sister, who complained when I dragged her unwillingly to services.

At sixteen I entered the University of Illinois, where I remained for two years. I earned my room and board by doing odd jobs, and often I was cold, hungry, and lonesome. I felt completely alone in the world, divorced from family, from all security, even from God. There was no one to guide my footsteps to the paths of the Spirit, and everything I read turned me away from it. The writing of Kropotkin attracted me, and I joined a small group of Socialists in Urbana and wrote radical articles.

My closest friend—and the first real one I ever had—was a Jewish girl, Rayna Prohme, who later achieved prominence as a Communist leader in China, and in Moscow, where she died. In *Personal History*, Vincent Sheean devotes most of a chapter to her work and influence. I read of her death with a sense of great personal loss.

I always felt that Rayna had those reserves of "spiritual energy" which Maritain speaks of. "It is to be noted," he writes, "that the reserves of spiritual energy that are to be found in human nature may be liberated by preaching and example and set in operation in the hearts of many without any sense of spiritual things other than that which they may find in the concrete experience of the fight for justice here below. . . . It follows from the idea of Catholicity that every just man of non-Christian denomination belongs to the invisible unity of the Church and on this ground only has a title to salvation. . . ."

So reading, my heart is comforted about Rayna, for most assuredly she loved truth and justice.

After two years at the university, struggling against loneliness, cold, hunger, and poverty, I came to New York, whither my family had now moved, and got a job on the New York *Call*, a Socialist paper. I left home to take a room down on the East Side. I wrote in behalf of the dwellers in

[123]

the slums, pleading for decent living conditions and for social justice for the laboring classes, then so largely un-
unionized. I joined the ranks of picketers in labor strikes and
fought conscription during World War I.

Many a morning, after sitting all night in taverns or coming from balls over at Webster Hall, I went to an early Mass
at St. Joseph's Church on Sixth Avenue. It was just around
the corner from where I lived, and seeing people going to
an early weekday Mass attracted me. What were they finding there? I seemed to feel the faith of those about me, and
I longed for their faith. My own life was sordid, and yet I
had had occasional glimpses of the true and the beautiful.
So I used to go in and kneel in a back pew of St. Joseph's,
and perhaps I asked even then, "God, be merciful to me, a
sinner."

So many nurses had joined the Red Cross and had gone
abroad that there was a great need for nurses at home.
Though still bitterly pacifist, I decided that nursing the
sick was not contrary to my beliefs, and so, in January 1918,
I signed up as a probationer in Kings County Hospital in
Brooklyn. There I met a Miss Adams, a probationer, who
brought to her work a joy and enthusiasm that was con-
tagious. She was a Catholic, and I was in such close association with her for the coming year that I came to admire her
greatly and to associate all her natural goodness and ability
with her Catholicism.

She didn't go to Mass more than once a week; she never
spoke of her faith. She had no Catholic literature in her
room aside from her prayer book, and she didn't use that
except on special occasions. She was the average sort of
Catholic whose faith was so solid a part of her life that she
didn't need to talk about it. I felt the healthiness of her
soul; I felt that it was strong and vigorous, but she did not
discuss it any more than she would discuss the health of her
body. I began to go to Mass with her on Sunday mornings,
even though it meant going without a few hours of much-
needed sleep. Mass was at five o'clock or five-thirty, and we

worked from seven to seven with half a day off on Sunday and half a day during the week.

I spent a year in Europe, but because I was associating at that time only with liberals, I had no vital contact with what was going on in those countries. My time in England, France, and Italy was spent with people who were interested only in art and literature and were not in any sense propagandists.

On returning from Europe, I came to Chicago and worked with Robert Minor on the *Liberator*. Minor was a former member of the I.W.W. who had become converted to the Communist cause. My sister was staying with me at that time in Chicago, and in midwinter we decided for personal reasons to go down to New Orleans and work there. We lived on St. Peter Street, across the street from the *cabildo* and the cathedral. I found work on a morning newspaper, the *Item*, and that winter I was occupied in straight newspaper work, writing interviews and feature stories.

Many evenings I had assignments, but when there were none, and I heard the cathedral bells ringing for evening devotions, I used to go to church. It was the first time I had been present at Benediction, and it made a profound impression on me. The very physical attitude of devotion of those about me made me bow my head. But did I feel the Presence there? I do not know. But I remembered those lines from the *Imitation:* "Who, humbly approaching to the fountain of sweetness, doth not carry thence some little sweetness? Who, standing by a copious fire, doth not derive therefrom some little heat?"

I wanted to know what the Benediction hymns were, so I bought a little manual of prayers at a religious-goods store down the street. I read the Mass. I had to be at the office by seven in the morning, and Sunday mornings I was too lazy to get up. But I learned a great deal from that little book. I did not know a single Catholic in New Orleans. If any of my associates were nominally Catholic, they did not let me know it. There was no one for me to talk to. But my devotion was sincere and I continued to make "visits."

Another girl, who is now secretary of the Communist affiliate, the League for Spanish Democracy in Chicago, was living with my sister and me. That Christmas she goodheartedly gave me a rosary for a present, and I learned to say it at the evening services in the cathedral. She was a Russian Jew and did not understand my interest in Catholicism. She just wanted to give me something she thought I'd like. I have not seen this friend since that winter, but I shall always remember her with gratitude and love.

That spring there occurred a reversal in my fortunes which brought about a very deep change in my life. During one of these crowded years I wrote a book, a very bad book, which one of the moving-picture companies bought on publication. I haven't the slightest idea why they bought it, since they never produced it. It was probably just one of many they extravagantly purchased to keep some other moving-picture company from producing it. They paid what to them was a very small sum, but which to me was the very large total of five thousand dollars, two thousand of which went to my publishers.

My reaction was that of many other radicals—now I could at last have a home of my own and a quiet spot off in the country where there would be time for study and writing and that small measure of security necessary for that work. I wanted to be by the water, so I bought a small bungalow with a plot of ground twenty by eighty feet on Raritan Bay on Staten Island.

Now that I had a place of my own to keep them in, Mother sent me some of my high-school books. The other day I came across these words, written on a faded slip of paper in my own writing. I do not remember writing them:

"Life would be utterly unbearable if we thought we were going nowhere, that we had nothing to look forward to. The greatest gift life can offer would be a faith in God and a hereafter. Why don't we have it? Perhaps, like all gifts, it must be struggled for. 'God, I believe' (or, rather, 'I must believe or despair'), 'Help Thou my unbelief. Take away my heart of stone and give me a heart of flesh.'

"It is interesting to note that these requests are mandatory. It is as though God expected us to demand these things as our right, not to plead for them as favors. 'Give us this day our daily bread,' not 'We beseech Thee to give us.'

"As to religious exercises, are not all those things silly? Yet to make the body strong, there must be physical exercise, discipline, and exertion. Then why not exercises for the soul, to be done whether we care for them or not, automatically if we must, at first—strainingly, gropingly, if we feel that way about it, but do them we must."

My child was born in March at the end of a harsh winter. In December, I had to come in from the country and take a little apartment in town. It was good to be there, close to friends, close to a church where I could stop and pray. I read the *Imitation of Christ* a great deal. I knew that I was going to have my child baptized a Catholic, cost what it may. I knew that I was not going to have her floundering through many years as I had done, doubting and hesitating, undisciplined and amoral. I felt it was the greatest thing I could do for a child. For myself, I prayed for the gift of faith. I was sure, yet not sure. I postponed the day of decision.

A woman does not want to be alone at such a time. Even the most hardened, the most irreverent, is awed by the stupendous fact of creation. No matter how cynically or casually the worldly may treat the birth of a child, it remains spiritually and physically a tremendous event. God pity the woman who does not feel the fear, the awe, and the joy of bringing a child into the world.

Becoming a Catholic would mean facing life alone, and I clung to family life. It was hard to contemplate giving up a mate in order that my child and I could become members of the Church. Fred would have nothing to do with religion, or with me if I embraced it. So I waited.

Those last months of waiting I was too happy to know the unrest of indecision. I was waiting. The days were slow in passing, but week by week the time came nearer. I spent some time in writing, but in general I felt inactive, incapable of going to meetings, of seeing many people, of taking up the threads of my past life.

And then the little one was born, and with her birth the spring was upon us. My joy was so great that I sat up in bed in the hospital and wrote an article for the *New Masses* about my child, wanting to share my joy with the world. I was glad to write it for a workers' magazine because it was a joy all women know, no matter what their grief at poverty, unemployment, and class war.

The article so appealed to my Marxist friends that the account was reprinted all over the world in workers' papers. Diego Rivera, when I met him some four years afterward in Mexico, greeted me as the author of it. And Walt Carmen, who was at that time editor of the *New Masses,* said that it had been printed in Russian newspapers and that I had rubles awaiting me in Moscow.

There was a Catholic girl in the bed next to me in the ward. "What you going to name your baby?" she asked me. "Teresa? I have a medal of the Little Flower here—you can have it if you want it."

I told her I didn't believe in such things, and she didn't take it amiss. "If you like someone, you like to have something to remind you of them," she said, and I was ashamed and took the medal.

Because of an attack of grippe after I left the hospital, Teresa's baptism was postponed for a time. Not being a Catholic myself, and not having been baptized myself until I was twelve, I didn't know the anxiety of Catholic mothers, that feeling almost that the baby had not yet been born until it had been baptized.

Deep moments of happiness gave way to a feeling of struggle, of a long, silent fight to be gone through with. There had been the physical struggle, the mortal combat almost, of giving birth to a child, and now there was coming the struggle for my own soul. I knew Teresa would be baptized, and I knew also the rending it would cause in human relations around me. I was to be torn and agonized again, I knew, and I was all for putting off the hard day.

Then one afternoon, as I wheeled her in her little carriage along the road which led down to St. Joseph's Home, a former estate of Charles Schwab which had been given to the Sisters of Charity, I met a Sister who was on her way to visit a neighbor of mine.

That estate had been one of my stumbling blocks. I could never pass it without thinking of Schwab's career as head of the Bethlehem Steel Corporation, of his work in breaking the Homestead strike, of how he, to that day, refused to recognize unions of workers in his Bethlehem Steel Corporation.

I could not but feel that his was tainted money which the Sisters had accepted. It was, I felt, money which belonged to the workers. He had defrauded the worker of a just wage. His sins cried to heaven for vengeance. He had ground the faces of the poor. "Let not the oil of the sinner fatten my head,"[1] I thought with the Psalmist. "He that offereth sacrifice of the goods of the poor, is as one that sacrificeth the son in the presence of his father. . . . He that sheddeth blood, and he that defraudeth the labourer of his hire, are brothers."[2] The words of the son of Sirach went through my brain, wearying me. Yet, strangely enough, in bitterness of soul these thoughts led me inevitably to the problem: how to have Teresa baptized.

That bitterness felt by so many in the radical labor movement toward what they call "organized religion" was mixed with the knowledge of the divinity of the Catholic Church. It was ever in my mind that the human frailties, sins, and ignorances of those in high places throughout history only proved that the Church *must* be divine to have persisted through the centuries. I would not blame the Church for what I felt were the mistakes of churchmen.

I could always console myself with Christ's words that the greatest enemies would be those of the "household."

I felt, too, that there were going to be many obstacles put in my path, and that this in a strange way was one of them.

That afternoon I was emboldened by a sense of compul-

[1] Psalms 140:5.   [2] Ecclesiasticus 34:24-27.

sion to speak to the Sister who was hurrying by me, to ask
her how to go about having a baby baptized. I had a warm
feeling as I approached her, a feeling that whatever the errors of Charlie Schwab, Sister Aloysia had no part in them in
her simplicity and poverty.

She was very matter-of-fact. She seemed to take things for
granted, and was not surprised that a mother of a new baby
would stop her in this casual fashion and ask her so stupendous a question. Of course a mother, no matter how heathen
she might be, would want her baby to be sure of eternal life!
She knew of me by reputation—indeed all the neighborhood
knew that we and our friends were either communist or
anarchist in sympathies.

But those same dear Catholic neighbors who heard sermons excoriating "the fiendish and foul machinations of the
Communists" (I have heard just such expressions used)
were kindly people who came to use our telephone and
bring us a pie now and then, who played with us on the
beach and offered us lifts to the village in their cars. Sister
Aloysia, too, had no fear, only a neighborly interest in us all.
Perhaps she had been praying for us these past two years as
she swept past down the lane on a visit to some of the Catholics at the end of the road. Perhaps her work-worn hand was
clutching that rosary which jingled at her side just a little
more fervently and comfortingly.

She felt my liking, and I was warmed by her interest. She
took me under her protection immediately. She did not make
little of my difficulties, nor did she think for a minute that
they were insurmountable. There was a hard row to hoe in
front of us was her attitude, but we could get through it.
She would hang onto that long, formidable-looking rosary of
hers, hang onto it like an anchor, and together we would
ride out the gale of opposition and controversy. All we had
to do was depend on prayer.

And as for practical details, we would just go ahead as
though it were very simple. Did I have any Catholic relatives?

Yes, there was Cousin Grace. She was married, and she

[130]

and her husband could be reached, though I had not seen them or any relatives for years.

All right, then, she herself, Sister Aloysia, would get in touch with the parish priest in Tottenville, a young man, very obliging. He had been coming down to offer up Mass at the Home, and she could see him after breakfast the next morning.

Somehow or other, with the irregularities of her parents not being Catholic, Teresa's baptism did not take place until late June. Sister Aloysia, in her anxiety that all should go well, dropped in every day to see if I were persisting in my determination. She also was quite frank in her anxiety for the baby's welfare. One morning she came rushing up on the porch. "She's not dead yet?" she wanted to know, and then praised God that the baby was living and also struggling toward her baptism. Sister was sure that the powers of darkness were struggling hard for my little one. "He's greedy for souls," she said, meaning the devil, and in this case I had more confidence and hope than she, because I assured her Christ must be even more so. Anyway, Teresa thrived lustily and was beginning to throw back her head and crow and gurgle, competing with the birds to make the morning joyful.

"Don't be afraid of this old black crow," Sister used to tell her as she bent over her crib. And Teresa used to open her mouth in a toothless smile, embellished by a delightful dimple which she has since lost.

But Sister Aloysia did not neglect me in her anxiety for the baby. "You must be a Catholic yourself," she kept telling me. She had no reticences. She speculated rather volubly at times on the various reasons why she thought I was holding back. She brought me pious literature to read, saccharine stories of the saints, emasculated lives of saints young and old, back numbers of pious magazines.

William James, agnostic as he was, was more help. He introduced me to St. Teresa of Avila and St. John of the Cross. And I already had St. Augustine and the *Imitation* and the Bible, from which I derived strength and comfort. But isolated as I was in the country, knowing no Catholics except my neighbors, who seldom read anything except newspapers and secular magazines, there was not much chance of being introduced to the good literature of the present day. Chesterton's paradoxes wearied me. Belloc's histories I enjoyed, but they did not inspire me. I was in a state of dull content —I was not in a state to be mentally stimulated. I was too happy with my child. What faith I had I held onto stubbornly. The need of patience, emphasized in the writings of the saints, consoled me on the slow road I was traveling. I would put all my affairs in the hands of God and wait.

Three times a week Sister Aloysia came to give me a catechism lesson which I dutifully tried to learn. But she insisted that I recite word for word, with the repetition of the question that was in the book. If I had not learned my lesson, she rebuked me. "And you think you are intelligent!" she would say witheringly. "What is the definition of grace —actual grace and sanctifying grace? My fourth-grade pupils know more than you do."

I hadn't a doubt but that they did. I struggled on day by day, learning without question. I was in that agreeable and lethargic and almost bovine state of mind, filled with an animal content, not wishing to inquire into or question the dogmas I was learning. I made up my mind to accept what I did not understand, trusting light to come, as it sometimes did, in a blinding flash of exultation and realization.

Finally the great day arrived and was a thing of the past. Teresa was baptized; she had become a member of the Mystical Body of Christ. I didn't know anything of the Mystical Body, or I might have felt disturbed at being separated from her.

But I clutched her close to me, and all that summer, as I nursed her and bent over that tiny round face at my breast, I was filled with a deep happiness that nothing could spoil. But the obstacles to my becoming a Catholic were there, shadows in the background of my life.

I had become convinced that I would become a Catholic, and yet I felt I was betraying the class to which I belonged, the workers, the poor of the world, the class which Christ most loved and spent His life with. I wrote a few articles that summer for the *New Masses,* but did no other work.

Sometimes I could get up to the village to Mass on Sunday, when I could leave the baby in trusted hands. But usually the gloom that descended on the household, the scarcely voiced opposition, kept me from it. There were some feast days when I could slip off in the middle of the week and go to the little chapel on Charlie Schwab's grounds. There were "visits" I could make, unknown to others. I was committed, by the advice of a priest I consulted, to the plan of waiting, and trying to hold the family together. But I felt all along that when I took the irrevocable step, it would mean that Teresa and I would be alone, and I did not want to be alone. I did not want to give up human love when it was dearest and tenderest.

Finally, with precipitation, with doubts on my part at my own unseemly haste, I made the resolution to bring an end to my hesitation and be baptized.

It was in December 1927, a most miserable day, and the trip was long from the city down to Tottenville, Staten Island. All the way on the ferry through the foggy bay I felt grimly that I was being too precipitate. I had no sense of peace, no joy, no conviction even that what I was doing was right. It was just something that I had to do, a task to be gotten through. I doubted myself when I allowed myself to think. I hated myself for being weak and vacillating. A most consuming restlessness was upon me, so that I walked around and around the deck of the ferry, almost groaning in anguish of spirit. Perhaps the devil was on the boat.

Sister Aloysia was there waiting for me, to be my godmother. I do not know whether I had any other godparent. Father Hyland, gently, with reserve, with matter-of-factness, baptized me and heard my confession.

A year later my confirmation was indeed joyful, and Pentecost never passes without a renewed sense of happiness and thanksgiving. It was only then that the feeling of uncertainty finally left me, never again to return, praise God!

It was human love that helped me to understand divine love. Human love at its best, unselfish, glowing, illuminating our days, gives us a glimpse of the love of God for man. Love is the best thing we can know in this life, but it must be sustained by an effort of the will. It is not just an emotion, a warm feeling of gratification. It must lie still and quiet, dull and smoldering, for periods. It grows through suffering and patience and compassion. We must suffer for those we love, we must endure their trials and their sufferings, we must even take upon ourselves the penalties due their sins. Thus we learn to understand the love of God for His creatures. Thus we understand the Crucifixion.

I pray that all who are groping for the truth will be led by the Holy Ghost from darkness into light. Even the little I see is light to me in the darkest of days and hours. And I could not breathe or live without that light which I have now—the light of Faith which has been given to me by a merciful God who is the Light of the world.

THE FLOWERING OF JUDAISM

David Goldstein

Widely known as a street preacher, lecturer, columnist, lay apostle, labor leader, and author is David Goldstein. Born in London in 1870 of poor Netherlands Jewish parents, he was brought by them the next year to America. He attended the public elementary schools of New York City, the Hebrew Free School, and the Spanish Jewish Synagogue, where he studied Hebrew. At the age of eleven he went to work, and soon learned the trade of a cigar maker; he took an active part in the Cigar Makers' International Union, where he was impressed by the propaganda of the Socialists and joined the Socialist Labor party.

He became a member of the National Board of Appeals, where he met Mrs. Martha Moore Avery, the first American woman of prominence in the Socialist movement. She entered the Church in 1903, and it was from her that Mr. Goldstein learned the principles and doctrines of the Catholic faith. That same year he resigned from the Socialist party, after eight years of active work on the lecture platform and in debate.

With the help of Mrs. Avery, he wrote *Socialism—The Nation of Fatherless Children,* in which he exposed the fallacy of the doctrines of Socialism. His continued study of Catholic teaching convinced him of its truth and showed him that the greatest influence for social justice and for the stability of the family was the Church founded by Christ and governed by Peter and his successors for nineteen hundred years. He was received into the Church in Boston in 1905 and soon was launched upon his great apostolate of spreading the knowledge of Catholic life and doctrine among the laboring classes and the general public.

The same tireless zeal that he had formerly shown for the advancement of Socialism he has since displayed for the dissemination of Christian truth. His next book, *Bolshevism: Its*

Cure, disclosed a menace to American liberty of which few were then aware. This was followed in 1945 by *Suicide Bent: Sangerizing Mankind.* Together with Mrs. Avery, he wrote *Campaigning for Christ,* telling the story of seven years' work by Mrs. Avery, himself, and associated speakers in combating Socialist propaganda with the Christian social Gospel.

In *The Campaigner for Christ Handbook* he answers the questions commonly asked at open-air meetings; at the suggestion of Cardinal O'Connell, he wrote the *Autobiography of a Campaigner for Christ.* Declining the attractive offer of a Southern university to teach sociology, Mr. Goldstein continued his apostolate of street preaching and lecturing, which brought him into most of the states.

He has been deeply interested in bringing to Jews the religious truths which have meant so much to him. In *The Jewish Panorama* he presents a well-balanced view of present-day Jewry, particularly in the United States. In *Letters of a Hebrew-Catholic to Mr. Isaacs* he seeks "to make plain to Jews (and Christians as well) that conversion from the Synagogue to the Church means love for, not denial of the faith of their fathers of old in Israel; it means passing from the caterpillar to the butterfly stage of Judaism, as Catholic Christianity is Judaism full blossomed."

In recognition of his magnificent apostolate of the pen and platform, Niagara University conferred upon him the honorary degree of Doctor of Laws, and in 1946 he received the Catholic Action Medal, conferred annually by St. Bonaventure's College upon a lay person who is outstanding in the field of Catholic action.

M Y JOURNEY into the Catholic Church was from the Socialist movement, through which I endeavored to further the welfare of wage earners who were subjected to sweatshop and other capitalist exploiting conditions such as would not be tolerated in our country today. Hence I am a convert from Marx to Christ, rather than from the Synagogue to the Church. Yet the conviction that the Catholic Church is of the living God came to me through study of the relation of Jewish to Christian teachings, the story of which will be unfolded.

It was Edward Bellamy's *Looking Backward*, with its minutely drawn picture of a civilization without political corruption, economic exploitation, and war; a collectivist society in which property would be held in common; in which men and women would be paid according to their needs instead of deeds, that captivated my youthful imagination and led me into the Socialist Labor party.

Say what one will about the Socialist movement, it has a marvelous though baneful attraction for the superficial man (such as I was) who discriminates not between condemning prevailing unjust economic conditions, which deserve condemnation, and having an adequate remedy, such as I imagined Socialism to have. Enthusiasm for the Socialist movement is due in great measure to the opportunity it gives a man to play a somewhat glamorous part in its propaganda, small though he may be intellectually and culturally.

My lack of proper standards of judgment kept me from appreciating the inadequacy of the substitution of collective for private ownership of the means of production and exchange as the remedy for the ills of society and the unworkableness of it on a democratic basis. I have in mind the failure in our country of about two hundred voluntary, democratically conducted, co-operative colonies, made up of selected persons, that demonstrated the wisdom of the Greek philosopher Aristotle, who said:

"This style of legislation wears a face and air of philanthropy. No sooner is it heard than it is eagerly embraced, under the expectation of a marvelous love to grow out of it between man and man, especially if the proposer goes on to inveigh against the evils of existing institutions, setting all down to the want of a community of goods. These evils, however, are due not to a want of community of property, but to the depravity of human nature. For experience teaches that disputes are far more likely to occur among people who possess property in common and live as partners than among those who hold estates in separate tenure. The life proposed appears to be altogether impossible."

My interest in Socialism caused me to pass, through study,

from the sentimental concept of it, as set forth in Bellamy's *Looking Backward,* to so-called "modern, scientific Socialism," as set forth in Karl Marx's *Das Kapital,* a book about which Victor Berger, the Milwaukee Socialist congressman, said: "All Socialists talk about it, but I bet that not more than one in a thousand Socialists has read it." He could have gone a step further and said that not many more than one in a thousand Socialists can explain the first half-dozen chapters of this so-called "Bible of the working class," if they were to read it. I myself would not have understood this intricate book, with its algebraic formulae that outline the laws of wealth production in a capitalist society, figured to inevitable climax in the "expropriated" working class "expropriating the expropriators," were it not for the late Mrs. Martha Moore Avery, president of the Karl Marx Class which we organized to acquaint our Socialist comrades with the "scientific" teachings of the father of modern Socialism.

The more I learned about Socialism, as set forth by its doctrinaires, the more I found myself at variance with its philosophy, especially as it relates to the family, a philosophy that led to the suicide of two "married" daughters of Karl Marx, leaving him without any descendants.

The growing consciousness that happiness in society depends primarily upon the stability of the family caused me to object to the sex doctrines set forth by internationally favored Socialist authors, such as August Bebel, Ernest Belfort Bax, Edward Carpenter, William Morris, and others whose books were officially recommended for the study of Socialism. These authors insisted that Socialism aims to make the individual, *not* the family, the economic unit of society; that men and women under Socialism would live together in marital relations and separate according to individual inclination without the intervention of the State or Church. I was convinced that such an unrestricted sex relationship would demoralize rather than improve the condition of the toiling masses, even if they did obtain all the goods and leisure Socialism promised and continues to promise after more than three decades of failure in the Land-of-Socialism-

[138]

Applied. My enthusiasm for Socialism caused me to dismiss the teachings of the above-named writers as their personal opinions, despite the circulation of their books by Socialist organizations.

I was brought to the realization of my misjudgment, after a long battle within the Socialist movement, upon the appearance of an English translation of *The Origin of the Family*, based in part upon notes of Karl Marx, written by his co-worker, Friedrich Engels. It was hailed in the Socialist press as "a great Socialist classic," one of the "most important additions to the literature of Socialism in the English language since the translation of *Das Kapital*." The quality of this book is seen in its condemnation of monogamy, which is declared to be "the first form of family life not founded on natural but on economic conditions,"[1] and its advocacy of "a more unconventional intercourse of the sexes and a more lenient public opinion of virgin honor and female shame."[2] The declaration is made therein: "A positive cessation of fondness and its replacement by a new passionate love makes a separation a blessing for both parties and for society"; but under Socialism men and women will be saved "the needless wading through the mire of a divorce case."[3]

I abhorred the divorce conditions in our country, which were a disgrace then and are still more of a disgrace today. Therefore, great was my aversion to an increase in the number of broken families that would inevitably result from permitting men and women to live in marital relations and to separate on the basis of mere sex fondness without even being subject to the civil law. I therefore set myself the task of studying the principles and history of the family, in order to meet my Socialist comrades with positive arguments against the sex teachings of the Socialist doctrinaires.

I was too indifferent to religion to think of studying the subject from the point of view of the Bible. Hence the thought of studying the attitude of the Catholic Church on marriage and divorce or any other subject never entered my mind. Such a thought might have occurred to me had I ever

[1] P. 79.   [2] Pp. 91–92.   [3] P. 99.

[139]

heard an exposition of Catholic teachings uttered by the Catholics with whom I worked for many years.

It was an accidental contact with a United States Government report, issued by the Department of Labor and entitled *Twenty Years of Marriage and Divorce in the United States*, that marked a turning point in my mental outlook. In it Carroll D. Wright, our first and foremost Labor Commissioner, a Unitarian, said: "Large and increasing as the number of divorces in the United States is, it is an undeniable fact that were it not for the widespread influence of the Roman Catholic Church the number would have been much larger. The loyalty of Catholics to the teachings of their Church, and the fact that one of the cardinal doctrines of their Church is that Christian marriage is a holy sacrament which, when consummated, can be dissolved for no cause and in no manner, save by death, has unquestionably served as a barrier to the volume of divorce which, except among the members of that Church, is, and during the past twenty years has been, assuming ever-increasing proportions throughout the country."[4]

This awakened in me an interest in the Catholic Church. It was the beginning of the blotting out of the inherited and acquired unfriendliness toward the Catholic Church which lurks in the hearts of many Jews in varying degrees even though they are friendly with individual Catholics. I was like a blind man whose sight was coming back. This caused me open-mindedly to examine the attitude of the Catholic Church toward Socialism. I studied *Rerum Novarum*, the Encyclical on the Condition of the Working Class, which Carroll D. Wright called "my constant companion." In it Pope Leo XIII warned the world from his moral watchtower in Rome of the danger that lurks in Socialism, while declaring that a remedy should be found, and quickly, to right the wrongs that the toiling masses suffer. It caused me to re-examine Socialism from an economic, political, sociological, and moral point of view.

[4] P. 123.

[140]

Thus was I led to a final battle within the ranks of Socialism; to the presentation of a set of resolutions to the Massachusetts Convention of the Socialist party, demanding that a halt be called to the circulation of books of a disruptive nature. It was an explosive occasion, noticed by the press throughout our country. Failing to get the Convention to adopt the resolutions, I resigned from Socialism, saying, in part:

"I had long hoped and often expressed the sentiment that the irrational literature and the economic absurdities spread broadcast among the people of our country would change in character with the growing power of the organization. But after close study of the teachings of the Socialist doctrinaires, their philosophy and so-called science, I must conclude that the Socialism I was preaching had no basis in fact: it was not the kind which the political Socialist movement stands for. It is my conviction that were the philosophical doctrines applied to a given country or to the civilized world in general, as promulgated by the founders of 'modern scientific revolutionary international Socialism,' namely Karl Marx and Frederick Engels, that economic justice, even to the degree which exists today, would be unknown."

This was the road I traveled that led to the realization that the grave issues confronting mankind are basically moral issues; that economic reform is secondary to the moral reform of society; in fact, it is dependent upon it; and that morality stems from religion. I was assisted in the understanding of this by Mrs. Martha Moore Avery, another convert from Marx to Christ, who, while in the Socialist movement, had sent her daughter Katharine into a French Canadian convent school for cultural reasons. She preceded her mother into the Church, became a Sister in the Congregation of Notre Dame, Sister St. Mary Martha, and at this writing is Superior of the Villa Maria Academy in the Bronx, New York. I became more and more interested in religion, especially the religion of the holy in Israel, as set forth in the

Old Testament, of which I had learned a little in a Hebrew school in preparation for my *bar mitzvah* (a sort of confirmation) and through the religious customs of my home.

I found the Judaism of the Old Testament to be an authoritative religion of God's making, as a religion must be to command the obedience of man without infringing upon his dignity as a human personality.

I found the religion of the Jews to stem from Moses, to whom God revealed His law; though Jews, as children of Israel, date back before the days of Moses to Jacob, whose name God changed to Israel.

I found that the Jews were genealogically divided into tribes, descendants of the twelve sons of Jacob. Foremost among them were the tribes of Levi and Judah. The tribe of Levi was the priestly division of Israel, within which existed the family of Aaron, the first high priest by the will of God. I learned later that the first high bishop of the Christian dispensation was Peter. The power of the high priest was great, his decisions being final, punishable in some instances by death.[5] "Judaism saw in the sanctuary," declares the Jewish Encyclopedia, "the manifestation of God's presence among His people, and the priest the vehicle of divine grace, the mediator through whose ministry the sins of the community, as of the individuals, could be atoned for."[6]

The holy office of the high priest passed on at death to the descendants of Aaron. "After the death of Aaron," reports Josephus, "his sons succeeded him immediately; and his dignity has been continued down from them to all their posterity. Hence it is the custom in our country that no one shall take the high priesthood of God but he who is of the blood of Aaron; while every one of another stock, though he were king, can never obtain the high priesthood."[7] Members of the tribe of Levi, who were not of the family of Aaron, were assistants who cared for the Temple, its tabernacle, and its sacred vessels.

[5]Deuteronomy 17.   [6]Vol. 4, p. 195.
[7]Book XX, Antiquities of the Jews.

The fame of the tribe of Judah centered in the existence within it of the family of King David, in which the Messiah, the Christ, would be born. I found the religion divinely set forth in the Old Testament expressed through a visible, authoritative spiritual society, as a religion of God's making must be. This I found entirely lacking in present-day Jewry, it being devoid of theological exactitude to the extent of even failing to be in agreement as to what constitutes a Jew.

I found the Orthodox group alone adhering, in principle and in hope, to belief in such things of basic import as a priesthood, sacrifices, and an expected personal Messiah. On the other hand, I found that Reform Judaism repudiates these Orthodox principles as well as belief in miracles; it also rejects the idea that the Books of the Old Testament are the word of God in the traditional sense of the term. In time I came to the realization that Reform Judaism, whose leaders with minor exception are the only rabbis known to the American public, are as far out of line with the Judaism of the Old Testament as is Unitarianism with New Testament Christianity. In fact, Reform Judaism is not Judaism at all, save in name. This was attested to by Rabbi Mendel Lewittes, who, writing in the *Jewish Advocate* on "Reform Judaism," said: "It is not merely a different form of Jewish worship, but a movement which has repudiated the fundamental principles of traditional Judaism."[8]

I found that all rabbis, Orthodox and Reform, are in agreement that an end had come in the first century of the Christian Era to the Aaronic priesthood, to the Temple, and to those Mosaic sacrifices which traditional Jews hold to be the highest expression of the love of God. This is so important to the understanding of present-day Judaism that it were best to let Jews themselves tell of it. The Jewish Encyclopedia, quoting authorities, says: "Judaism saw in the sanctuary the manifestation of God's presence among His people, and in the priest the vehicle of divine grace, the mediator through whose ministry the sins of the com-

[8] Boston, December 7, 1944.

[143]

munity, as of the individual, could be atoned for . . . [that] through the Temple Israel is cleansed of its sins, that the chief purpose of altar and priesthood is to make atonement for, and effect the forgiveness, of sin, as stated again and again in Talmud and Midrash."[9]

The Encyclopedia of Jewish Knowledge says: "The fall of the Temple and the disappearance of the high priesthood occurred at the same time. That form of intercession, ground for possible belief in human symbols of divine authority, vanished. Nothing remained but the sublime faith in the invisible omnipresent Creator."[10]

The same thing is reported in *Mid-Channel*, by Ludwig Lewisohn, professor of English literature, Brandeis University, Waltham, Massachusetts. He writes: "With the destruction of the Temple the sacrificial cult of Jews was destroyed. For among the people there was but one temple and one altar, hence the Jewish people were suddenly laicized. Priests and sacrifices and tangible mysteries were no more."[11] In *The Brandeis Avukal Volume* (1936), Rabbi Louis Epstein, of Brookline, Massachusetts, writes: "In the course of time the priest and sacrificial cult gave way to rabbinical orders." But rabbis are not priests, as Joseph Leftwich, former editor of the Jewish Telegraph Agency, says in *What Will Happen to the Jews?*, without being questioned by any Jewish reviewer of his book. "The Rabbi is not a priest. The priesthood passed with the Temple. Even the rabbinical diploma, unlike the Christian ordination, confers no sacred power and is not a license. It is simply a testimonial of ability of the holder to act as a Rabbi if he wished to be elected" by some congregation.

Rabbi Epstein, quoted above, goes on further to let us know that no one speaks with authority in Jewry, saying: "When a dispute of the interpretation of the law arises, there is no authoritative body to give final decision. Authority is contained in a dead-letter book, not in any living individual or organized body."

Surely, I concluded, a "laicized" ruled Judaism, a Judaism

[9]Vol. X, p. 195.   [10]P. 364.   [11]P. 259.

with "a dead-letter book" as its only authority, is not Old Testament Judaism. I found further evidence that it is devoid of a priesthood, sacrifices, and Temple, vital to Old Testament Judaism, in the fact that the Orthodox Jews, the intensely religious division of Jewry, prayed daily for the reinstitution of the Aaronic priesthood, with their sacrifices, and for the coming of a personal Messiah. This impressed me as pathetic, for—as I discovered to my amazement— there is no genealogical evidence whatsoever to prove the existence of a family of Aaron from which an Aaronic priesthood could possibly be reinstituted, and there are no genealogical records whatsoever to prove the existence of a family of David, in which a Messiah could possibly be born. Thus Orthodox Jews remain like

> An infant crying in the night;
> An infant crying for light;
> And with no language but a cry.

It was this religious catastrophe that prompted me to conclude that present-day Judaism is not, and cannot possibly become, the Judaism of my Israelitish fathers of old. It was the claim of the Catholic Church that Christianity is the fulfillment, the perfection, of Old Testament Judaism that gave me the key to understanding that the end of the Aaronic priesthood, the Levitical sacrifices, and the Temple was providential and not accidental; that it was a blessing, and not the calamity that Orthodox Jewry believes it to be. This finally led me to the baptismal font of the Catholic Church with love of the faith of my fathers of old in my heart. God had not abandoned His chosen people! The promised Messiah had come. Jesus is His name! I "found Him of whom Moses in the Law, and the prophets, did write, Jesus," as did Philip, one of the Twelve Jews who became Apostles.[12]

I found that Jesus was born in the family of David of the tribe of Judah, as Moses[13] and Ezekiel[14] said He would be born. I found that God promised "a sign," that something

[12]St. John 1:45.   [13]Genesis 49.   [14]Ezekiel 34:23.

unusual would take place. "A virgin shall conceive, and bear a son, and his name shall be called Emmanuel"; that signifies "God with us," that is, with the children of Israel, as was Jesus who was born of the Virgin Mary.[15]

I found that Jesus was born in the time foretold by Daniel[16] nearly five centuries before Mary, the Lily of Israel, brought him forth in the City of David. I found Jesus to be the fulfillment of the prophecies of Isaiah, whom the Jews classify as "the greatest of the prophets." Isaiah said about seven centuries before the Christian Era that "God Himself will come and save you," the children of Israel;[17] that he "shall be called Wonderful, Counsellor, God the Mighty, the Father of the world to come, the Prince of Peace";[18] who was to "sit upon the throne of David . . . for ever";[19] and that he would be adored by kings.[20]

I found that Jesus was conspired against; betrayed; sold for thirty pieces of silver; led like a sheep to slaughter; suffered His hands and feet to be pierced; and withal rose from the dead as foretold by Isaiah,[21] by Zacharias,[22] and David.[23]

I found Jesus to be the "Prophet" of whom Moses told the children of Israel: "The Lord thy God will raise up . . . like unto me," to whom Israel should give ear.[24] This likeness to Moses was seen in Jesus being meek, yet courageous; a mediator, lawgiver, and deliverer; and still more, in that He, "God with us," was the Prophet of prophets.

I found that during the days of Jesus in Palestine, and the days when the Apostles, inspired by the Holy Spirit, preached things Christian, that Mary, Joseph, John the Baptist, the Apostles, and thousands of other Jews were convinced that the hope of Israel had been fulfilled in Jesus the Messiah, who instituted the "new covenant" foretold by Jeremiah.[25] I was strongly convinced that nearly all of the Jews of those days would most likely have cried out

[15]Isaiah 7:14.   [16]Daniel 9:25–26.   [17]Isaiah 5:4.
[18]Isaiah 9:6.   [19]Isaiah 9:7.   [20]Psalms 71:2.
[21]Isaiah 2:10, 53.   [22]Zacharias 2:12–13;   [23]Psalms 21.
[24]Deuteronomy 18:15.   12:10; 13:6–7.   [25]Jeremiah 31:31.

to Jesus, as did a multitude of them during His triumphal ride through Jerusalem:

Hosanna to the Son of David
Blessed is He who comes in the name of the Lord,

were it not for official Jewry, which was subservient to the political power in Rome. The high priests, whose office was hereditary and tenable for life, were appointed and deposed by the Romans at their pleasure. The Herodian priests, including Caiphas and Annas, and the members of the Sanhedrin were the enemies of the people as well as of Jesus. This is recorded in the *Talmud;* in *Jesus of Nazareth,* by Professor Joseph Klausner of the Hebrew University, Jerusalem; in *The Nazarene,* by Sholem Asch, and in other Jewish writings.

Surely, I reasoned, God our All-Merciful Heavenly Father did not leave His children without a safeguard against the changing whims and fancies of men. After an end had come to the guidance He gave the Jews through their priesthood, He gave them a religion which binds man to Him. Surely God did not leave man without the consolation of the sacrificial means of paying homage to Him and atoning for their sins! If Christianity is Judaism full-blossomed, as its foremost proponents claim it to be, I concluded that this should be evidenced in the existence of a spiritual society superior to the one that guided the Jews in pre-Christian times. Then must this spiritual society have a priesthood and sacrificial worship of a higher order than was enjoyed by the children of Israel. This I found in the Christ-established Catholic Church, with its Christ-instituted priesthood according to the Order of Melchisedec.[26]

I found the Church to be as superior to the Temple as Jesus is to Moses. I found this to center in the superiority of Christian to Jewish principles; in the Church being universal—Catholic—whereas the Temple was for an exclusive people, the children of Israel; and in having altars all over the world, whereas the Mosaic law permitted but one Altar,

[26]Psalms 109.

[147]

in a central sanctuary, the Temple.[27] This Temple containing the Holy of Holies was destroyed by the soldiers of
Titus in the year 70 A.D., thus fulfilling the prophecy of
Daniel,[28] and the prediction of Jesus that "not a stone upon
a stone" would be left of the Temple.[29]

I found that Jews held, as did the Council of Trent, that
"priesthood and sacrifice are indissolubly united." Hence
the end of Israel's priesthood meant that an end had come
to offering the sacrifices called for in the Book of Leviticus.
Thus Jews could no longer "make atonement for their sins
. . . as Jehovah commanded Moses."[30]

I found that belief in the Mosaic-commanded sacrifices still
abides in Orthodox Jewry. This is apparent particularly on
Yom Kippur, the day of contrition, confession, and re-
generation, when services are held in commemoration of the
days when the Jews had a priesthood, including the recitation of prayers patterned after those that were said in the
Temple. The consciousness of needing to atone for sin by
the shedding of blood is evidenced in the custom among
eastern European Jews of substituting an animal for sacrifice in place of forfeiting the life of a sinner. It is called
Kapparah (means of atonement).

The man takes a rooster (the woman a hen), swings it
three times around his head, saying in Hebrew: "This
rooster is killed as an acknowledgment of being worthy of
death for sin." The entrails are cast upon the roof of the
house, so some raven or crow may carry them into the
wilderness, together with their sins, to place upon the head
of Azazel, the scapegoat, considered in Jewish apocalyptic
literature to be the name of the ramlike demon of the desert, the personification of uncleanness. This practice is not
to be scoffed at, as it is by Reform Jews, it being a recognition of the principle, though not the practice, that is set forth
by St. Paul in his Epistle to the Hebrews, that "without the
shedding of blood there is no forgiveness."[31]

I found that the Mosaic law called for a bloody sacrifice

[27]Deuteronomy 12.   [28]Daniel 9:26.   [29]St. Matthew 24:2.
[30]Leviticus 16.   [31]Hebrews 9:22.

daily, mainly a lamb without blemish. But in the Christian religion only one Lamb was sacrificed, the unblemished "Lamb of God" who offered Himself as a victim on the Cross "for the sin of the world."[32] He is the Lamb who Isaiah said would be "led as a sheep to the slaughter."[33]

I found that the Christian sacrifice took place but once *in a bloody manner;* that was on Mount Calvary. It began at the Last Passover Supper in the upper chamber in Jerusalem, during the time at which Christ proclaimed the "new covenant of My blood which shall be shed for you,"[34] and ended on Mount Calvary.

I found that this Bloody Sacrifice on the Cross is continued in the Mass, though in an *unbloody manner,* "in remembrance" of Christ, as He commanded.[35] It is the "clean oblation" Malachias foretold.[36]

I found that the last remnant of the Judaism of my forebears had disappeared with the destruction of the Temple by the soldiers of Titus, which was the one and only place in which communal sacrifices could be offered in honor of the One True God and to atone for sin. This loss is appreciated by observing Jews, though unfortunately through eyes that are closed when it comes to the question of the cause thereof. Rabbi David Levi exclaims in his *Siddur* (book of daily prayers):

"Sovereign of the universe! Whilst the Holy Temple was established, if a man sinned, he brought an offering, and made atonement for himself; but now because of our iniquities, we have neither sanctuary, nor altar, nor offering, nor priest to atone for us; there is nothing left but the commemoration of them. O may that be our expiation, and we will render prayers of our lips instead of offerings."

The bemoaning of the final, sacrificial, worshipful ending of Judaism with the destruction of the Temple is seen in the Talmud story of the High Priest who, upon seeing the Temple in flames, went up to the roof of the sanctuary "with a group of the flower of the priesthood." There, holding the

[32]St. John 1:29. [33]Isaiah 53:7. [34]St. Luke 22:20.
[35]St. Luke 22:20. [36]Malachias 1:11.

[149]

keys of the Temple in his hand, he said: "Holy One, Blessed be He, Creator of the Universe, since we are not worthy to be your faithful custodians, we transfer the keys of your house to You," and with these words the keys were thrown up. "Something in the form of a hand descended from heaven and grasped the keys." Those keys of the doors of the Temple were useful no more, not merely on account of the destruction of the building, but because keys symbolical of greater power had been given in Jewry to Simon Bar Jona by the Messiah, Jesus, who changed Simon's name to Peter, the Rock upon which the Church of the New Covenant was built; just as God changed the name of Abram to Abraham, to signify his new spiritual office, father of the multitude.

I found that the principles of Judaism, set forth in the Old Testament, which Moses personified, had been elevated to higher intellectual and moral heights, personified by Jesus as revealed in the New Testament. The Commandments, for instance, though unchangeable as is the God who gave them to man, had been elevated in their application by Christ. I found likewise that the means instituted by Christ for the attainment of salvation were greater and more efficacious than were those recorded by Moses, even though the latter were of divine origin.

I found the beauty which abided potentially in Judaism full-blossomed in Christianity, just as the potential beauty in the caterpillar is unfolded in the butterfly. Therefore, when a Jew becomes a Catholic, he no more denies the faith of his fathers of the days when Judaism was the Mosaic religion in its fullness than the butterfly, if it had the power of reasoning, could rightly deny the caterpillar from which its beauty evolved.

Thus was I in conscience bound to go to the baptismal font, as I did, to receive the sacrament instituted by the Messiah for Jews and others to be incorporated into His Mystical Body—the Church. Forty-four years have passed since, by God's grace, I was regenerated. They have been years of ever-growing understanding and love of Jesus

Christ and the Catholic Church that He established. I found Jesus, the Messiah, to be what He professed to be: "the Way, the Truth, and the Life." I end the story of my spiritual Odyssey with the words which express the deepest yearning of my heart and soul:

> Thou art the Way, the Truth, and the Life;
> Grant Israel that Way to know,
> That Truth to keep, that Life to win,
> Whose joys eternal flow.

ON A FIRM FOUNDATION

Jocelyn M. C. Toynbee

Jocelyn M. C. Toynbee, the sister of the noted historian Arnold Toynbee, has won wide recognition because of her scholarly research in the classics, which she has made her lifework. A teacher, lecturer, and author, she has made important contributions to our understanding of Greek and Roman art, life, and culture.

Born in London in 1897, Miss Toynbee was educated at the Girls' High School, Winchester, at St. Mary's College, Paddington, and at Newnham College at Cambridge. She received her M.A. degree from Cambridge University and her Doctor of Philosophy degree from Oxford.

She is a lecturer on the faculty of classics at Cambridge University and the director of studies in classics at Newnham College, Cambridge. She is a Fellow of the Society of Antiquities of London and of the Royal Numismatic Society, and a vice-president of the Society for the Promotion of Roman Studies. In 1948 she was awarded the medal of the Royal Numismatic Society.

She has contributed scholarly articles to the *Journal of Roman Studies, Numismatic Chronicle, Papers of the British School at Rome, Classical Review, Classical Quarterly, Archaeologia, Antiquity*, the *Antiquities Journal, Journal of the Royal Archaeological Institute, Month, Studies, Dublin Review, Cambridge Review, Burlington Magazine, Greece and Rome*.

Her favorite diversion is travel on the continent of Europe, where she takes deep interest in studying historical monuments and records of ancient cultures.

SO FAR as I am consciously aware, my conversion—or, more precisely, the offer of the grace which ultimately led to my conversion—dates from a May morning in 1929, when I sat down in my room in Newnham College, Cambridge, and opened *The Times*. My eye was caught by a letter signed by some Anglican clergymen in London, who, being forbidden by their bishop to reserve what they in all good faith believed to be the Blessed Sacrament, declared their resolve to ignore the bishop and to appeal beyond him to Catholic authority.

As an Anglo-Catholic, I was indeed used to such incidents. I was accustomed to regarding bishops of the Church of England as being, with a few exceptions, deficient in Catholic-mindedness, or even hostile to Catholic doctrine.

As an Anglo-Catholic believing the Church of England to be a branch of the Catholic Church, I was faced with the dilemma of having to recognize as Catholic the Low-Church Anglican bishops who glory in the name of Protestant and who have no desire at all to be called Catholic. I was thus obliged to think of those persons as being Catholic bishops in spite of themselves, i.e., without their realizing the fact. Thus I was forced to believe that, as an Anglo-Catholic laywoman, I was better informed about the true character of those persons than they themselves were!

For roughly fifteen years, since I as a student had decided that I was High Church, or Anglo-Catholic, I somehow managed to accept that strange point of view. But on that May morning in 1929, I knew that I could not be satisfied with accepting it any longer. Where was Catholic authority, if not in the Anglican episcopate? It was no longer possible to think of it as existing vaguely somewhere in a nebulous Catholic Church composed of mutually exclusive communions or branches.

It must be located precisely, if it existed anywhere; and there was one place in which I knew at that moment that I was in conscience bound, come what might, to search for it, and that was in the Roman Catholic Church. I knew that I must begin immediately to study that Church as

[153]

deeply and fully as I could, that I must embark on a journey which might lead me out of Anglicanism to either agnosticism or Roman Catholicism, with no possibility of a third alternative.

And so I set out upon my journey with one all-important question in the forefront of my mind: By what authority was I a "Catholic," or even a Christian at all? On whom was I ultimately relying for all that I believed and did?

The stages of a journey of this kind have so often been described that I need give only the barest outline of them here. The whole Anglican position had first to be examined anew; and, in particular, the grounds of the Church of England's opposition to Rome. Anglican books must be read and Anglican clergy questioned before Catholic books were opened or Catholic priests approached. And as long as doubts left room for any belief in its reality, Anglican practice had to be maintained with even greater care than before. One must make every effort to know, with all possible thoroughness, what it was that one might eventually be called upon to leave.

Most illogically, as I later came to see, but then in all sincerity, I continued with Anglican practice for many weeks after I had come to regard the Anglican arguments for rejecting the "Roman" claims as completely unconvincing and unsatisfactory. I continued it after I had begun to study the Catholic answers to those Anglican arguments and to investigate Catholic doctrine systematically, and even after I had had all my outstanding problems solved in a talk with a Catholic priest.

By January 1930, I had learned to understand and accept the full Catholic doctrine of the Church and of the Papacy and all the other elements of Catholic teaching which usually offer stumbling blocks to Anglo-Catholics. I still clung to the possibility, however, that Anglican orders might after all be valid. I remained sidetracked by the thought that the bull *Apostolicae Curae* was not technically an infallible pronouncement. I failed to perceive that its argument all turned on the Church's infallible teaching on the content of the sacraments and on the intention with which they are administered.

When I seemed to have reached an impasse, I took the advice of a Dominican Father, then lecturing in Cambridge, to make a novena to the Holy Ghost, and went daily to communion in the Anglican Church. Were those nine last Anglican communions, made in deep doubt, but with the one desire of coming to know the truth, real Spiritual Communions, through which God gave me the grace of enlightenment? At any rate, on the ninth morning the solution of my dilemma was suddenly clear to my mind; next morning I went to Mass in the Catholic church, sought instruction the following day, and was received a month later on March twenty-ninth.

The points from which souls start on their homeward journey to the Catholic Church are indeed multifarious. They range from atheistic Communism, at one extreme, to "Anglo-Papalism," at the other. Each type of journey has its own particular problems; and while all souls outside the visible unity of the Church are objects of the convert's apostolate, it is legitimate for him to feel special solicitude for those who still remain at the point from which he once started.

What, then, after twenty years in the Catholic Church, would I say to Anglicans and Anglo-Catholics? I would assure them that, if they believe (as they surely do) that Christianity is the infallible Revelation to man of Him who is Truth Itself, their faces are already set toward the Catholic Church: barriers which they seem to see erected between themselves and her are really imaginary. In our eyes, indeed, they are already, if validly baptized, one with us in virtue of their baptism. Since there is only one Church and only one baptism, they were all members of the Catholic Church until such time as they formally adhered to Anglican denials of Catholic doctrine and forms of worship conducted outside Catholic unity. Thus an Anglican, in becoming a Catholic, does not, as is so often thought, repudiate his baptism: he returns to that to which it admitted him.

[155]

The Anglican is saved, not by his denials of, or opposition to, Catholic doctrines, but by those Catholic beliefs which he holds and which he ultimately received from the Roman Catholic and Apostolic Church. All the positive, affirming things which he believes, he believes in common with Catholics: the differences enter when he begins to deny, to be negative. As a Catholic, I am now positive, where as an Anglican, I was negative. I am positive now, for instance, about the visible unity, the indivisibility, and the divine nature of the Christian Church; positive about her power, as the Mystical Body of Christ, to preserve and transmit, intact and unerringly, the infallible truth which God entrusted to her and commanded her to teach with His Own Voice; positive about the Pope as the God-appointed mouthpiece of the Church's infallibility.

Our very denial of the validity of Anglican orders is necessitated by the denial voiced by the founders of the Anglican Church of vital Catholic doctrines, denial of the true, real, and objective presence of Our Lord in the Holy Eucharist and of the sacrificial nature of the Mass as the re-enactment in an unbloody manner of the Sacrifice of Calvary. The first Anglican bishops did not intend to transmit to their ordinands a power in which they themselves had ceased to believe, namely, the power to offer the Holy Sacrifice of the Mass, the primary power which, when He ordained them at the Last Supper, Our Lord gave to the Apostles, the first Catholic priests; and so they cut off the Church of England from Apostolic continuity. Yet what Catholic would dare to deny that Anglican communions, orders, and absolutions, while not channels of true sacramental grace, can be used by God as the means of offering actual graces to those who receive them in all sincerity and in inculpable ignorance of where His True Church is to be found?

To the convert from Anglo-Catholicism, the Catholic Church is, in a special sense, a place of liberation. Here is freedom from the tyranny of private judgment as the criterion of what one may, and may not, believe; freedom from the stifling task of trying to reconcile Anglican formularies with the Catholic doctrines which those formularies explicitly deny; freedom from the paradox of relying on Rome's authority for what one has selected of Catholic faith and practice while being committed to the belief that Rome has erred. Here is freedom from the limiting notion of a "Catholicism" specially adapted to the English-speaking race; freedom from the dilemma of having to regard as "Catholic" bishops and clergy who would repudiate the name and have no intention whatsoever, when they celebrate the Anglican Communion Service, of offering Mass.

Here, on the firm foundation of certain knowledge of God's Revelation and of knowledge imparted by the lips of a Living Church, can be built that spiritual life of worship and service of God which is the essence of perfect liberty for man. Here is access to inexhaustible riches of faith and devotion. Here we can draw, uninhibited, upon the plenitude of sacramental grace; here, unrestricted, we can have recourse to the intercession of the saints. By the gift of faith in the Catholic Church the soul is released, as it were, from a cage, and can explore at will all the manifold streets and mansions of the City of God. Truly can we say with the Psalmist: "The snare is broken and we are delivered. Our help is in the name of the Lord who made heaven and earth."

THE PEARL OF GREAT PRICE

Daniel Sargent

Daniel Sargent has won recognition as a poet, historian, and biographer, and his numerous productions in these three fields have secured for him a goodly audience on both sides of the Atlantic. Born of Unitarian parents in 1890 in Boston, he was educated at Groton and then at Harvard, where he received the A.B. and A.M. degrees. He was elected to membership in Phi Beta Kappa, an honorary scholastic fraternity, and was chosen as class orator.

In 1916 he joined the ambulance corps of the French army. Upon the entrance of the United States into the conflict, he served with the United States Artillery in the First Division in France as a first lieutenant, later rising to the rank of captain. After the war he was a faculty member of Harvard for fifteen years, teaching history and literature; then he withdrew to devote his full time to writing.

In 1920, Mr. Sargent married Louise Coolidge, who had been reared as a Unitarian but who became a Catholic in Ovieto, Italy, in 1915. Her husband was received into the Catholic Church on Palm Sunday in 1919. The Sargents have a son and a daughter.

Mr. Sargent's study of medieval literature, especially the works of Dante, awakened an interest in the Catholic Church and caused him to examine her credentials and her doctrines. He acknowledges his indebtedness likewise to the writings of two eminent Catholic philosophers, Maurice de Wulf of Louvain and Jacques Maritain, now at Princeton University.

He has written six books of poetry: *Our Gleaming Days, The Door, The Road to Welles-Perennes, The Song of the Three Children, My Account of the Flood,* and *God's Ambuscade.* Even more numerous are his prose works, of which the following have achieved wide circulation: *Christopher Columbus, Thomas More,*

Four Independents, Catherine Tekawitha, Our Lord and Our Lady, All the Day Long, Mitri or *The Story of Prince Demetrius Augustine Gallitzin, The Assignment of Antonio Claret,* and *The Life of St. John Eudes.*

Mr. Sargent was elected president of the American Catholic Historical Society for 1935, and in the following year he was elected president of the Catholic Poetry Society of America. His favorite recreation is mountain climbing, and of his books of poetry he prefers *The Song of the Three Children,* while of his prose works he likes best *Our Lord and Our Lady.*

T HE MERCHANT who found a precious pearl in a field and who spent all his fortune in order to buy it probably was actively hunting for pearls. I was not like him when I found the Catholic Church: I was not looking for churches.

I began life not merely having a disinterest in churches, but an antipathy for them. My parents were Unitarians of Boston, and Unitarians of Boston resented the very word *church.* It reminded them of the Church of Rome, which had persecuted their Calvinistic ancestors, and also of their Calvinistic ancestors who had persecuted them as Unitarians. If the Unitarians accepted the title of church for themselves, it was only for convenience. Quite rightly, they conceived of a church as claiming some relationship with Heaven, and they claimed no such thing for themselves. They prided themselves on being a mere association of "common-sense" human beings.

My parents and I had some very agreeable acquaintances who were sure that they belonged to churches. I had a charming uncle who belonged to the Episcopal Church and who had books on his shelf proving that it was descended from the Apostles. He used to banter with my parents, asking them if they had been "to meetinghouse" on Sundays, as they had. And we had likable Irish Catholic maids and a wonderful Catholic coachman who was a family oracle when it came to questions of the weather. But, leaving out personalities, we disliked churches. A church was an association of men, who in their arrogance considered themselves as superior. Imagine anyone talking about "*the* Church"!

Fortunately, we were not too distressed about there being churches. The Unitarian ministers told us that there was no creed, but they gave us one: "I believe in the Fatherhood of God, the Brotherhood of man, and in the progress of mankind upward and onward forever." According to this formula, we could feel assured that someday in the general improvement there would be no churches.

At the age of thirteen I was sent to a boarding school not far from Boston—Groton—which was conducted by an Episcopal minister, the Reverend Endicott Peabody. It was classed as a church school, but though I stayed there for six years, it made me feel no more friendly toward churches.

Let me say that this was not because I did not esteem Mr. Peabody, but because I esteemed him without thinking him really a churchman. It is true that on my first Sunday at the school I heard him recite the Apostles' Creed (which I had never heard in all my life before) and nearly fainted with surprise when he announced "I believe in the Catholic Church," but I never became convinced that he really meant it. I considered him as safely "unchurchy"—that is, without frills. So far as his sermons were concerned, there might never have been the Incarnation, and thus there could not be a church. He taught us an awe of God, and a respect for courage, fair play, and cleanness of life.

In the classroom our studies sometimes bore on the Church. One teacher of considerable ability taught a fascinating course of science. In it he traced life up from the amoeba, through apes and men, and even to insects, who in the race of survival of the fittest would, he surmised, supersede man. In this exciting plot there was no place for "the Church" at all.

Then there was a course in medieval history, and in it the Catholic Church had to be spoken of. It was, and was spoken of without abuse. Yet there was no indication of what the Catholic Church believed. Therefore the story of the Middle Ages was a series of facts with no motives and with no plot at all.

Upon my graduation from Groton, I had the following thoughts concerning churches: God had established no church. He had created the amoeba and left it to make good of itself. The amoeba had done fairly well. It was men, not God, who had established churches. If the members of a man-made church found that it had become important, they called it in arrogance *the Church*. To belong to a church that called itself the Church tended to make a man obnoxious. Catholics called their church *the Church*, but it was in loyalty to a lost cause and pardonable. Endicott Peabody, my schoolmaster, called his Episcopal Church *the Church*, but it was because he had been brought up in England, where the English used ancient formulas after they had lost their meaning. Occasionally to Groton, which was a Low-Church school, there came High-Church Episcopalians who talked of *the Church* as if it meant something, but by us boys they were considered play actors. Unitarians remained to my mind as right in claiming to be no more than an association. I was content with the Unitarians, but wished that their sermons were less literary.

I entered Harvard College. There I took some courses in philosophy, which led me to a stone wall: one could not know anything, not even that a butterfly was a butterfly. But the courses in literature did give me some comprehension of what the Church had been. I might cite a course on Chaucer, but a course by Barrett Wendell on the traditions of European literature was more striking in this respect.

Barrett Wendell was not a Catholic, and never became one. He maintained the attitude to all religions that a tourist might devote to the political parties in a foreign country, but he greatly admired the Catholic Church and had a widely traveled aversion for the self-important and brash sectarians of the last five hundred years. In his survey of literature from Homer to Whitman he never hid his respect for the wisdom of the Catholic Church. In adopting his per-

spective, I caught little sight of Catholic doctrines but much
of the Catholic spirit. I found in Catholic writers, generally,
a composure and fundamental joyousness which served to
enable me to perceive the Catholic Church as different from
all others.

I thank Barrett Wendell for this, and I thank him for
another thing: he urged me in my fourth year at Harvard,
when I was in the graduate school, to take a course in
Dante. He said:

"You can take it without knowing Italian. I took it without knowing it from James Russell Lowell, who didn't know
it either."

I did take the course in Dante. It was given by the
philologist, Charles H. Grandgent, who was self-effacing;
but Dante was not. In the *Divine Comedy*, I found a story
of creation which made the tale of the "up from the amoeba"
puerile and trivial. I learned of the pilgrimage of every
man through grace to glory. It was in terms of this pilgrimage that the common words of all our European languages had found their meaning. In forgetting that pilgrimage, those words had continued to be used, but without
meaning, separated from their context: sin, virtue, penance,
freedom, peace, progress. Among those words was the word
Church. I discovered at last what Catholics thought the
Church was.

I saw, for instance, that there could not be more than one
Church. There had to be only one Church, or no Church.
God, with his perfection of love, had to establish a Church,
because His Son had come to earth, to join men to Him by
means of a Church. There could not be two Churches coming from Calvary. The picture of a one Church had been
hideous to me; now it became beautiful.

Dante's *Divine Comedy* had been singularly vivid. When,
for instance, I had arrived with Dante at a realm of light
above the skies, and stood in the calyx of a flower, the Rose
of Paradise, I could scarcely think that I was not there
myself. And it seemed to me that, with my own eyes, I saw
St. Bernard come to my side and point out to me the elect

in the petals of the Rose. When he prayed to the Blessed
Virgin for Dante, it was as if he was praying for me:

> *O Virgin Mother, daughter of thy Son!*
> *Created beings all in loveliness*
> *Surpassing, as in height above them all.*

The *Divine Comedy* had been so vivid that it could
neither fade from my mind nor stay there as a mere fairy
tale. It must have planted the thought of becoming a Catholic, for I remember once dining with a friend, also an admirer of Dante, and saying to him: "Since I have read
Dante, I cannot help thinking that someday I will become
a Catholic." To which he answered, staring in amazement:
"I admire the word pictures by Dante, but regard the theology in his poem as nearly spoiling them." Yet I do not remember mentally debating the step of becoming a Catholic. I certainly passed no sleepless nights arguing pro and
con. I experienced no struggle. I made no attempt to study
the Catholic Church as it still existed about me, to determine
if it were as divine as Dante depicted it.

It would have been easy so to do, for Boston had many
Catholic churches, even though they were not conspicuous
in my haunts and though I had never, in my memory, laid
eyes on the Catholic cathedral; also I was making various
trips to Europe, where the Catholic churches were more
conspicuous and where I could not help visiting them as a
tourist. In Italy, I even met a priest or two and conversed
with them on architecture or literature. I was studying and
teaching, and books of Catholic theology were at my elbow.
Yet two years passed and I had avoided any real acquaintance with the Church.

Yet the acquaintance came to me, and it came to me
gratis, without my looking for it. It came to me through
my experience in World War I, in its confusion and stress,
in and about the battle front, where I spent nearly three
years.

It was while I was studying in Marburg, Germany, in the
summer of 1914 that the war broke out. I left Germany,

[163]

pained at a conflict which had ended the genial amity of Germans, French, Russians, and English at the *pension* where I was staying, yet excited at what seemed to me a terrific game that was beginning. I returned to the United States, never intending to take a remote part in it. But after a year or more I enlisted in the American Ambulance Service, the members of which carried the French wounded from the battlefield to the hospitals in little Model-T Fords. My motive in so doing was partly restlessness, but also an antagonism to German philosophy, particularly that of Nietzsche, against which it seemed the French were fighting. I wished to help the French, and embarked for France via England in January 1916.

My first experience did not bring me to an appreciation of the divine marks of the Church, but it no doubt prepared me to perceive them. After passing through England, I boarded a neat little channel steamer named the *Sussex*. It slid happily with romantic me in it over the glassy sea toward France. Then there came a shock as if we had struck a cliff and a roar as if a volcano had burst up under us, and I understood that we had been torpedoed. The forward half of the ship had disappeared, and with it the dining saloon containing those passengers, not greedy, who had gone to lunch at the second sitting. I was greedy. I had been to lunch, and was alive. Yet there seemed too little likelihood that I should remain alive. There was no shore in sight. I do not think that any passenger or ship's officer thought the ship could stay afloat. Most of the lifeboats were damaged. Those which were not went drifting off filled with women and children. Fortunately there was no wind, no swell.

There followed eleven hours in which it was very hard not to meditate on the fact that men are mortal, I among them. It was different from lying abed, dangerously sick with a fever, for my body was whole and my head healthily clear. I tried to avoid the meditation and tried to think of trivial things as a distraction, busying myself for a half hour taking camera pictures, with a friend's camera, of how we

[164]

looked when still alive. But some meditation was forced on me. I was not Christian enough to look beyond death. I had the common attitude: "Don't think about death." My thoughts, at least most of them, ended with frigidity and fishes. But the meditation revealed to me how contrary to human nature was mere stoicism. We are not made to bury our heads in the sand like ostriches.

We were rescued late at night and taken to France. The feel of the solid land was so assuring that for the moment I regained the impression that I would live happily forever after.

But there was a war going on, and after several months in a quiet sector I became acquainted with the full fury of it at Verdun in June 1916, where the battle which caused more carnage than any other in history was at its height. We in our ambulances would glide through the demolished city of Verdun after dark and cross the Meuse up to an obliterated village, Bras, where we would find the wounded. The road there, simply by its stench, made the circles of Dante's Inferno seem salubrious. The detonations around it were like the end of the world. On this road, I remembered Dante well enough to recite the prayer *Vergine Madre*. There was no dear earth left. There was only Heaven.

It was at Bras that I had my first glimpse of French Catholic chaplains under fire. I remember one in particular—bearded, beskirted in a cassock, with a V-shaped fatigue cap on his head—who used to help us load the stretchers into the Fords and who was singularly efficacious and unperturbed.

Years later, after my conversion, people said to me, as if ferreting out why I had become a Catholic: "So you found the Catholic chaplains better than the Protestant ones?"

Better! I had never thought of it in terms of better or worse. The Catholic chaplains were different. They went about their work more unself-consciously, bringing with them not their virtues but God's Sacraments. They were never in the way. They did not stand with their own personalities between the dying men and God. I had caught sight of the divinity of the Church, not in a book, but in a drama of which I was a part.

From then on the Catholic Church became vivid and living about me. I could scarcely see anything else, whether I was driving along the roads, or unloading the wounded in a hospital, or buying cigarettes in a village, or reading a newspaper. I saw France as a building which had been constructed by the Church. Part of the building was in ruins, but even the ruins spoke of the Church.

And not only did I everywhere see the Church, but I everywhere admired it. Everything that was admirable in France showed the touch of the Church.

While my eyes were open this way I enjoyed several visits of leave in Paris. They were somewhat hilariously spent, for Paris was a resplendent city and it was a joy to be alive there, yet in my hilarity I did not fail to see the Church. Tourists can go to Paris and see Notre Dame, and yet not see the Church at all. I did not often enter Notre Dame, yet I passed it often, and, in passing it, I did not regard it merely as a beautiful monument: it seemed what it had been to the men of old, a "sermon in stone." In its portals I saw, sculptured, Christ enthroned, Our Lady crowned, the elect going to heaven and the damned to hell. Once upon a time I had stared at such things as an outmoded myth. Now there was nothing truer. All other knowledge seemed comparatively unimportant. The Church had become to me the perennial and ever-patient teacher.

It was during one of my leaves in Paris that I bought and read and reread two books, then recently published, which sharpened my gaze at the Church. Both had been written by young Frenchmen who had just died in battle. One was *Le Voyage du Centurion* (*The Voyage of the Centurion*), by Ernest Psichari, and the other was *Morceaux Choisis* (or *Selected Verse*), by Charles Péguy. They were not so vivid as Dante's *Divine Comedy*, but they were contemporary and they made a deep impression on me.

The first, that by Psichari, was the veiled account of the

[166]

author's conversion to the faith which had come over him during his campaigns as a soldier in North Africa on the borders of the Sahara Desert. Brought up an agnostic, and inheriting skepticism from his grandfather, the apostate Ernest Renan, he had begun by feeling a sense of inferiority before the Mohammedans, who prayed as he did not. And the Mohammedans always referred to him as a Christian, as if a Frenchman could not be anything else, which humbled him even more. In the silence of the desert, with the earth so simple beneath him and the sky more simple above him, and the babble of politics stilled, mere literature having become the affair of dilettantes, he recognized the Church.

The second book was not the account of a conversion. Péguy, a baptized Catholic, was a poet who in his own life had shown a singular hesitation to become a wholehearted Catholic, but I knew nothing of that. I found his poetry Catholic, and more Catholic than that of other Catholic poets, precisely because in it was the image of the Church. He was not writing of his individual emotions. He was celebrating the march of mankind, of the children of Eve through time. And the drama everywhere in his poems was the story of the Catholic Church, of the wedding of earth in heaven. It is true that he was always talking of characters whom most of us associate with the past—Our Lady, St. Genevieve, St. Joan of Arc, and St. Louis—but to him they were of the present, and not far off. Heaven was as near to him as the France of Clemenceau and the Sorbonne, and nearer. He had the simplicity of a child, and I saw the Church, present and past, through his eyes.

In October 1916 my section of ambulance drivers took steamer from Marseille to Salonika, there to serve the French forces fighting around Monastir against the Germans and Bulgarians. During my voyage thither, and my nine months in Macedonia, Albania, and Greece, I enjoyed an experience which was not wholly a distraction: it was a preoccupation with the ancient Greeks. I could scarcely escape it, for we visited the Aegean Isles, coasted along the shore of Attica, saw Mount Olympus from Salonika, and ran our cars on one occasion into horse-breeding Thessaly. Much Greek history came back into my mind, especially Homer's *Iliad,* which I read and reread as I had *Le Voyage du Centurion.*

But what has this to do with the Catholic Church? Only this: that it put an end to the superstition, still lurking in my mind, that we were leaving the men of old far behind, that we were becoming a new kind of men, according to the formula preached by our Unitarian ministry, that we were progressing "onward and upward forever." The manner in which I was traveling, not as a tourist but as one engaged in a war, gave me a comradeship with the ancient Greeks in their wars, particularly with the men of the *Iliad.* Death was the same to us as it had been to them, and sleep, and far-away home. Human nature was not changing. I was as much a contemporary of Achilles as I was of the French generals who, in motorcars, not chariots, occasionally drove by with gold oak leaves round the band of their caps. There had been only one event that had changed human nature, and that was the Incarnation, the birth of Our Lord at Bethlehem, of the Blessed Virgin. By that, the clumsiest private soldier in any army could become divinized to a glory which far outshone that of endless ambrosial laughter on Mount Olympus. The Greeks had looked forward to the Incarnation, and we looked back to it. Otherwise we were the same.

In December 1916 we were stationed at Monastir. On Christmas Eve a Frenchman said to me: "Come to the Midnight Mass at the Chapel of the Sisters of Charity." I had never in my life attended a Mass, although I had stared in detachment at Masses going on. I accepted the invitation and, in the still darkness—for the enemy for once had let up their bombardment—I walked to the chapel. It was very small, and there were not fifty of us in it. There were some Sisters of Charity present in their blue robes, with their white cornucopia hats. A French priest before our eyes took off his soldier's jacket and put on his vestments with simple dignity. And the altar candles were lighted, and the Mass began.

I have read of how St. Patrick converted pagans in old

[168]

Ireland simply by celebrating Mass, in all its splendor, before them in a grove, and I have asked myself can such a conversion be a real conversion. It can, especially where the pagans have already, as is common to all men save disinherited Christians, a sense of offering sacrifice. I was a disinherited Christian, yet the sight of the Mass sent its light all through me. I discovered there and then what a sacrifice was, and recognized this sacrifice as no invention of man, but as God's own act—Christ offering himself to God, the Father.

Several Frenchmen whom I knew kneeled to confession openly on this occasion and then received Holy Communion. They were not among the "naturally pious." That is what impressed me most about their action. Here was a Church not for those who felt good, but for those who knew they were not.

By the time the snow was melting on the hills about Monastir, I had gained through more than a year of war a soldier's acquaintance with the Catholic Church. It was certainly not that of a theologian, but it served to convince me that the Catholic Church was of divine origin. First and last, it was not a church which bore any resemblance to other so-called churches. Its excellence did not depend on the merits of its clergy or its laity, although I found them admirable. It had the confidence of a body which derived its authority from outside itself; and all its actions, even its defects, bore witness to that. It was calmly, not emotionally, confident.

Moreover, this authority did not frighten me. It was what I thought the Church had to have, and I welcomed it. An authority which was true promised a freedom. It liberated one from enslavement to human beings who, perhaps by intellectual prowess, sought to impose their ideas on others, ideas which changed with every generation, like the teachings of the philosophers. I was tired of being preached to by mere human beings, on subjects concerning which they had no more authority than I. My rebellion to "churchmen" had brought me to wish for a church. I had seen the Catholic

Church, and its authority, and had no doubt that its authority was true.

The rest of my story is chiefly a tedious account of my delays in accepting the pearl which I had become convinced was divine, but I tell it to show how God finally made it impossible for my delays to go on.

In August of 1917, I was back in Paris, and there received a commission as first lieutenant in the Field Artillery of the United States, which was now in the war. I was sent to a battery in the First Division of the A.E.F. Without planning it, I began in my new task to live as if I were a Catholic without being one. That is, I always defended the Catholic Church against my fellow officers when they found fault with such trivial things as the way Catholics conducted their funerals. Also I attended Sunday Mass whenever possible.

In the month of December it was always possible to attend Mass, for we were in winter quarters in a little village on the upper Meuse, named Chassey, where our battalion interpreter, a French Jesuit with the English name Gurney, regularly celebrated it. I always was present at Sunday Mass, standing up and kneeling down with the Catholics. Since the Mass at Monastir, I could not conceive of the world without its central act, the Mass.

I became quite friendly with Father Gurney, partly because he was very affable and well liked by all of us, and also because I worked with him in conducting a Christmas party for the village children. He became at times very confidential with me, as he had to, in order to explain how delicate was his position because of the animosity of the anticlerical schoolmistress. But I was not confidential with him in anything important. I asked him no questions concerning the faith, and I am not sure that he did not consider me a Catholic.

At any rate, some of the enlisted men of the battery took it for granted that I was. One day when we were on the road to the front again, the battery farrier, a Catholic, informed me that Father Gurney would celebrate Mass at 4 A.M.—the next morning.

[170]

"But I am not a Catholic," I replied.

He stepped back in amazement, as if I had struck him. He had a right to be amazed. I ought to have been amazed at myself.

The spring of 1918 was a busy one for the First Division, for the Germans had broken through near Amiens, and we had been offered to the French by General Pershing to help ward off a disaster. During these actions, at times ferocious, when I was sometimes acting in liaison with the infantry, I found myself in situations where death seemed as inevitable as it had on the *Sussex*. Since I was now well aware of what Eternal Life was, it might be thought that I would have been prompted by those situations to join the Catholic Church, which led to Eternal Life, while the opportunity was still open, but I did not. At most I merely said to myself that I would become a Catholic "someday."

Before the end of the war I was back in the United States as an instructor in the School of Fire at Fort Sill, Oklahoma, and there the "someday" nearly arrived. There sat at my officers' mess two Catholics, who had no idea that I was thinking of becoming a Catholic, and they certainly did not take me for one, for I had decided not to attend Mass any more until I was actually a Catholic. They were cheerful and frank about their faith, however, and did not hide the fact that they went to Sunday Mass. They even used to regale us with stories of their chaplain—a Father McCarty, I believe. He was regularly late for their Sunday Mass, they said, and when they complained to him he answered: "I can't be late for it. It's I that celebrate it."

I was delighted with the account of the priest and wanted to attend one of his "late" Masses. I wanted also to be able to kneel before a statue of Our Lady and really belong to her—*Vergine Madre*. I felt that if I could do that, there would be nothing but joy in existence. So I decided to end my delay and become a Catholic.

I approached Father McCarty's lodgings with cautious detours, and finally, with dry mouth—frightened at I knew not what—I knocked on his door.

[171]

"Come in."

It was not Father McCarty. It was his orderly.

"Father McCarty is not in. He won't be back till tomorrow. What can I do for you, Lieutenant?"

"Nothing."

"Not a message?"

"Not a message."

My courage had spent itself. I continued my delay, and I left Fort Sill and returned to civil life at Boston without becoming a Catholic.

Protestants who live in Boston and who consider themselves Anglo-Saxons may be deterred from entering the Catholic Church because it seems to them that they will be changing their race to Irish. I had no such feeling, yet for a month after my return home I did no more than occasionally pray in a Catholic church and refuse to join my parents at the Unitarian place of worship. I circled twice round a Catholic rectory, but did not enter.

Finally I tried more elaborate methods. I called on an acquaintance of mine in New York who I knew was a Catholic and asked to be introduced to a Catholic priest. He considered me an intellectual and sent me to a learned Jesuit he knew, Father Wynne, editor of the Catholic Encyclopedia.

I entered Father Wynne's businesslike office, and found a businesslike Father Wynne, who was very direct. He asked me if I had any difficulties. I had none but, wishing to be intellectual, asked him if the Pope was considered really infallible, or pragmatically so, like the Supreme Court. He said that the Holy Father was really infallible. I was delighted with his uncompromising answer, and by the fact that he did not try to accommodate me and act as a good salesman for the Church.

Father Wynne gave me a letter to Father Martin J. Scott, S.J., of the Immaculate Conception Church at Boston—a priest not perhaps widely know to Protestants, but familiar to Catholics as the priest who has authored many pamphlets of wide circulation. I called on Father Scott.

[172]

Said he: "State your reasons for thinking that Jesus Christ is God."

I thought and thought, stammered and couldn't say a word.

Afterward he confided to me that he had thought I was so stupid that he wondered how I had ever found his door.

Certainly I was stupid, but one reason for this particular stupidity was that I had not come to the Church by first learning that Christ was God. I had begun by finding the Church to be divine, and inferred that its founder must be divine. I had never put to myself the question that Father Scott put to me. That Christ was divine was self-evident.

Father Scott gave me several months to learn a little theology, and on Palm Sunday in 1919 I was baptized.

If it be asked what joy I had there and then, I can only say that the joy is unique and there are no words capable of describing it. But an unhappy story comes to my mind, which I had read in childhood, and which I now retell because it sets off by contrast the joy that was mine.

There was once a man who entered into a beautiful garden, where every flower surpassed every other. He picked a fruit that was more beautiful than the flowers. He tasted and it turned to dust, and all the leaves turned over, with the words "April Fool" written on them.

My experience was the contrary. I had entered the garden of creation. I was very sensitive to its beauty. In it I had seen a pearl so beautiful that I could not believe it was real. It was the pearl of great price. After a delay I had at last dared to take it for my own—in baptism. Immediately all creation had shouted out: "It's true!"

INTO THE LIGHT

Dale Francis

A journalist, editor, and free-lance writer for many magazines, Dale Francis is a versatile young writer of promise. Into his thirty-three years he has already crowded the work of a student, soldier, minister, news reporter, lecturer, and writer.

Born in 1917 in Newark, Ohio, Mr. Francis was educated in the public schools of Hamden and Troy in that state. He attended Ohio Northern University and Bluffton College, receiving an A.B. degree from the latter. While in college, and after graduation, he served as a minister in various pulpits. He also worked on newspapers in Troy, Lima, and Dayton, Ohio.

Upon the entrance of our country into World War II, Dale enlisted in the army and served four years with the Air Corps in Ohio, Texas, Hawaii, Tinian, and Guam. His service in the army brought him for the first time into sustained contact with a Catholic priest and started him on a line of investigation and study which ultimately led him into the Church.

Upon the invitation of Bishop Vincent S. Waters, Mr. Francis organized the North Carolina Catholic Laymen's Association and founded the North Carolina *Catholic,* a weekly newspaper of which he became editor. In September 1947 he came to the University of Notre Dame, where he pursued graduate studies for a Ph.D. degree and acted as assistant in the department of public information. In 1949 he was appointed director of the University Press, in which position he has charge of all the official publications of the University of Notre Dame.

In 1943 he married Barbara Hoole, and they are the proud parents of a baby boy. In addition to his duties at the university, Dale assists Barbara in looking after the baby and still finds time to contribute to the *Commonweal,* the *Sign, Information,* the *Marionist, Integrity,* the *Ave Maria,* and other magazines of wide circulation.

O N THE DAY I knelt in an army chapel and became a Catholic I was certain that mine was an intellectual conversion. I'd come to the Church through pure reason, I would have said, and believed what I said.

Now, nearly five years later, I know how small a role my intellect played, how great was the role of grace.

How do you begin to tell the story of the most important thing in your life? I became a Catholic on June 15, 1945, but I was years on the road. It began in my home, of course. My parents believed in God and taught us to believe. My mother knelt in prayer each night and taught us to kneel in prayer. My father lived a Christian life that found its expression in his kindness to others, his devotion to his family.

We all of us have a God-ache, and the God-ache was with me early. I must have been no more then five when I used to go into a spare room we had and kneel there in secret before a picture of Jesus cradling a lamb in his arms.

It was about this time I first heard the word "Catholic." I was looking through the mail-order catalogue, deciding for the hundredth time what I wanted for Christmas, when I came to a picture of a crucifix. This is what I want, I told my mother, and she said that those were for Catholics. I heard more about Catholics soon afterward. The Ku Klux Klan was strong in our town, and one night they marched to the Stanton home and burned a cross. "They're Catholics," someone told me.

I didn't understand all this, but I was afraid of the Ku-Kluxers. Once we went to a funeral, and sitting on one side of the church were the men dressed in their white robes and the peaked caps with the slits for eyes. On the other side were the women and children and my dad. The next day at school one of my classmates jeered at me, "Your dad isn't a Ku-Kluxer," and instead of feeling ashamed, I was proud, though not half so proud of it as I am now.

We moved when I was eight from the little town where the only Catholics were the Stantons to another city where there were more Catholics. I went to Sunday school, joined the Loyal Temperance Legion, wrote a poem about Jesus.

When I was in the fourth grade I started to read all the books I could find. Because I'd always been interested in things religious, I started reading the only Catholic magazine in the public library, *Columbia*, and it was in it that I learned for the first time about the sign of the cross.

It intrigued me, and I practiced it in secret. I used it in public for the first time in a way that must have startled some good nuns. I'd always been in awe of nuns. I'd stare at them and tip my hat and wish that I could speak to them. One day I saw two Sisters coming down the street toward me. I decided to act as if I were a Catholic, let them think that I was really one with them, and so as I came up to them I smiled, bowed, and made the sign of the cross, then went on my way confident that they had recognized me as one of their own.

Every Sunday my brother and I went to Sunday school. It was not always enlightening. We liked the singing of hymns before the classes began, but the classes were more social than spiritual. Our teachers were earnest young men who knew only the meager lessons that had been given them by other earnest young men. They had difficulty keeping order, and the class periods frequently became only periods for the exchange of jokes and gossip. My brother and I both decided that it was wrong, that we didn't like it. He stopped going to Sunday school and didn't return until he was a young man, although through those years he was always a believing Christian, while I, in an effort to escape that decision, became one of the earnest youngsters who taught those who were younger.

I knew very little except that the God-ache was in me and that it wanted to be satisfied. When I was seventeen I was baptized in the Baptist Church, and when I came up from the water I felt a tingle through my spine.

I hadn't decided exactly what I wanted to be—a newspaperman or a minister. From the time I was fourteen I had been working at the Troy *Daily News*, writing about high-school sports in the winter and handling a sports column in the summer. Since it did not seem likely that I could afford to go to college, the decision was made for me. On graduation from high school, I got a job as a reporter on the Lima *News,* a newspaper in a city of about forty-five thousand people. In a year's time I was on the staff of the Dayton *Herald,* writing a daily column and doing fairly well for a fellow of nineteen.

It was here that I came in contact with Catholics again. When Lent came around, I talked to the managing editor. I told him that Lent was too often ignored, that we should observe it. I convinced him that we should run a daily Lenten sermon on the front page. I was given the assignment. In my innocence, I contacted the various Protestant ministers in the city. The days went by and the Catholics waited. Finally they protested with great vigor. Why had we carried daily Lenten sermons and never asked for one from a Catholic priest? In a vague way, I'd known Catholics observed Lent, too, but it had never occurred to me to ask a Catholic priest to write one of the sermons. The incident had its good side—to appease its Catholic readers, our paper hired a man on a part-time basis to serve as Catholic reporter.

It was while I was in Dayton that I came into the Real Presence for the first time, too. I was sent on an assignment with the photographer to get a picture of the Christmas crib at the University of Dayton chapel. I'd like to be able to say that I *felt* the Real Presence, but I did not. I found myself talking in whispers, but that was all.

That spring I went through a spiritual conflict. I felt myself drifting away from things I wanted. I decided that, if I was ever to be a minister, I'd better make the decision immediately. So I told the editor that at the end of summer I would leave the paper, go to college, and begin my preparation for the ministry. I enrolled at Ohio Northern University.

I have neither praise nor criticism of Ohio Northern. I only know that I never felt at home. I liked the professors and I liked my fellow students. It was just that I somehow never felt at home. The next year I transferred to a school that fitted me better.

Bluffton College is a Mennonite school. There was a seriousness of purpose at Bluffton which I had not found at Ohio Northern. The whole atmosphere was exactly what I wanted.

It was this year that I became a licensed minister, too. The superintendent of the Lima district of the Methodist Church was a man who had been a friend of mine in my home town. He introduced me to the superintendent of a district in the western part of Ohio, and I was invited to give a trial sermon at Fort Recovery, Ohio. The people at that Ohio village and at the country church that was the second point on the circuit liked my sermon, and I was invited to become their pastor.

Mercer County, Ohio, is as densely Catholic an area as you'll find anywhere in the country. Every Sunday, as I drove to the country church at Erastus, I passed St. Anthony of Padua Church, and I wondered each time why it was that so many were there while we were hard put to draw forty to our morning service. I didn't trouble myself, however, to find out why.

It was while I was a student at Bluffton, whose professors teach only good solid Christian philosophy, and while I was a minister at Fort Recovery, where I should have been growing in grace, that I began to fall farther and farther away from the fundamentalist position.

Part of it was a revulsion to other fundamentalists. I intensely disliked a shouting religion, and most of the fundamentalists were shouters. One day I heard a Unitarian minister give a good, quiet sermon that I liked. It was a social message and it appealed to me. I lost all concern with any of the fundamental beliefs; my religion became one of doing good. The divinity of Christ, eternal life, the existence of a personal God, all these things were for me matters of secondary importance. The greatest thing was to live a life of service.

Soon the divinity of Christ became even less than some-

[178]

thing of secondary importance. It seemed to me not even logical. So I evolved something that seemed much more logical. Christ was born an ordinary man, but through living a life in conformity with God's will He became divine. Mixed up? Sure I was mixed up. Fortunately, I knew I was mixed up. Unfortunately, I wasn't able to find any help out of the labyrinth.

Three things happened that might have brought me closer to the answer. A lady from the country church came to me with a question. A Catholic had given her a list of all the popes, she said. Did I think the Catholics could really trace their popes clear back to St. Peter? I shrugged my shoulders, lightly discarded nineteen hundred years of history, and told her it was not likely.

Then I attended Mass for the first time. It was the midnight Mass on Christmas Eve 1938, and St. Gerard's Church in Lima was crowded. My friends and I stood in the rear of the church. I was stirred by the Mass, and I told one of my closest friends next day that I wished we had it.

Finally one of the ladies in the Fort Recovery church gave me a Catholic missal and prayer book. I don't believe she was interested in the Catholic Church; as I recall, I believe she was more a Christian Scientist than a Methodist, but she gave me the missal because she thought I'd be interested in seeing it. I hardly glanced at it, but for nearly three years I carried it in my overcoat pocket. I do not know why.

In the spring of 1941, I faced another decision. I now had to finish my theological training and prepare for ordination. For three and a half years I had served as a minister at Fort Recovery. I loved the people and I think they liked me. Yet I was certain that something was wrong.

I was confused. I was only half a believer. I felt God tugging at me, but I didn't know where He wanted me to go. I only half believed in the divinity of Christ, and yet, in all the years at Fort Recovery, I never once presided at the distribution of Holy Communion, although I had been given permission. When I received the bread and wine at services I attended, I tried to make it become a reality for me; I tried to imagine what it was like for the bread and wine to become in reality the body and blood. The very thought overpowered me, and somehow it seemed wrong even to think of presiding at the distribution of the bread and wine, saying the words He had said.

As I said, all this I felt when I was only half a believer in Christ at all. I do not pretend it was reasonable. I tell it only because it is true; I do not know how to explain it.

In my confusion, I decided I would take a church near Columbus, Ohio, and go to Ohio State, and afterward, for I dreaded the thought of ordination, become a social worker for the Methodist Church. I was assigned a church, but two weeks later my father was critically injured in an accident. I went to his bedside, but my message to the district superintendent somehow didn't get through, and he, thinking that I had changed my mind, assigned another man to the church. When I returned he said he would find me another place. However, relieved after the first disappointment that the decision had been made for me, I told him no and returned to the Dayton newspaper.

For the next six months I substituted at different churches on Sundays, working as a reporter on weekdays. Then came Pearl Harbor. I enlisted the next day and, after a two-week period for straightening up my affairs, I entered the service.

It was in the army that I first came into close contact with Catholics, particularly with Catholic priests. The first contact wasn't pleasant. In an effort to make the USO's Sunday entertainment more Sunday-like, I'd introduced a hymn and a prayer. The Catholic chaplain called me in and told me that if that wasn't stopped he'd forbid the Catholic men to attend. I couldn't understand. After all, the prayer we said was the Lord's Prayer. He told me in no uncertain terms that the Our Father was properly said in a way different from the way we said it. I went away not certain what the fuss was about, but convinced that Catholics felt very strongly about such things.

There was Catholic literature to read in the chapels. I read a few pamphlets and was impressed. But not impressed enough. It was about this time that a girl I had known in college wrote to me and told me she was planning on becoming a Catholic. She wanted to know what I thought. I told her. There were many excellent things about the Catholic Church, but then it really wasn't the thing for educated people—it was too filled with superstition, too confining and narrow. She wrote back and thanked me, saying that she knew she could trust my keen insight in such matters and thanked me for saving her from a great mistake.

Two years later this young lady received another letter from me. I was by this time much better acquainted with the Church. I wrote to her in a much different tone. She became a Catholic nearly two years before I did.

My own way to the Church was slow and tortuous. Little things happened to move me along the way. A fellow crossed himself in the mess hall before eating and shocked me into the realization that I was thanking God too little. The *Catholic Digest* went on sale on the newsstands, and I started reading it. The pamphlets in the chapel took more and more of my time.

I met the girl who was to become my wife, too. At one time I hesitated to tell people I had married a Catholic before I myself became one. A couple of years after I'd become a Catholic, I was talking to a minister and he said, "Just answer one question: Did you marry a Catholic?" I told him I had. "That's enough," he said smugly. "That explains it all."

It explains a lot, all right, but not in the way he meant. He was talking as though I'd become a Catholic as a kind of convenience or just to please my wife. To have become a Catholic for either of these reasons would have been unthinkable for me. When I was married I was rid of my prejudices against the Catholic Church but I was firmly convinced that I would never join her.

Yet marrying Barbara explains a lot; she is a good Catholic. During the years when my decision was being made, hers was the major influence. She knew her faith and it was of prime importance. She attended daily Mass and she lived a good Catholic life.

[181]

It was in the army that I met Father Emeric Lawrence, too. In civilian life he was a Benedictine monk teaching at St. John's in Minnesota. He was the first priest to whom I ever talked about religion. We used to talk late into the night, about many things. I started attending Mass. For several weeks, while the post was without a Protestant chaplain, I substituted at the Protestant services, but I attended Mass beforehand. I was stationed in Texas, and when I did not preach the sermon at the Protestant chapel I almost always had an invitation to speak at a Protestant church somewhere in the area. It was understood, though, that I attended Mass before. Once when a Colorado City minister asked me to speak at his church for him he told me that Mass was being celebrated at eight o'clock at the town's only Catholic church and I'd be able to attend and still be back in time for services at his church.

There came for me now two years of unrest and indecision. When I finally made my decision it seemed as simple as ABC. My thinking went something like this.

Either there was a God or there was not a God. One of the two was right. Now, the unity of nature made it ridiculous for me to suppose there was no God. If the stars in the heaven ran with such precision that men could calculate their positions years in advance, then there must be a Mind greater then the minds of the men who made the calculations. There was a God. I was certain of that.

Well, after that I faced another problem. God was either a personal God or not a personal God. There was a chance that He had supplied the wisdom for the universe and left things there. But this was not true if God came to earth. This was not true if Jesus Christ was more than man, if He was God. I reserved my decision on the matter of a personal God for the decision on the divinity of Christ.

I was certain of one thing. Christ wasn't just a good man. He said He was God. If He wasn't God and said that He was, then He was an impostor and a liar. He couldn't be merely a good man, because good men don't lie. So He had to be God, or just a deceitful man. I decided I'd believe He was God if I could believe in the resurrection. There was the proof. I reserved another decision.

Now, did Christ really rise from the dead? That could just be a fanciful story, I reasoned. So I started making deductions. I tried to figure it out the way I might have had I been covering it as a newspaperman.

Christ said He was God, and His Apostles apparently believed Him. Well, if they were really convinced, they should have stuck with Him when He was threatened with crucifixion. But, even though they'd seen His miracles, they bolted in the crisis. Only one even stayed around at all. Peter denied Him three times. While He lived, and they could reasonably hope that with His power He could free Himself, they were afraid. Then He was killed.

That should have been the end of the story. But it wasn't. A short time later His Apostles were openly proclaiming their devotion to Christ. Frightened Peter was no longer afraid. He even suffered death gladly.

Something had happened. The men who were frightened while Christ lived should have become more frightened with His death. Instead they were now willing to dare all things. Something had happened in the meantime, and that must have been the resurrection of Christ. It had to be something that big to make the difference. So I came to believe in the resurrection of Christ—and, with it, in His divinity—and, with that, in a personal God.

So I believed that Jesus was more than man. Truth was on the earth while He was here. Now, God, being infinitely wise, certainly knew that truth had to be maintained. I'd played that game where a sentence is whispered from one person to another and ends up by being entirely different from the way it started. Since I was aware of the way man exaggerates things, I know, of course, that God knows this too.

So I was sure that God would somehow protect the truth, see to it that it was maintained inviolate on earth. He would do it, it seemed to me, in one of two ways. Either through guidance by the Holy Ghost or through the Bible. I quickly made my decision on this. I'd seen the Bible interpreted too many different ways: there was no unity there, and there would have to be unity in God's guidance. It had to be through the Holy Ghost.

But how? One of two ways—either personally or through a Church. Now, I knew some people who claimed that the Holy Ghost guided them personally, but all of them were being led in different directions. That couldn't be. Besides, there had to be continuity, and that wouldn't be possible if guidance came only from humans. God's guidance must be continuous, it must stretch back to Christ. So it had to be through a Church.

All right, was it the Catholic Church or one of the Protestant churches? It couldn't be, as some of my Protestant friends said, all churches. They believed too many conflicting things. The truth couldn't contradict itself. I read much and I studied much. I found the teachings of the Catholic Church to be unchanged in fundamentals over the centuries. There was unity, there was continuity. No Protestant church could offer me the same.

I wasn't ready to submit yet, though. I wanted to make more certain. I came to the Holy Eucharist. I found Christ saying that we had to eat of His Body. Figuratively speaking, I thought hopefully. No, He said it again to the people who asked Him if He really meant what He said. The Bible told me that after that there were some who walked with Him no longer. So I ran into another incontestable fact. Christ either meant exactly what He said about eating of His body or He meant it figuratively. If he meant it as a figure of speech, then He was responsible for turning some people away from following Him. After all, He had only to tell them he was speaking figuratively. But He didn't. So, if He meant it figuratively, He was guilty of turning people away from God. But that couldn't be, since He was God. So I had to face it. He must have meant exactly what He said. It overwhelmed me, but there was no way out of it.

By this time I was on my way for sure. Born Catholics can't understand it, but I think most converts can, when I tell you there is something of a panic that overcomes you as you approach the necessary decision. After all, it is a tremendous decision. I could switch from being a Baptist to being a Methodist without a second thought; but becoming a Catholic—that was the great and final decision. I grasped at straws, seeking to hold myself back.

At this time I found a book in which appeared the essay, "Why I Am Not a Catholic." I read it, liked it, and held onto it. I wanted to know more about the author who had put my own thoughts and fears so well into words. His name was William Orchard. After writing this admirable essay he had become a Catholic. I gave up.

I made my decision known to my family. They had not been with me on my long journey. I was not surprised that they were disappointed. I would have been disappointed with myself four years before. They asked me to wait for six months, just to be sure. I did as they wished. I read some arguments against my decision. They did not affect me, for my decision had been made. I had, through my studies, made out the dim outlines of the True Church, but the light of grace had brought the truth of the Church into blazing clarity. Having come into the light, I could not now return to the shadows.

On a June morning in an army chapel outside of Big Spring, Texas, Father Thomas McDonald baptized me conditionally and I received Holy Communion.

For this I thank God with all my heart.

THE MARITAINS FIND GOD

Raïssa Maritain

The leading Thomistic philosopher of our day, Jacques Maritain, is recognized as one of the outstanding thinkers of the twentieth century and has received honors from many universities in Europe and America. Certainly no other contemporary has done so much to interpret the philosophical system worked out by St. Thomas Aquinas and to apply it to the problems of our times. He has caused the impact of Thomistic principles upon contemporary philosophy to be felt in all the important schools of philosophy on both sides of the Atlantic.

Born in Paris in 1882 of a nominally Catholic father and a Protestant mother, he was educated along the rationalist humanitarian lines then prevalent in France. He attended the Lycée Henri IV and the Sorbonne, where he met Raïssa Oumansoff, whom he later married. Both of them were deeply affected by the rationalism, positivism, and skepticism which then dominated the Sorbonne.

The Maritains formed close friendships with Ernest Psichari and Charles Péguy and came under the influence of Henri Bergson, then lecturing at the Collège de France. After years of fruitless searching for intellectual peace, they came in contact with Léon Bloy, an ardent Catholic and a writer of singular power and genius; he interested the Maritains in the study of the lives of the saints and mystics, and was thus chiefly instrumental in leading them to an understanding of the Catholic faith. When they were baptized on June 11, 1906, Bloy acted as their godfather.

In 1907, Jacques Maritain received the Michonis scholarship to Heidelberg University, where he spent two years studying biology under Hans Driesch. He was the first to publicize Driesch's theory of vitalism in France, publishing his study of Darwinism and neo-vitalism in 1910 in the *Revue de Philosophie*.

Returning to France, he studied the philosophy of St. Thomas under the scholarly Dominican, Père Clerissac. Jacques came to perceive in Catholicism not only a divine revelation, but also a philosophy which could foster, direct, and regulate speculative thinking. He decided that henceforth his true vocation lay in the exposition of the great philosophical system of St. Thomas and in bringing its timeless truths to grips with contemporary problems. In 1913 he published a lengthy critique of the philosophy of Bergson, and in his lectures at the Institut Catholique he pointed out the inadequacy of the metaphysics of Bergson, Descartes, and of German idealism as compared with Thomism.

In 1917, Maritain was requested by the bishops of France to work out a manual of philosophy for use in seminaries; accordingly, he published his *Introduction to Philosophy*, which prompted the Congregation of Studies in Rome to confer upon him the title of Doctor *ad honorem*. He soon became the center of the Thomistic revival in France, and the numerous philosophical works issuing from his busy pen spread his influence throughout Europe and America.

During the upheavals of recent years Maritain has kept himself free from entanglement with political parties and has proclaimed the freedom of the philosopher to treat, as a philosopher, the problems of contemporary politics. Many students consider *The Degrees of Knowledge* his most profound work in speculative thought, while *True Humanism*, dealing with the practical problems of our social structure, has been most widely acclaimed.

For some years Professor Maritain taught regularly at the Pontifical Institute of Mediaeval Studies in Toronto and at the University of Chicago. In addition, he lectured at Louvain University, at the Angelicum in Rome, at Geneva, in Milan, in Germany, Ireland, and England. In 1936 he made an extensive lecture tour through South America. During World War II he taught one semester each at Columbia and Princeton, with shorter courses at Toronto and Chicago.

In 1945 he was appointed French ambassador to the Vatican. He is at present teaching Thomistic philosophy in the graduate school of Princeton University and continuing his contributions to the leading philosophical journals.

His books in English are: *The Angelic Doctor, Art and Scholasticism, A Christian Looks at the Jewish Question, The Degrees of Knowledge, France, My Country, An Introduction to Logic, Freedom in the Modern World, An Introduction to*

Philosophy, Prayer and Intelligence (with Raïssa Maritain), *A Preface to Metaphysics, Religion and Culture, An Essay in Order, Scholasticism and Politics, Science and Wisdom, Some Reflections on Culture and Liberty, The Things That Are Not Caesar's, Three Reformers: Luther, Descartes, Rousseau, True Humanism, The Living Thoughts of St. Paul, The Twilight of Civilization, Education at the Crossroads, Ransoming the Time, Existence and the Existent, The Person and the Common Good, The Rights of Man and Natural Law,* and *Christianity and Democracy.*

*   *   *   *   *

A small, slender woman, dark and vivacious, Raïssa Maritain is deeply interested in philosophy, literature, art, and music. Sympathetic and thoughtful, she possesses a genius for friendship and has won the devotion of many talented men and women. She was born in Russia in 1883 of Jewish parentage and was raised under the influence of her grandparents in an atmosphere of strict orthodoxy.

When she was ten her parents moved to France, where they felt that greater opportunities would be offered to their two little girls. Raïssa Oumansoff was a brilliant student and entered the Sorbonne at the age of seventeen; she followed courses in science and in 1904 married Jacques Maritain. Her story henceforth is inextricably bound with the life of her husband, as they have studied and written together over the years.

She has collaborated in many of his philosophical works, and her name is signed with his to *Prayer and Intelligence* and to *Situation de la Poésie.* Until 1939 they lived in a modest villa in Meudon, just outside Paris, where their home became a focal point for Catholic intellectual life in France.

A notable group assembled there each fall to make a week's retreat under the direction of a Dominican priest. Students from various lands, as well as leaders of various youth movements, came there for advice, encouragement, and guidance and always left heartened and encouraged.

She has written several poetical works, *La Vie Donnée* and *Lettre de Nuit,* also a child's life of St. Thomas Aquinas, and *The Prince of This World,* translated by Gerald Phalen. Her memoirs, *We Have Been Friends Together* and *Adventures in Grace,* translated by Julie Kernan, tell of the Maritains, friendship with Bergson, Psichari, Péguy, Léon Bloy, Georges Rouault, Pierre Termier, and other intellectuals of the period in France. They are charmingly written and combine warmhearted friendliness with a capacity for objective appraisal.

Adventures in Grace, published in 1945, was the Catholic Book Club selection for July of that year. She has likewise written *Le Mystère d'Israel* and *Histoire d'Abraham.*

While Mrs. Maritain has captivated with her charm and hospitality those who know her personally, she has reached a much wider audience through her writings, bringing to them her words of healing and of light. In the following account she tells of the conversion of both her husband and herself to the Catholic faith.

A T ABOUT THE AGE of fourteen I started asking myself questions about God. Now that I knew how unhappy or wicked men could be, I wondered if God really existed. I recall very clearly that I reasoned thus: If God exists, He is also infinitely good and all-powerful. But if He is good, how can He permit suffering? And if He is all-powerful, how can He tolerate the wicked? Therefore He is not all-powerful or infinitely good; therefore He does not exist.

This conclusion, which was to lead me to despair later on, still remained in the realm of ideas proposed rather than affirmed. A distressful idea, which I did not really accept. . . . I instinctively held myself back and preserved myself from despair. I waited; I laid my hope in the solution of science, of that science which was promised me, of those scientists who, a little later, would be my teachers. And, morning and evening, I continued to pray in secret to the God who was disappearing from my mind but whom my heart would not abandon.

This was the beginning of a great drama, and in that drama I was alone. My parents were of no help. They had given up nearly all their religious practices, and the influence of my forebears was far away! Yet my parents kept their faith in God; they did not believe that their child could lose that faith; they lived in this quiet assurance.

Nor did I come in contact with any religious instruction in school. All the little girls were making their First Communion. On the appointed day they came, serious in mien and dressed all in white, and presented holy pictures to their fellow students. And the teachers, as well as the other pupils, greeted them with joy, embraced and congratulated them. But in all this I saw only a business of ritual and custom—I had no notion of the Sacrament, and no one thought to tell me about it, believing, no doubt, that, like other children of my own age, I had received adequate explanations of such things. I had no regard for holy pictures, the significance of which was beyond me, and I continued in my total ignorance of Christianity. Yet I had read *Polyeucte:* I had recited again and again the celebrated "Stanzas," and had loved it more than all the other works of Corneille. How could it happen that I had not received therefrom at least some little enlightenment? Probably the whole business, as far as I was concerned, remained in the realm of those beautiful tales of which great writers know the secret, and whereof I did not see the connection with truth and life.

At fifteen I took a course in the history of philosophy under Dr. Charles Rappoport. He himself was a Kantian, but he did nothing to make me prefer Kantianism to any other system. I, for my own part, was in no haste to reach conclusions or to choose. Therein also I waited and withheld my decision. It was already an immense joy to know that others besides myself had sought truth and had not scorned to devote their lives to that search. How many treasures had revealed themselves to the activity of the human intelligence! I thought that one day among them all I would find my own treasure—absolute truth, unshakable truth! I should know the meaning of life and the truth about God. But I also believed that no certitude of this sort could be obtained without the proof and approval of science.

It can thus be seen that my tutor had failed to tell me about the hierarchy of knowledge. In my "degrees of knowledge," I placed at the top a dominating physical science, weighing and measuring all things and holding the keys to all the enigmas of the universe.

Philosophy and religion, the conduct of private life, the structure of society—I believed that all these depended on the discoveries of natural and physical science. I owed this conviction to the intellectual climate in which I lived. All the students and teachers who visited my parents thought the same. They were believers in scientism, determinism, positivism, materialism—and I went along with them. Or, rather, with that feeling of expectation which never left me and which made everything provisional for me, I believed them, but still without any considered acceptance of their theories.

At seventeen I began my studies at the Sorbonne. There the scientists insofar as they philosophized at all, were generally partisans of such philosophical theories as mechanism, epiphenomenalism, absolute determinism, evolutionary monism—doctrines which deny the reality of the spirit and the objectivity of all knowledge which goes beyond the cognition of sensible phenomena.

All these theories constituted a more or less acknowledged system which Jacques, in one of his first books several years later, was to designate by the name of *Scientism*. "Scientism," he said, "sees in mathematics the universal instrument and supreme standard of knowledge . . . It replaces the intelligence with the entirely material perfection of technical procedures. It substitutes for intelligibility the mere possibility of being reconstituted or reconstructed by means of mathematical elements of spacial representations. Thus scientism imposes on the intelligence the very law of materialism: those things alone are intelligible which are materially verifiable. Thus it comes about that scientism signifies a universal mechanism. The thesis that everything can be reduced to extension and movement, and that no other laws exist except mathematical functions, was not for our scientists even something that required demonstration; it was of the essence of thought itself."

They were indeed obliged to recognize that thought had its proper needs, even when they disowned it; and they were certainly obliged constantly to fall back on the intelligence, since it is impossible to state the most insignificant fact without abstraction and generalization, or to affirm or deny the least thing without implying confidence in the processes of the intelligence and in the principles of its activity.

Thus the scientists openly reveal what is within their competence, with an implicit reference to common sense. And this is the best philosophic attitude that they can have, and the most effective means of teaching.

I wondered how the remarkable men of science whose courses I attended and whose books I read could consent to remain in so confused and vague a state of mind without being upset thereby, especially when every intelligible reality faded away like some mirage when you thought to approach and grasp it, and when the sacrosanct "facts" themselves dissolved into the dust of purely empirical assertions, for that which was generally denied by the prevailing philosophy was the objectivity of our knowledge, our very ability to grasp the real.

This created a singularly rarefied atmosphere for the intelligence, an infinite uneasiness. We swam aimlessly in the waters of observation and experience like fish in the depths of the sea, without ever seeing the sun whose dim rays filtered down to us. We could only yield to the gods of science, without the least help from any testimony of the mind. Jacques would draw pictures of grimacing little men who through some inordinate effort hoisted themselves up from the ground with their own hair as a halyard. He had always known how to join kindness and quiet mirth with the most serious of feelings. But I got out of my depth, and, being too weak to struggle against all these giants of science and philosophy or to defend the rightness of my deepest intuitions, I took refuge in sadness.

But still I had, for some short time at least, to lay aside these metaphysical problems. Within the limitations of positive science, the scientific instruction given us was of a very high order. And had we directed our studies toward the physicomathematical rather than toward the natural sciences, we would undoubtedly have been fascinated by the magnificence of the discoveries of so great a galaxy of scientific genius; perhaps this would for a long time have hidden from us our hunger for metaphysical knowledge. It would have been wonderful, for instance, to attend the classes of Paul Appell, or of Marie and Pierre Curie, scientists of genius and heroic workers, who had opened the way to a new science and a new therapeutics. But in the Faculty of Natural Sciences, less rich in men of genius, Jacques and I followed with particular interest the courses of Félix Le Dantec, the most appealing and brilliant of our professors.

He had noticed the attention with which we listened to him, and, becoming interested in such studious pupils, he decided to know us better. One day when Jacques and I were waiting for a trolley at the corner of the Rue Soufflot and the Boulevard St. Michel, he came up to us and began to talk as though to old friends; and he invited us to come to his home, which we did rather frequently thereafter.

We had long conversations with him, and he expounded to us his philosophy, which was materialism. He told us, and he said as much to anyone who wished to listen to him, that it was impossible for him not to admit the truth of materialism, but that after all it is a faith just as undemonstrable as the credo of Christians. And this was scandalous to those of his colleagues who were less disposed than he to admit it.

I knew nothing of the Christian credo; yet I wanted none of this materialist faith. I said to myself that doubtless someday or other I would have to come to it; that no one was offering us a more coherent doctrine, and that since all the others led at best to Montaigne's *"Que sais-je?"* they were no less disillusioning. Sadness pierced me, the bitter taste of the emptiness of a soul which saw the lights go out, one by one.

Le Dantec, however, full of enthusiasm, promised us a brilliant scientific future if we would work in the direction he advised. We were to synthesize living matter, and, by doing so, to demonstrate that life was nothing more than some specific chemical combination. He loved this kind of simplification; for him the intelligence was merely "a flabby material which functions at a temperature of thirty-eight degrees," and consciousness was "an epiphenomenon."

But these handsome vistas did not beguile us. What good was the synthesis of living matter, what good this power over the physical universe, if the very reason for life and existence, if the entire moral universe were to remain unanswerable riddles?

Le Dantec also professed an atheism from which, he insisted, he could never be dissuaded. He told us that he had never been capable of religious faith, even in his childhood. He had studied his catechism faithfully; he had always been at the head of his class in religious instruction; yet never had he known what it was to believe in God.

It is a rare thing to meet an atheist so convinced, so absolute, so calm. For several years I had been sinking toward atheism; indeed, I believed that I no longer believed in God; but what suffering this caused me, what desolation of all my being, what devastation! To Le Dantec this was something astonishing, but not a ground for antipathy—quite the contrary! He seemed never to have come across such a problem, and for such reasons! He had become very much attached to me, and I thought I must tell him that I was—still secretly —engaged to Jacques. Thanks to me, our meetings became more and more infrequent, and soon ended completely. Afterward I greatly wished it had been otherwise. This man —good, generous, loyal—merited complete confidence; through clumsiness I put an end to a precious friendship; but I was too young at the time to think of all this, and I acted in the brusque and awkward way of those who have as yet had but little human experience.

Already I had come to believe myself an atheist; I no longer put up any defense against atheism, in the end persuaded, or rather devastated, as I was by so many arguments given out as "scientific." And the absence of God unpeopled the universe.

If we must also give up the hope of finding any meaning whatever for the word truth, for the distinction of good from

[194]

evil, of just from unjust, it is no longer possible to live humanly.

I wanted no part in such a comedy. I would have accepted a sad life, but not one that was absurd. Jacques had for a long time thought that it was still worth while to fight for the poor, against the slavery of the "proletariat." And his own natural generosity had given him strength. But now his despair was as great as my own.

This life which I did not choose for myself—I no longer wished to live in such a shadowy light. For the comedy is sinister and is played upon a stage of blood and tears.

Our complete understanding, our own happiness, all the sweetness of the world, all man's art, could not make us accept without some reason—in no matter what sense of the word—the misery, the unhappiness, the wickedness of men. Either the world could be justified, and this could not be if real knowledge did not exist, or else life was not worth the trouble of a moment's further notice.

Were there but one solitary heart in all the world to feel certain sufferings, one solitary body to know death's agony, that would demand a justification; and were there only the suffering of one single child, even if animals alone were left to suffer on the earth—that, all that, would still demand some explanation.

In no case is the state of things acceptable without some true light on existence. If such a light is impossible, existence also is impossible and life is not worth living.

If . . . if . . . and we went on adding dark stanza after dark stanza to this dirge of our distress. But there was always this conditional mood in our souls. There was always that little ray of hope, that door half open on the road to daylight.

Before leaving the Jardin des Plantes we reached a solemn decision which brought us some peace: to look sternly in the face, even to the ultimate consequence—insofar as it would be in our power—the facts of that unhappy and cruel universe wherein the sole light was the philosophy of skepticism and relativism.

[195]

We would accept no concealment, no cajolery from persons of consequence, asleep in their false security. The epicureanism they proposed was a snare, just as was sad stoicism; and estheticism—that was mere amusement. Neither did we wish, because the Sorbonne had spoken, to consider that the last word had been said. The French university world was then so hermetically sealed within itself that by the very thinking of this simple thought we showed some little merit.

Thus we decided for some time longer to have confidence in the unknown; we would extend credit to existence, look upon it as an experiment to be made, in the hope that to our ardent plea the meaning of life would reveal itself, that new values would stand forth so clearly that they would enlist our total allegiance and deliver us from the nightmare of a sinister and useless world.

But if the experiment should not be successful, the solution would be suicide; suicide before the years had accumulated their dust, before our youthful strength was spent. We wanted to die by a free act if it were impossible to live according to the truth.

It was then that God's pity caused us to find Henri Bergson.

He taught at the Collège de France, whose buildings face those of the Sorbonne. We had only to cross the Rue St. Jacques and take several steps down the Rue des Ecoles; but this was not so easy as one might think. A mountain of prejudice and distrust existed between these two institutions—particularly so on the part of the Sorbonne philosophers with respect to Bergson's teaching. These feelings were so strong that it was almost as difficult for the young students to think of going from the Sorbonne to the Collège de France as from the Sorbonne to the Church of St. Geneviève, its near neighbor.

Once a week we attended a course of lectures in which Bergson interpreted Greek texts. It was given at the Collège de France in a small room and for a small number of students. We would find ourselves so near the table where he placed the text to be studied that we were almost able to read it with him. And it seemed to us that this proximity, this intimacy, brought us nearer at once to the master commentator and the master who was commented upon. It was as though we were all absorbed into the luminous cloud of their wedded intelligences.

The year I attended this course, Bergson was expounding Plotinus; we felt that he was personally very much interested, but we had no idea of the great role which Plotinus would one day play in his life. We knew of it only very much later. Bergson's explanation made the difficult text lucid, and under his direction everything seemed to me easy to understand. These special courses were infinitely precious to us. They were an introduction into those regions to which we seemed to aspire naturally, where we can breathe freely, where our hearts burn within us, and where we begin to foresee that there exists a spiritual realm "from which descend all perfect gifts."

I began to read Plotinus with great joy outside of class. Of this reading, one single dazzling memory stands out for me and throws all the rest into shadow. One summer day in the country I was reading the *Enneads.* I was sitting on my bed with the book on my knees; reaching one of those numerous passages where Plotinus speaks of the soul and of God, as much in the character of a mystic as in that of a metaphysician—a passage I did not think of marking then and which I have not looked for since—a wave of enthusiasm flooded my heart. The next moment I was on my knees before the book, covering the page I had just read with passionate kisses, and my heart burning with love.

Every time I have thought to evoke this memory, I have found it ever living and vibrant within me, even though an hour after the spiritual event I have just related I had ceased to give it further thought, nor did I reflect upon it or draw any conclusion from it at the time.

I took up my life once again exactly at the point where it had been before; I remained outwardly unchanged and I continued to seek after that which I had unexpectedly found, or rather He who in a flash had made Himself felt in me and had then disappeared.

One day, trembling all over, I went to Bergson to ask his advice about my studies, and even more, no doubt, about my life. It was the first time I had ever done anything of this kind. A few words of what he said to me are forever engraved in my memory: "Always follow your inspiration." Was this not to say, "Be yourself, always act freely"? Much later, when I reminded him of this advice, which I had set about following indeed, Bergson, smiling at his imprudence, said kindly: "That was not advice I could have given to many people."

Nevertheless, such advice would have been entirely within the spirit of Bergson's doctrine of freedom. In fact, for Bergson, to follow one's inspiration (if it is truly inspiration, that is, the personal or divine counsel which springs from the depths of one's self) is to act according to what we really are, or according to the best in ourselves—that is, to act freely.

The danger consists in mistaking for this welling-up from the depths, for this great breath of the soul, some fugitive breeze or other from without, which skims lightly over the consciousness and flatters it.

However this may be, Bergson had given me confidence in my essential tendencies, had opened my mind to the inwardness of life, had freed me from the fear of not acting in accordance with the purest ideals of scientific positivism.

It was only after reading Plotinus that I read Plato, and then Pascal. These great voices filled my soul with their resonance to the infinite. Still confusedly, I perceived in them the heralds of a world new to me. Everything has been said about the beauty of Plato's *Dialogues*. It is indeed their beauty and the poetry that lives in them which assure their perennial appeal, perhaps even to a greater extent than the philosophy they set forth. And their inspiration, too, is often surprising, whether its source be in Socrates or be higher than Socrates. After having read these dialogues, I could take up Pascal without feeling the transition too great. And after having read Pascal, I could come back to Socrates with even more admiration.

I think it was during this same year that for the first time I read a Christian mystic, Ruysbroeck. *L'Ornement des Noces Spirituelles,* translated from the Flemish by Maurice Maeterlinck, fascinated without greatly enlightening me. One sentence, however, haunted my memory, and uplifted me, I do not know why. To rid myself of the obsession, I finally carved it on the door of the country house in which we lived during the summer. I quote the sentence from memory, but doubtless without much difference, if any, from the original wording: "Simplicity of intention is the principle and the completion of all virtue."

Jacques and I had been engaged for at least two years when we decided to get married without waiting for the end of his studies.

Our engagement took place in the simplest way, without any proposal. We were alone in my parents' living room. Jacques was sitting on the rug, close to my chair; it suddenly seemed to me that we had always been near each other, and that we would always be so. Without thinking, I put out my hand and stroked his hair; he looked at me and all was clear to us. The feeling flowed through me that always—for my happiness and my salvation (I thought precisely that, although then the word "salvation" meant nothing to me)— that always my life would be bound up with Jacques's. It was one of those tender and peaceful feelings which are like a gift flowing from a region higher than ourselves, illuminating the future and deepening the present. From that moment our understanding was perfect and unchangeable.

One day we read *The Woman Who Was Poor,* by Léon Bloy, and for the first time found ourselves before the reality of Christianity. Up to that time, in reading Corneille or Pascal, or even Ruysbroeck, something, I do not know what, masked from me Christianity's real being, placing it in some realm of art and imagination. Reading *The Woman Who Was Poor,* we passed through the literary form as the spirits, they say, pass through walls, to go directly not to the author but to the man, the man of faith illumined by rays of that strange thing, so unknown to us—Catholicism—and, so to speak, identified with it.

This time magnificence of language meant little to me. For my taste, here was something only too magnificent! Those endless endeavors to note minutely ugliness or mediocrity, that fixed predilection for violence and force, the perpetual hyperbole, could have been tiresome in the end and could have diminished, everything considered, the credibility of the story. But all was saved by a shining sincerity, an unswerving uprightness, a genuine, deep, inexhaustible lyricism, by the exquisite tenderness of a heart made to love absolutely, to cling entirely to what it loved.

By every evidence, we were in the presence of a very great writer; but, again, this was not what held us at that time. What struck us so forcibly on first reading *The Woman Who Was Poor* was the immensity of this believer's soul, his burning zeal for justice, the beauty of a lofty doctrine which for the first time rose up before our eyes. Faith, poverty— "One does not enter into Paradise tomorrow—nor in ten years; one enters it today, when one is poor and crucified!"— and sanctity: all these equally exalted, indissolubly united— "There is but one sadness: not to belong to the saints"; courage and independence of character where we would have expected to find obsequious conformity, the "darkness of the Middle Ages," bourgeois pharisaism.

We wrote to Bloy, whose profound faith and genius impressed us so deeply, and were invited to visit him. In his preface to the *Letters of Léon Bloy to his Grandchildren,* Jacques thus describes our first visit:

"June 25, 1905, two children of twenty mounted the sempiternal stairway which leads up to Sacré-Cœur. They carried in themselves that distress which is the only serious product of modern culture, and a sort of active despair lightened only (they did not know why) by the inner assurance that the Truth for which they hungered, and without which it was almost impossible for them to accept life, would one day be shown to them. They were feebly upheld by a sort of esthetic morality in which the idea of suicide—after certain experiments that remained to be attempted and which were probably too beautiful to succeed—seemed to offer the sole escape. Meanwhile they were cleansing from their minds, thanks to Bergson, the scientific superstitions on which they had been nourished at the Sorbonne—although they were well aware that Bergsonian intuition was but a too flimsy refuge against the intellectual nihilism logically resulting from all modern philosophies.

"Moreover they considered the Church, hidden from their sight by inept prejudices and by the outward appearance of many 'right-thinking' people, as a rampart of the rich and powerful whose interest it was to maintain the 'darkness of the middle ages' over minds. They were going toward a strange beggar who, distrusting all philosophy, cried divine truth from the housetops, and who, while being a Catholic integrally obedient, condemned his times and those who have their consolation here below with far more liberty than all the revolutionaries in the world. They were terribly afraid of what they would meet—they had not yet become used to literary men of genius; moreover it was something entirely different which they were now seeking. Not a shade of curiosity was in them, but another and graver feeling filled their souls: compassion for unsheltered greatness.

"They crossed a little old fashioned garden, then entered a humble house, its walls decorated with books and lovely pictures, and first encountered a great white figure of kindness, impressive in her peaceful nobility—this was Madame Léon Bloy. Her two little daughters, Véronique and Madeleine, gazed upon the visitors with great, surprised eyes. Léon Bloy seemed almost timid, he spoke but very little and very softly, trying to say something important to his young callers which would not disappoint them. What he uncovered for them cannot be told; the tenderness of Christian brotherhood, that trembling both of mercy and of fear with which a soul marked with the love of God is seized when it faces another soul. Bloy appeared to us as the opposite of other men, who hide grave failings in the things of the spirit and so many invisible crimes under a carefully maintained whitewash of the virtues of sociability. Instead of being a whited sepulcher, like the Pharisee of old, he was a fire-stained and blackened cathedral. The whiteness was within, in the depth of the tabernacle.

"Once the threshold of this house was crossed all values were dislocated, as though by an invisible switch. One knew, or one guessed, that only one sorrow existed here—not to be of the saints. And all the rest receded into the twilight."

At a moment when everything filled us with despair we had placed our confidence in the unknown (which we did not think of in capital letters). We had decided to extend existence credit, in the hope that it would reveal new values to us, values which could give a meaning to life—and here is what life brought us! First Bergson, and then Léon Bloy. Bergson traveled uncertainly toward a goal still far off, but its light had already reached both him and us, and without our knowing it, like the rays of a star across a desert of unimaginable skies; Léon Bloy had lived for many years united to his God by an indestructible love which he knew to be eternal in its essence. Life cast him upon our shores like a legendary treasure—immense and mysterious.

Nevertheless we did not feel ourselves strangers in the house of Léon Bloy; our passage from his books to his life was without a break. All here was as he said: true the poverty, true the faith, true his heroic independence. And he and his wife had adopted us from the first. We went down from the heights of the Rue de la Barre and the Sacré-Cœur enriched by a unique friendship, so gentle on the part of this violent man that all fear had left us from the day of our first meeting, and our respect became daring and familiar, like that of children who feel that they are loved.

Of course, having seen Léon Bloy, we could no longer limit ourselves to a literary admiration, nor even to an active compassion. We had to go further; we had to consider the principles, the sources, the motives of such a life. This time we were brought face to face with the question of God, both in all its power and in all its urgency.

We read Bloy's book, *Salvation Through the Jews,* in the country during the month of August 1905. It revealed St. Paul to us, and the extraordinary ninth, tenth, and eleventh chapters of the Epistle to the Romans, from which Léon Bloy took the inscription for his title page and the support for his exegesis.

"I speak the truth in Christ . . . I suffer a great sorrow and in my heart I have unceasing grief. For I wished to be an anathema from Christ, on behalf of my brethren, my kinsmen according to the flesh, who are Israelites, whose is the adoption as the children and the glory and the covenants and the giving of the law and the liturgy and the promises, whose are the fathers, and from whom is Christ according to the flesh."

But the first line of that great lyrical and scriptural poem which is *Salvation Through the Jews* has a still higher reference: "Salvation is of the Jews." Christ's words in the Gospel of St. John, Chapter 4, verse 22.

"Like other unfortunates, I have wasted several valuable hours of my life," writes Léon Bloy immediately after quoting this verse, "in reading the anti-Jewish lucubrations of M. Drumont, and I do not recall that he quoted these simple and formidable words of Our Lord Jesus Christ, reported by St. John in the fourth chapter of his Gospel.

"Yet surely it amounts to something, this testimony of the Son of God! . . ."

For me, this testimony was, above all, the revelation of the union of the two Testaments. We pass from one to another by means of Christ. He Himself says this; He, who is Salvation, He comes of the Jews. Through Him the Old Testament flows into the New, which is not opposed to it, which is its accomplishment, its perfection.

Léon Bloy's scriptural exegesis in *Salvation Through the Jews* is a torrent of splendid texts: St. Paul, Jeremiah, Ezekiel, and the Catholic liturgy speak of Israel in stirring terms, of its vocation, of its most mysterious destiny, its perpetual sufferings, its ignominious present, its glorious future. Léon Bloy's exegesis is a fiery furnace of analogies and of symbols which prolong into the infinite the meaning of divine realities. At times Bloy reduces the Jewish people to the level of vermin; at times he exalts them to a likeness and representation of the Paraclete.

"Israel is therefore by privilege invested with the representation and with one knows not what occult protection of this wandering Paraclete of Whom it was the abode and the hiding place. To anyone who is not destitute of the faculty of contemplation, to separate them seems impossible, and the deeper one's ecstasy, the more narrowly do they appear soldered to one another . . ."

Léon Bloy was persuaded, and with reason, that "apart from supernatural inspiration . . . and after the eleventh chapter of St. Paul to the Romans," his book was "the most energetic and the most pressing Christian testimony in favor of the First-born Race."

"If their lapse," said the Apostle, "is the enriching of the world, and their diminution the enriching of the Gentiles, how much more their fullness!

"If the loss of them be the reconciliation of the world, what shall the receiving of them be, but life from the dead?"

"*Salvation Through the Jews*, which might be considered a paraphrase of this chapter of St. Paul, points out from the first line that the blood shed upon the Cross for the redemption of humankind, as well as that which each day is shed invisibly in the Chalice of the Sacrament of the Altar, is naturally and supernaturally Jewish blood—the immense river of Hebrew blood whose source is in Abraham and whose mouth is in the Five Wounds of Christ."

Thirty years later Pope Pius XI was to give final expression to this supernatural view when he said: "By Christ and in Christ, we are the spiritual descendants of Abraham. No, it is not possible for Christians to have any part in anti-Semitism . . . Spiritually we are Semites."

In vivid phrase and with historical accuracy Bloy showed that *Catholicism is the flowering of Judaism*, the religion of my childhood, and that "the Apostolic Roman Church for nineteen centuries had protected the Jewish people; in favor of whom its most sorrowful Liturgy speaks to God on Good Friday; from whom came the Patriarchs, the Prophets, the Evangelists, the Apostles, Christ's faithful Friends and all the first Martyrs—without even daring to speak of the Virgin Mother and of our Saviour Himself, Who was the Lion of Judah, the Jew in his essential plenitude—an ineffable Jew!—and Who likely had spent a whole previous eternity yearning to spring from this people.

"The thought of the Church in every age has been that holiness is inherent in this exceptional, unique, and imperishable people which is protected by God, preserved as the apple of His eye in the midst of the destruction of so many peoples, for the accomplishment of His ulterior designs. The very abjection of this race is a divine sign, the very manifest sign of the permanence of the Holy Spirit over men so despised, who are to appear in the glory of the Consoler at the end of time."

Addressing himself directly to those who hold to anti-Semitism, he said to them: "Imagine that people about you spoke continually of your *father* and your *mother* with the greatest contempt, and treated them only with insults and with outrageous sarcasm. What would be your feelings? Well, that is exactly what is happening to Our Lord Jesus Christ. We forget, or rather we do not wish to know, that Our Lord made man was a Jew, the Jew par excellence, the Lion of Judah; that His Mother was a Jewess, the flower of the Jewish race; that all His ancestors were Jews, along with all the prophets; finally that our whole sacred liturgy is drawn from Jewish books. How, then, can we express the enormity of the outrage and the blasphemy involved in vilifying the Jewish race?

"Formerly the Jews were detested, they were gladly massacred, but they were not scorned *as a race*. On the contrary, they were respected and feared, and the Church prayed for them, remembering that St. Paul, speaking in the name of the Holy Spirit, promised them all things, and

[205]

that they should one day become the light of the world. Anti-Semitism, an altogether modern thing, is the most horrible blow which Our Lord has received in His Passion that continues forever; it is the most bloody and the most unpardonable, because He receives it *upon the face of His Mother* and from the hands of Christians."

Ignorant as we were both of Judaism and Christianity, we could not, when we first read these pages, have understood all of Léon Bloy's complex symbolism. But its beauty was obvious. And these lamentations of a heart made disconsolate by injustice, these aspirations toward the glory of truth—were they not to some degree present in us, sufficiently so for us to recognize them in the heart of the sorrowful old writer?

In answer to an enthusiastic letter of mine, expressing appreciation for his noble message to the world in *Salvation Through the Jews,* Bloy wrote me in 1905, saying among other things: " 'I am not a Christian,' you say, 'I can only seek, and mourn.' Why do you continue to seek, my friend, since you have found? How could you like what I write if you did not think and feel as I do? You are not only Christian, Raïssa, you are a fervent Christian, a well-beloved daughter of the Father, a spouse of Jesus Christ at the foot of the Cross, a loving servant of the Mother of God in her anteroom as the Queen of the world. Only you do not know, or rather you did not know, and you were sent to us to learn.

" . . . The importance, the *Dignity* of souls is beyond utterance, and your souls, Jacques and Raïssa, are so precious that it took no less than the Incarnation and the agony of God to ransom them—exactly as my own . . . *Empti estis pretio magno*—you have been bought at a great price. That, my friends, is the key of everything, in the Absolute. We have been ransomed, like most precious slaves, by the ignominy and the willing torture of Him who made heaven and earth. When we know this, when we see and feel it, we are like Gods, and we do not cease from weeping.

"Your desire to see me less unhappy, my good Raïssa, was a thing which was in yourself, profoundly, in your substantial being, in your soul which prolongs God, long before the birth of Nachor who was the grandfather of Abraham. Strictly, it is the desire for the Redemption, accompanied by the presentiment or the intuition of what it cost Him who alone could pay the price. That is Christianity, and there is no other way of being a Christian.

"Kneel down then at the edge of this well and pray for me thus: My God who hast bought me at a great price, I humbly ask Thee to put me in union of faith, hope, and love with this poor man who has suffered in Thy service and who perhaps is suffering mysteriously for me. Deliver him and deliver me for the eternal life which Thou didst promise to all those who would hunger after Thee."

On our return from the country, we stopped three days in Chartres to visit the cathedral. Those days were spent in very close contemplation of the architecture, the statuary, and the glass of the most French of churches, which has always remained for us the most beautiful cathedral in the world. Indeed, we spelled it out letter by letter like a Bible.

Since that first visit we have gone several times to Chartres, and each time the cathedral has presented a new aspect to us. Sometimes it was all beauty, sometimes all piety. The last time we circled its outer balconies, high above the ground, through an unbelievable entanglement of arches and buttresses. And it left us with the memory and image of a fantastic and all-powerful vessel in the broad sky of France.

But in its first aspect, in its plastic language, it was for us a master teacher of the theology, of sacred history, and of exegesis. It repeated what *Salvation Through the Jews* had just told us: that the two Testaments are united in the person of Christ; that the Old prefigures the New and is its basis, just as the New is the fulfillment and the crown of the Old.

The cathedral told us this by means of its gigantic windows, in which the four great Prophets carry the four Evangelists upon their shoulders. It told it through its majestic statues of the kings and the patriarchs and the Apostles,

David and Solomon, and John the Baptist, who bears upon his heart a Lamb, worn as a medallion.

The book of the cathedral revealed to us sublime and familiar and tender things. I am thinking, for instance, of a sculptured group representing the creation of man. Christ is fashioning him with love, this first man, whose head, still vague, rests upon the knees of God. I can still see the beautiful, pensive face of "God creating the world." We see only this august countenance; the creation is as yet wholly in the mind of God, but we can perceive its unmarred beauty; it shines through the expression of the divine features, like the bottom of a lake whose waters are crystal clear.

And the windows of Chartres! Who does not know their beauty? We saw them from below and from above, circling the nave by the triforium. We were surfeited with splendor. Alone, having taken leave of our chance guide, we went to rest ourselves near the naïve images about the altars, close to the Virgin Mother dressed in satin and gold, lighted by the flame of the candles and the oil lamps. There everything was so humble, so calm. The majesty of the place, the sacred presence of the Mysteries, all of which the heart felt, blended into a pure repose of love and simplicity. And we were inclined to believe that the unity and harmony of so much lofty beauty could have as its foundation only the unity of truth.

It was, I think, only a short time later that, while on a journey and watching the forests glide by my car window, I had for the second time the feeling of the presence of God. (The first time was the violent and fugitive feeling I had had while reading Plotinus.)

I was looking out the window and thinking of nothing in particular. Suddenly a great change took place in me, as if from the perception of the senses I had passed over to an entirely inward perception. The passing trees suddenly had become much larger than themselves; they assumed a dimension prodigious for its depth. The whole forest seemed to be speaking, and to speak of Another, became a forest of symbols, and seemed to have no other function than to *signify* the Creator.

Jacques, who later on was to allude to this vividly felt impression in one of his books, finds in it a case of "metaphysical experience." "At the sight of something or other," he says, "a soul will know in an instant that these things do not exist through themselves, and that God is." It also often happened, before I knew the things of faith, that I experienced through a sudden intuition the reality of my being, of the profound, first principle which placed me outside nothingness. The violence of this powerful intuition sometimes frightened me, and first gave me the knowledge of a metaphysical absolute.

It is not my intention to put down in these recollections the things which touch and interest me alone, but I believe that what I have just related is useful in understanding what follows.

Jacques and Vera, my sister, each followed their own roads in those approaches to faith which are like a morning twilight, when the light of dawn still seems uncertain, and when, without realizing it, the soul is already attracted and more acted upon than acting—the while it bestirs itself in inner searches and trials, in doubts and hopes. It is about my own road that I tell something in these recollections, and about what was common to the three of us. . . . I would like to note that Jacques later told me that everything had changed for him when, thinking that it was fair to put to a test by an act of the soul the promises of the unknown God, he started praying in the following way: "My God, if You exist, and if You are the truth, make me know it," and then one day decided to kneel down to recite the Lord's Prayer for the first time.

We were happy at this time, although as yet nothing was clear to us. Some intimation of light had been given us, we felt. A beneficent constellation reigned in our sky. Plotinus, Pascal, Péguy, Bergson, Léon Bloy bathed our souls with their spiritual influence. It may be remarked that Léon Bloy did not know Péguy and Bergson; neither did they know him. We brought them together in ourselves, by loving them. Their influences were harmonious, their dominants were the same. Our shadows were gently, slowly lifting under their light. Vera was with us in our great secret. It was not that we jealously hid our friendly relations with Bloy. On the contrary, we spoke of him to our parents and to Péguy, and Péguy began to take umbrage at it. The secret involved only our search for truth in that phase which required the gathering of all our strength in silence and in peace. No controversies. We had none with Bloy; we had no discussions with him. He did not argue with us. By a tacit agreement, Jacques and I asked of Léon Bloy only the example of his life, a trusting, tranquil communication, in terms that were his own, of what he believed, of what he loved, of what he held for the absolute truth.

We reserved to ourselves the examination together, at home, of these data on the life, the doctrine, and the sources of Catholicism. We felt a certain humility at our incredible ignorance of this complex world of religion, whose beauty began to unveil itself to our eyes. We weighed against it the things that science offers as most certain, the philosophical discoveries of Bergson, our most constant and deepest aspirations.

Little by little, the hierarchy of spiritual, intellectual, scientific values was revealed to us, and we began to understand that they could not be inimical to each other. In varying degrees, all participate in the mystery in which all science finally ends, all participate in the light from whence descends all knowledge. And we saw clearly that the truth of one could not be the enemy of the truth of the others. Once we recognized as inoperative the objections of rationalistic skepticism and pseudo-scientific positivism, which, in destroying the value of reason, themselves destroy the value of every argument situated within their frame of reference and directed against the affirmation of a religious absolute, once this was recognized, the veracity of faith became a plausible hypothesis. We thought that faith itself could be considered as a higher gift of intuition, and that by invoking the idea of an absolute truth, faith would also imply and permit the elaboration of a doctrine of knowledge which would assure the human intelligence its grasp on reality.

Thus neither our interest nor our difficulties consisted in the solution of the objections which are raised to the indivisible whole of Catholic doctrine. The difficulty was in entering into the mystery proper to this doctrine; in finding the center around which all the rest is organized and orientated. The path of religious experience was out of our reach, since it presupposes faith. And how could we adhere to dogmatic propositions which presuppose a rational inquiry, the content of which, we were told, although superior to reason, is supremely reasonable, but to which one adheres only when motivated and illumined by faith—an adhesion of a unique kind, foreign to any form of adhesion known to us, whether philosophical, scientific, or simply of opinion?

So months were to pass, and we might have been permanently halted by these insurmountable difficulties if Léon Bloy had sought to use with us an apologetic of demonstration. On what bases? Our reason was equipped to destroy, not to construct, and our confidence in reason, as well as in historical criticism, was very much shaken. But he did not even think of such a thing. He placed before us the fact of sanctity. Simply, and because he loved them, because their experience was near his own—so much so that he could not read them without weeping—he brought us to know the saints and mystics.

How often, his face streaming tears, did he not read us pages from St. Angela of Foligno, in Ernest Hello's beautiful translation! "It is not for fun that I have loved you!" We felt that Léon Bloy had experienced the bearing of these words of God to St. Angela. He also spoke to us frequently of Ruysbroeck the Admirable, and often repeated this sentence of his, weeping the while: "If you knew the sweetness that God gives, and the delicious taste of the Holy Spirit!"

Without the confidence we had in Léon Bloy, would we ever have been willing to open one of these books? They had such a bad reputation at the Sorbonne, where they were beginning to be studied—but with what bias, and with what distrust! At the very beginning Léon Bloy made us read Schmoger's three thick volumes on the life and visions of Anna Catherine Emmerich, a nun from Dulmen in the Rhineland, one of the greatest mystics of the nineteenth century, which brought forth so many such.

The *Revelations* of Anna Catherine Emmerich gave us a picture of Catholicism that was crowded and vivid, moving and yet familiar. They taught us countless things—we, who knew nothing of Catholic history, dogmas, theology, liturgy, mysticism. At that time a sober catechism would probably have done nothing to make us understand. In our ignorance, we had the greatest need for the help of images, for that sort of portrait of the Church, drawn in the four dimensions of height and length, of width and depth. And, at the same time, we were shown heroic Catholicism—sanctity in its terrible trials, in its humility and its divine charity, in its asceticism, in the beatitude wherein it reaches its fulfillment, in its pure harmony, in its power and in its beauty.

We learned that sanctity invisibly unites all the living members of the Church, and that this *Communion of Saints* is the bond and the life of the Church's mystical body and gives it its note of sanctity, independent of the imperfections and faults of some, or of most, of the members of the visible Church—the Church whose head is Christ, whose soul is the Holy Spirit, but whose members are born sinners like all men since the Fall; the Church which exists wherever there is a holy soul, militant on earth, suffering in Purgatory, or glorious and blessed in eternal life.

There was, however, one catechism which we read during the first months of our relations with Léon Bloy: it was the *Catéchisme Spirituel,* by Father Surin. The reading of this book at once had a decisive effect on us, though we did not yet know it. We blessed our first total ignorance which allowed us suddenly to discover this treatise, so long a classic of spiritual life, in all its pristine freshness. The scattered notions regarding contemplation which we had found in Plotinus, in Pascal, and in Léon Bloy here had their center of fullness and efficacy. This charter of sanctity, grasped for the first time, seemed to us, by its organic logic, to be the only one capable of dealing with the inner life, of awakening that life dormant in each of us, of making us really alive and human in our spirit as well as in all our acts. But we had to realize too that the perfection which is the goal of all the labor of the ascetic can be truly attained only by means of a passive life of the spirit in which God Himself guides the souls He wishes to fill with His gifts.

Thus it was necessary for us to abandon the hope of attaining, solely by the application of our will, that union with God which gives the saints all their perfection and beatitude. It was necessary, then, to believe in God. Faith in the existence of God was still very weak in me, I thought. But there burned within us the desire for that marvelous life where "all is but order and beauty," love, calm, and truth. How powerless, uncertain, and aimless seemed our own interior life, and that of even the best among us, as against the lives of those souls full of grace and strength!

How we thirsted for that contemplation, of which Father Surin says that it "is an operation by which the soul looks upon universal truth," and that through this contemplation "the mind, raised up to a high notion of eternal truth, returns therefrom with marvelous tastings, and with marks of great price and profit, which are not known so much in themselves as in their effects; so that a man, accustomed to these operations, is fruitful in wisdoms and in virtues." Indeed, "through contemplation the soul attains to evangelical perfection, not only as the result of the good impulses it receives, but formally, in the very act of contemplation . . . The soul tends only toward that Truth which it knows, and in the manner in which it knows It, that is to say universal, stripped of its individual qualities; this is what maintains the soul in a perfect purity and gives it an eminent wisdom whereby it discerns all things, not being imbued

[213]

with a taste for any; inasmuch as its practice is to strip itself and ceaselessly to deprive itself of all that is individual and particular, and to strive toward that which is unnamable and impenetrable." And then this, which created in my heart an immense emptiness, together with an infinite longing toward that which could fill it: "It sacrifices to the unknown God, Who is greater than the known God, because what one knows of God is nothing compared to what one does not know."

Thus, through the love of truth, the soul is filled with wisdom, and when it has arrived at the perfection of love it also arrives at the perfection of liberty.

"It lets itself be moved of the Holy Spirit: this is why it does not know what it is to feel constraint . . . As such persons dwell in love, they do what they wish; they freely say what others dare not have thought, because they fear nothing . . . They also have but one desire. They are like the birds of the skies, situate on high, that is to say in God, which brings it about that they have no limitation. Where is the Spirit of the Lord there is liberty."

Truth. Love. Liberty. Beautiful words, which give the soul a foretaste of Paradise! Who could have invented you if reality itself had not begotten you! It is reality which gives you that savor which the heart of man cannot resist. Where you live, God lives with you, even if we do not know it.

What a wonderful conjunction of the action of God and the heroic docility of the soul, what a perfect union of asceticism and of contemplation this spiritual catechism established! Later we learned about the extraordinary life of its author, and we saw that in order to write about contemplation Father Surin had but to draw upon his own experience.

The city of God was becoming visible on our horizon, its outlines vague as yet, but already dazzling.

Later on Jacques and I met at the home of Léon Bloy, an eminent scientist, whose friendship, deep faith, and profound scholarship were sources of help and co-operation to us. Pierre Termier, one of the most renowned scientists of his day, member of the Institut and widely honored, was also a very great and very humble Christian. To us, who had never met a scientist of this kind, his very existence was an apology for the faith. Poetry dwelt at his hearth as the companion of science. Pierre Termier, whose considerable scientific work is beyond the grasp of those ignorant of geology, has also written several books of a general sort on science, on scientists, on the beauty of the earth, of whose surface and depths he knew so much. *The Vocation of a Scholar, The Joy of Learning, To the Glory of the Earth* are the works of a great humanist.

In February 1906, I fell dangerously ill, and this illness was for Jacques, for Vera, and for myself something like a break in the unnoticed flow of time, of our time which was fleeing, of time in which one lets oneself live, without the will's making itself heard. Generally we live with faculties half asleep. A whole life can slip by in such fashion. From the day when the question of the truth of Catholicism had been put to us by Bloy, eight months had slipped past, and we were not yet thinking of any decision. A deep work had been wrought in us, it is true, but only in the speculative order. All that had preceded our meeting with Bloy, and all that had followed—reading, reflection, new friendships—had at once led us to agree that none of the objections to Catholicism was decisive, and also had given us a burning desire for the happiness and holiness of the saints.

My illness, which lasted for several weeks, was for Jacques a special occasion for decisive reflections, and gave him the feeling that the time had come to awaken from sleep. It was during those days of anguish that he had thrown himself on his knees, as a person casts himself into the sea to save another, and had for the first time said the Lord's Prayer. His resistance gave way, and he felt himself ready to accept Catholicism, if he must.

He told me all this after my recovery; before, I would not have been able to hear or to understand him; I was too

[215]

ill to think of anything. On February fifteenth Bloy wrote me:

"My very dear Raïssa: We are thinking a great deal of you here at home, and thinking of you with tenderness. This morning at early Mass I wept for you, my friend. I asked Jesus and Mary to take whatever might be meritorious in my tormented past and to apply it mercifully for your recovery, to impute it to you with strength and power, for the peace of your body and the glory of your soul. And such sweet tears flowed that I believed I had been heard . . . You are greatly loved, supernaturally cherished. Hear me. You will be cured and will know immense joys."

"You will be cured . . ." I did not greatly like the idea of prayers for my cure, when I myself had not prayed in a disinterested way since I had lost the faith of my childhood. You lack simplicity when you are far from God.

One day, when my illness was at its worst and I was suffering terribly, Madame Bloy came to see me and sat down at my bedside. She told me to pray, and said that she was going to give me a medal of the Blessed Virgin. I could not speak, but I felt extremely vexed at what seemed to me a great indiscretion. As Jeanne Bloy heard no answer, she placed the medal around my neck. In a moment, and without truly realizing what I was doing, I was confidently appealing to the Blessed Virgin, and then fell into a gentle and healing sleep.

My convalescence began, and it was a time of long conversations between Jacques and myself. Yet I still did not feel that a decision was urgent. And it was only on April fifth that we told Léon Bloy of our desire to become Catholics, surrounding this desire, it is true, with all sorts of naïve restrictions. He noted the date in his Journal:

"The miracle is accomplished. Jacques and Raïssa want to be baptized! Great rejoicing in our hearts. Once more my books, the occasion of this miracle, are approved not by a bishop nor by a doctor, but by the Holy Ghost."

On April sixth he wrote to Pierre Termier:

"After leaving you yesterday, I rushed to their house.

I believe I told you that they were waiting for me, and had something to tell me. They did indeed, and I am still gasping.

"They were at the uttermost of the desert and they asked for baptism! In their ignorance of liturgical forms, they thought that I could baptize them myself, Raïssa not having received this sacrament at all and Jacques having received at best a counterfeit. I had to explain to them—and with what rapture!—that since they were not in danger of death and since it was easy to obtain a priest, they must receive baptism as it is conferred by the Church and not the simple rite administered *in extremis* by a lay person . . ."

We still thought in very truth that all this could be a matter between ourselves and God and our godfather. We dreaded all externalization.

While the spectacle alone of the sanctity and that of the beauty of Catholic doctrine had occupied our thoughts, we had been happy in heart and mind, and our admiration had grown by leaps and bounds. Now that we were preparing ourselves to enter among those whom the world hates as it hates Christ, we suffered, Jacques and I, a kind of agony. This lasted for about two months. Once, during those months, I heard in my sleep these words, said to me with a certain impatience: "You are forever seeking what you must do. You have only to love God and serve Him with all your heart." Later I found these words in the *Imitation,* which I had not then read.

Léon Bloy had sent us to a priest of the Sacré-Cœur Basilica, "the very image of a child and martyr, whom you will love," he had written to Pierre Termier. Father Durantel awaited our decision.

Our suffering grew greater every day. Finally we understood that God also was waiting, and that there would be no further light so long as we should not have obeyed the imperious voice of our consciences saying to us: You have no valid objection to the Church; she alone promises you the light of truth—prove her promises, put Baptism to the test.

We still thought that to become Christian meant to aban-

[217]

don philosophy forever. Well, we were ready—but it was not easy—to abandon philosophy for the truth. Jacques accepted this sacrifice. The truth we had so greatly desired had caught us in a trap. "If it has pleased God to hide His truth in a dunghill," Jacques said, "that is where we shall go to find it." I quote these cruel words to give some idea of our state of mind.

I see in a letter from Bloy to Termier that, on May twenty-first, we had given him "complete assurance" that we would soon enter the Church. My sister was also ready, and I believe even that she had been so for a long time. Yet on June first Bloy wrote Termier that "nothing has yet happened with the Maritains."

Suddenly our decision was made. Purely for reasons of convenience—I had a journey to take—we chose the eleventh of June for the baptism of all three of us. And on June ninth Bloy was writing to Termier:

"The object of this further letter is above all to inform you that Jacques Maritain, his charming wife Raïssa, and the latter's sister, Vera, will be baptized at Montmartre on Monday, the eleventh, the Feast of St. Barnabas. My wife, Véronique, and I will be the godparents. You are among those who can understand the deeply hidden greatness and splendor of such an event.

"It is something to think that when I die I shall leave, kneeling beside me and weeping from love, people who knew nothing of such an attitude before they met me."

On June eleventh all three of us betook ourselves to the Church of St. John the Evangelist in Montmartre. I was in a state of absolute reserve and could no longer remember any of the reasons for my being there. One single thing remained clear in my mind: either baptism would give me faith, and I would believe and I would belong to the Church altogether, or I would go away unchanged, an unbeliever forever. Jacques had almost the same thoughts.

"What do you ask of the Church of God?"

"Faith."

We were baptized at eleven o'clock in the morning, Léon

Bloy being our godfather; his wife was godmother for Jacques and Vera, his daughter Véronique for me. An immense peace descended upon us, bringing with it the treasures of faith. There were no more questions, no more anguish, no more trials—there was only the infinite answer of God. The Church kept her promises. And it is she whom we first loved. It is through her that we have known Christ.

I think now that faith—a weak faith, impossible to formulate consciously—already existed in the most hidden depths of our souls. But we did not know this. It was the Sacrament which revealed it to us, and it was sanctifying grace which strengthened it in us.

FINDING CHRIST'S CHURCH

Christopher Hollis

Christopher Hollis, author, historian, educator, economist, and member of Parliament, has packed achievements in many fields into his first half century. Born in 1902 at Aldridge, Somerset, England, the son of the Right Reverend George Arthur Hollis, Bishop of Taunton, he was educated at Eton and Balliol College, Oxford. At the age of twenty-two he entered the Catholic Church.

"When I was a boy at school," he wrote, "I was taught by Mr. Aldous Huxley, and he used to tell us that in the modern world the scale of the stage was so great that there would never again be great figures as were the figures of the Victorian and previous centuries. We had to write essays on this. Mr. Huxley was a very good teacher. I learnt much from him, and it has taken me all the rest of my life to discover that everything that I learnt was untrue."

From 1924 to 1925 he toured the United States, New Zealand, and Australia as a member of the Oxford University Debating Society. While in attendance at Oxford, he was elected president of the Oxford Union. From 1925 to 1935 he was assistant master at Stonyhurst College. In 1929 he married Margaret Madeline King, and to this union were born two sons and a daughter.

From 1935 to 1937 he was engaged in economic research at the University of Notre Dame, and taught there in 1938. In 1939 he was a master at the famous Downside School, conducted by the Benedictines. Since 1937 he has served as a member of the editorial board of the *Tablet*, and in 1939 became a director of Burns, Oates and Washbourne, a long-established London publishing company.

During World War II, Mr. Hollis served as flight lieutenant in the Royal Air Force. In the elections of 1945 he won in the

Constituency of Devizes and is serving with distinction in the House of Parliament.

Mr. Hollis is a prolific writer; besides contributing to important English, Irish, and American periodicals, he has for years conducted a column, "Men and Movements," for the *Tablet* of London. He has authored some sixteen books on history, politics, and economics. Some of his better-known biographies are: *Erasmus, Thomas More, Lenin, Dryden, Dr. Johnson,* and *St. Ignatius.* In *American Heresy* he presents an interpretation of the course of democracy in the United States; *The Monstrous Regiment* corrects the popular misconception of the Elizabethan period; *Breakdown of Money* is a stimulating and provocative study in modern finance.

For many years Mr. Hollis has been deeply interested in promoting a better understanding between peoples and has written many articles and books on this general theme. Reflecting his deep interest in this subject are his books: *Foreigners Aren't Fools, We Aren't So Dumb, Foreigners Aren't Knaves,* and *Our Case.* His most popular book is probably *The Death of a Gentleman.*

American readers have come to know him through his books, and particularly through his thought-provoking articles on a wide range of subjects in the *Commonweal.* He writes with freshness and originality, and his learning, candor, and sincerity have won for him a wide and appreciative audience of readers both in the United States and abroad.

I HAVE BEEN ASKED to write an article explaining why I joined the Catholic Church. There are two ways in which that question could be answered. It might be answered by a psychologico-historical account of the stages of my progression. It might be answered by a philosophical account of why I do accept what I now accept. I doubt if I am capable of answering the question in the first way, and even if I were, I cannot flatter myself that the answer would be of much interest. On the other hand, it may be objected that to answer in the second way is to explain why I am a Catholic rather than why I became a Catholic. However, it is that second answer which alone I am capable of making and which I propose to give here.

There has never been a time, since I was at all capable of understanding them, when I have found any difficulty in accepting the arguments for the existence of God. Nor if God was the author of the laws of nature did it ever seem to me metaphysically impossible that He should, on special occasions, interfere with the workings of His own laws or give to men a special revelation of Himself. On the other hand, while willing to accept God's existence, I was not willing to accept the claims of a particular revelation unless compelled to do so by overwhelming evidence. My mother still tells the story of how, when I was very young, she expounded to me for the first time the doctrine of the Trinity. I turned on my heel and, saying, "Really, Muvver, you can't expect me to beleeb all dat," walked from the room.

I found myself then in the world and compelled by curiosity, and by the desire for standards by which to regulate my conduct, to see how far I could come toward explaining the mystery of it. It seemed clear that both those who said that the unaided reason was utterly futile and those who said that it was all-competent were in error. Unaided reason could clearly get me a certain way, but not all the way. It could teach me that there was a God, an unlimited Being, and that by consequence of His being unlimited He was the Creator, Omnipotent and Omniscient. He created me with happiness as my end, and at the same time He demanded of me virtue, and yet it was clear that in this world virtue often did not lead to happiness. It seemed to me probable, therefore, that in a future existence virtue and happiness would somehow be equated. How, I could not say. I was left like Plato, when he recounts the vision of Er, the son of Armenius, to say, "This must be the sort of thing that is going to happen. I cannot tell the details nor exactly how."

So far reason led me. It was not very far or very satisfying, and it was natural, therefore, if I wanted to know more of the mystery, to examine the title deeds of those who claimed the possession of a special revelation. At first sight, it seemed that such an examination would involve a study of every religious system known to man. But I soon learned that the overwhelming majority of so-called revealed religions were not in reality revealed religions at all, even in their claims. Some, like Confucianism, were ethical systems, perhaps admirable, but not possessed of any evidence at all that they were more than the products of the minds of intelligent men. Others claimed a supernatural origin, but placed that origin not at a definite historical date, but in mythical times which there was no serious reason to imagine ever had existed. There were only three of the great religious systems of the world which claimed to date their foundations from revelations of God which took place on definite historical dates. Those three were the Mohammedan, the Christian, and the Jewish.

As I have said, it did not seem to me that either a revelation or a miracle was an impossibility. On the other hand, I quite agreed with Hume—and still do agree with him—that the a priori probabilities are strongly against any particular claim to revelation being a true claim. If a man says that God is speaking through his mouth, it is obviously very probable that he is lying or mistaken. We are only entitled to accept the supernatural explanation of the facts if there is no natural explanation that can possibly account for them. On this criterion it did not seem that the Mohammedans were able to make good their claims. I do not imagine that there will be sufficient Mohammedans among my readers for it to be worth while stopping to examine in detail the evidence for the Mohammedan miracles. What about the Christian claims?

The postwar generation prided itself a little on having outgrown the old formulae of Matthew Arnold that miracles did not happen. It was inclined to admit that they may have happened, that the world was a very much queerer place than Matthew Arnold imagined, but that whether they happened or not did not very greatly matter. M. Coué had just come into fashion, and I was brought up in a generation which was not indisposed to pay to Jesus Christ the great compliment of admitting that he was perhaps one of M.

Coué's forerunners. Now it did seem to me that some of the miracles of the New Testament might have happened as reported, and yet might really not have been miracles at all—the miracles of healing, for instance. But there were others for which this facile explanation was not at all sufficient: for instance, the feeding of the five thousand with the loaves and fishes. If it ever took place as reported, then no explanation which science could furnish could possibly explain it away as a merely natural phenomenon. If it happened, then the finger of God was there.

In the Christian creed three miracles are mentioned, and a man's attitude toward the Christian revelation must stand or fall with his attitude toward those three miracles. They are the Virgin Birth, the Resurrection, and the Ascension. There clearly was no evidence for the Virgin Birth which would compel one to accept it and deduce from it the Divinity of Christ. If one accepted it, one did so because Divinity was acceptable on other grounds. It was impossible to believe in the Ascension unless one first believed in the Resurrection. Therefore the crucial question was that of the Resurrection.

One had to approach the question exactly as one would have approached any other historical question—to consider the evidence for and against, exactly as one would have considered the evidence for and against Julius Caesar's crossing of the Rubicon. Did Jesus Christ ever exist? Was he "crucified, dead and buried"? It had been vigorously questioned, but not, as I thought, at all convincingly. There was a good deal of evidence of what the early enemies of the Christians said about them. They denied the Resurrection, but they never, it seemed, denied the existence of Christ or the crucifixion, as they obviously would have done had it been possible for them to do so.

"He was crucified, dead and buried." What happened then? Any one of a hundred explanations was more probable than that of the Resurrection. For a time the answer seemed satisfactory. And then one started to ask oneself, "Yes, but which one of a hundred explanations?"

[224]

The skeptics were usually content to explain that it was extremely improbable that a dead man would rise again from the dead. Very rarely did they seem to see that, if they rejected the Resurrection, then they were under obligation to explain what had become of the body after Easter Sunday. When they did attempt to explain it away, their explanations were feeble.

This is the greatest problem with which the mind of man has ever been faced, a problem to which every intellect of ability has given itself since the foundation of the Christian religion. I am not pretending that I have anything new to contribute toward its solution, or anything to say that has not been said ten thousand times before by people incomparably wiser and better than myself. I am not even pretending that I am doing proper justice to those who have rejected the Christian explanation. I am merely giving a record of the sort of arguments which seemed to me convincing.

If the Resurrection did not take place, then after Easter Sunday the body of Our Lord must have been in one of five places. It may have been either in the possession of the Romans, or in that of the Jews, or in that of His disciples; it may have been still in the tomb, or in some other nearby tomb; it may never have reached the tomb at all and was mislaid on its way between the cross and the tomb. The more that I pondered on each of these five lines of explanation, the more completely impossible did all of them seem to me to be.

The cardinal and certain fact was that Jesus's disciples began to preach the doctrine of His Resurrection quite a few days after Easter Sunday. They preached it neither in Galilee nor in Rome, but in Jerusalem—about a quarter of a mile from the spot where it was alleged to have taken place. Their preaching met with enormous hostility.

Those facts seem at once to destroy the possibility that Our Lord's body was in the possession either of the Jews or of the Romans. Had it been so, they would clearly have produced it, and the whole Christian case would have collapsed ignominiously. They would have done the same had it remained still in the tomb of Joseph of Arimathaea or in some other nearby burial place. Either it was never put into the tomb or else, as the Jews seem to have suggested, the disciples stole it away and had it in their possession.

Now, almost every one of the first disciples of Our Lord suffered martyrs' deaths. It was the purpose of their enemies to exterminate the Christians. We may be sure, then, that those enemies must have brought every pressure they could bear in order to induce some of those disciples to deny the Resurrection and, if there had been an imposture, to confess it. We may be sure that every method would have been used to make any confession widely known. There is no record or whisper, whether from the side of friend or enemy, of any such imposture. We may, then, fairly say that the disciples, rightly or wrongly, were passionately convinced of the truth of the Resurrection.

What convinced them? It is quite clear to anyone who reads the Gospels that it is impossible to say they were convinced of it because they expected it. It is one of the most amazing touches in an amazing story that the Jews apparently had an uneasy feeling that something of the nature of a resurrection might be going to take place; but Our Lord's disciples, in spite of all that He had said to them, did not expect it for an instant.

What convinced them? It is impossible to exaggerate the importance of the point that the empty tomb was not in itself sufficient to convince them. If we went to a place where we were told that the body of a friend was and were unable to find it, we would not conclude that our friend had risen from the dead. We would conclude either that we had mistaken the place or that somebody had moved his body. So it was with the Apostles. So little had they expected the Resurrection that even the discovery of the empty tomb did not lead them to guess what had happened. They were convinced that Our Lord had risen again not because of failing to find His dead body, but by seeing His risen body.

That being so, we may then clearly restate our proposition

thus. The disciples were certainly convinced that they had met Our Lord after He had risen from the dead. And if that be admitted, then we can say the following of such speculations as those of Kirsopp Lake, which maintain that He was never put in the tomb at all. First, that they are entirely without evidence. Second, that if they could be proved to be true, they would not touch the main difficulty: Where was He between Easter and Ascension? This question also disposes of the objection that one or two of the disciples may have stolen the body while the others honestly believed that He had risen and died for their mistaken faith. All, or practically all, had *seen* Him; they had not merely heard that He could not be found.

What is the explanation? Skeptics today do not seem quite certain whether: (1) science has proved that bodies do not rise from the dead and therefore there was no Resurrection or (2) whether spiritualism has proved that bodies do rise from the dead and that therefore the Resurrection was no miracle. As for the spiritualist argument, granting the most extreme claims, there is no evidence as strong as that for the Resurrection. No spiritualist has been able to produce phenomena in any way resembling those commemorated on Easter Sunday.

I therefore reached the conclusion that there was only one possible explanation of the facts: Jesus Christ had risen from the dead on the third day. That Resurrection could only have been the result of a direct interference of God in the affairs of this world. I believed on Platonic principles that God could not be a deceiver. Therefore there seemed to me no explanation of the facts save that the Resurrection was a sign from God that the teaching of Christ was true. What, then, was that teaching?

If we apply to the Gospels and the Acts of the Apostles the ordinary critical tests that we would apply to any other document two thousand years old, the conclusion is that they can be accepted as historical records. It is only the authority of the Church, that can justify us in ascribing to them absolute verbal accuracy. I therefore did not seek to

[227]

deduce Christ's teaching by picking out isolated texts. From them, I should very likely have derived only a vicious and partial notion. The fair method of discovering Christ's teaching was to discover what His disciples taught about Him immediately after His death. They taught, above all, three things—that Christ was God, that He had founded a Church and a sacramental system.

Just as the skeptic who rejects the Resurrection is under obligation to explain what then happened to the body, so the skeptic who rejects the Divinity of Christ is under obligation to tell us who was, then, the creator of that fiction. Either Christ was a madman, self-deceived, or else somebody else invented for Him those claims of Divinity which He did not Himself put forward.

The second alternative is utterly untenable. If Christ did not Himself claim divinity, the claim was certainly made for Him almost immediately after His death. The amazing impostor who first thought of putting forward that claim was able not only to persuade those who had known Him intimately of its truth, but also to persuade the Evangelists that Christ had said many things He can never have said. It is hardly possible to believe that any merely human inventor would ever have thought of inventing so many claims for Him.

It is incredible that an impostor who wanted to persuade people that the Son of God had come down on earth would have described how God chose as the chief of His disciples, as the guardian of His sacred doctrine, a man who was afterward to deny Him and to fail at a test which the average schoolboy would emerge from with flying colors. It is just possible that a novelist who set himself down to tell the story of Christ would invent the character of Judas; it is quite inconceivable that he would invent the character of Peter. The date of the Gospels is irrelevant to the argument. Whatever their date, it is incredible that their story should be mere fiction.

The other alternative is that Christ claimed to be the Son of God and was mistaken. Quite apart from the evidence of the Resurrection, is this alternative any less impossible than the other? Is the tremendous figure of the Gospels the figure of a madman? Does a madman call to all that are weary and heavy-laden and promise that he will give them rest? Is it the life of a madman from which people of every nation and class have drawn their comfort and their inspiration for nearly two thousand years? It does not seem probable. The difficulties of believing in the Divinity of Christ are considerable, but the difficulties in rejecting it are insuperable.

This essay is the account of my own conversion. Other minds, far richer and deeper than my own, have been troubled for many years by this question: Where is the Church of Christ to be found today? Though I was brought up in the Church of England, that question was one to which I never doubted the answer. If Christ was the Son of God, I did not doubt that the Roman Church was the Church of Christ. The "churches" were all agreed that Christ had founded a church; none ventured to assert that He had founded the present variety of "churches." All were agreed, too, that His church was imperishable, that "the gates of hell" were not to prevail against it. That being so, the "one, holy, Catholic and Apostolic Church," of which the Creed speaks, must be in existence somewhere today, and must have been in existence continuously ever since the times of the Apostles.

There seemed to me to be nowhere that this Church could be found save in the obedience to Rome. The very definitions of the Church, as given by those outside this obedience, are a denial of her unity. She alone is Catholic. And, if she be not apostolic, certainly no other is, for all others can trace their ancestry back to the Apostles only through her. If Christ was God, the Church must exist, and if the Church exists, the Church of Rome cannot but be the true Church.

Is she holy? The mark of sanctity does not admit of the almost mathematical demonstration which one can give to the three other marks. Wide generalizations about the superiority of one age or of one nation to another cannot of their nature be substantiated. They serve little purpose; they are not to the point. It may or may not be true that the average Catholic is better than the average non-Catholic. Whether it be true or not, it has very little to do with the Church's mark of holiness. It is certain that Christ did offer a possibility of mystical companionship with him even while we are still on this earth.

In every Catholic society, throughout the whole history of the Church, there has been found this phenomenon of sanctity—a few sacrificing everything that this world offers for the sake of this tremendous invitation. The many living their life on in this world and occupied with the things of this world, but at least understanding that "Mary hath chosen the better part" and honoring her for the part which she chose. In her worst days, this desire for holiness has never quite perished from the Church; in the days of their noblest and most philanthropic vigor, it has never been found among other Christian bodies.

This is why I accepted the Catholic Church. Some may object that there is too much argument and too little faith in my answer. I can only reply that when asked the question "Why?" it is only possible to answer with "Because." Nor does the teaching of the Church demand acceptance of that opposition between reason and faith of which the Sunday papers talk. The arguments are in favor of the Church. The tremendous conclusion to which reason leads is that the Incarnation really did happen. But just because that conclusion is so tremendous, feeble man is apt to fall back before it and hide himself in negations of reason. It is then that the gift of faith is needed to enable our imaginations to accept the conclusions of our reasons. We cry in the great paradox of the paralytic's father, "Lord, I believe; help thou mine unbelief."

With the gift of faith, doubts vanish, but difficulties remain, and must always remain. Those difficulties are sometimes found among Protestants. Yet they seem to me at least as hard to refute on a Protestant hypothesis as on a Catholic hypothesis. I was often told, for instance, that the Catholic

Church relied upon force. This objection seemed to be based on three charges—that the Church in the past had persecuted those who refused to accept her teaching, that today she compelled the faithful to accept her teaching without question, that she compelled the faithful to go to Mass, whether they wanted to or not. It is true enough that the saddest of all the records of history are those which tell of the appalling cruelties which, at one time and another, man has wrought upon man in the name of Christ. Yet Catholics have not been the only Christians to be guilty of such cruelties. Nor have Catholics been the only Christians to insist upon an absolute obligation to worship God.

At the time of the Reformation none of the reformers, of whatever school, dreamed of denying that there was an absolute obligation to worship God on Sunday. Protestant ministers continued to insist on that obligation until it was so widely neglected among their followers that continued insistence would only expose them to ridicule.

The same applies to the larger question of freedom. An Anglican clergyman whom I greatly respected used to tell me that he did not believe it to be the will of God that we should take our faith upon authority; he thought that God wished us to think things out for ourselves. Such a theory, before I was received into the Catholic Church, seemed to me to be quite probable. I could quite imagine that that might be God's plan. When I looked in the New Testament, however, I did not find there any record of Christ talking as my friend talked. I did not find Him saying, "These are a few observations that have occurred to me. I should be very grateful if you would go away and think them over and see if you can find anything in them." I did find him teaching "with authority," hurling dogma at the heads of His audiences, commanding them to accept His teaching and holding out to them the appalling threat of eternal damnation if they refused acceptance.

The same also applies to the general problem of hell. To this day I find it extremely difficult to see how it is not contrary to the nature of a loving God to condemn a soul to all eternity. I am familiar with the normal dialectic on the subject. Yet it does not wholly remove my difficulty. Nevertheless, it is clear that nothing could be more fantastically false to history than to suggest that there was a historical "Jesus, meek and mild" followed by a priesthood which invented the appalling doctrine of hell. If one thing is clear about Christ, it is that He taught the doctrine of hell with terrifying energy. The Church has continued to teach it only because, in view of Christ's words, she has been left with no alternative. If you believe in Christ, then you must believe in hell. If you cannot believe in hell, then you cannot believe in Christ.

When I was at school, among my school fellows were two Protestants. One term one of them returned after the holidays and said that his parents had read the New Testament and, as a result, he and they had become Roman Catholics. The other lad thought this a very strange story. At the time I did not see why it was so particularly unlikely. When, some years later, I came to read the New Testament myself, I found why it did not seem strange at all.

THE WHITE PEBBLE

Thomas Merton

Few writers in our day have been catapulted so suddenly into fame as has Thomas Merton, the author of *Seven Storey Mountain* and *The Waters of Siloe*. The former, one of the outstanding best sellers of recent years, has made his name a household word on both sides of the Atlantic and has awakened widespread interest in the life and personality of this gifted young author. Its enduring popularity bids fair to stamp it as one of the most remarkable books of the decade.

Born in 1915 in a small town in the Pyrenees, near the Spanish border in southern France, Thomas Merton was the son of two artists. His father, Owen Merton, a New Zealander, was achieving a reputation as a powerful and original landscape painter when his career was cut short by his untimely death in London in 1930. His mother, an American from Ohio, had died ten years previously in New York, where the Mertons had gone during World War I to be with her family.

Thomas traveled with his father to Bermuda and then to France, where he studied at the Lycée of Montauban and acquired a fluency in French. The Catholic culture of the Middle Ages surrounded them on all sides and awakened in both of them an interest in Catholicism, though it was confined chiefly to the cultural sphere. Owen Merton died in the Anglican faith in which he had been reared.

At the time of his father's death, Thomas was at Oakham School in the English Midlands, where he received the customary English classical education with the addition of much French and German literature. He did considerable traveling in Italy and learned Italian. In 1932 he won an exhibition at Clare College, Cambridge, and after a year of reading modern languages at the university, he left England to rejoin his younger brother and his grandparents in the United States.

He continued his studies at Columbia University, where he took an active part in campus activities and won a prize for poetry. In 1938 he entered the graduate school of English and wrote a thesis on "Nature and Art in William Blake" for a Master of Arts degree. This brought him in contact with Jacques Maritain's *Art and Scholasticism,* whence he passed on to the reading of Thomas Aquinas and other masters of Christian thought. Meanwhile his interest in poetry brought him in touch with the thought of Father Gerard Manley Hopkins, S.J., Crashaw, and others. This resulted in his application to Father Ford, chaplain of the Catholic students, for instruction in the Catholic faith. He was received into the Church on November 16, 1938, and received his M.A. degree from Columbia in 1939.

With the intention of devoting himself to an academic career, Mr. Merton continued in the Columbia Graduate School and taught English in the University Extension; during this time he wrote book reviews for the New York *Times* and the New York *Herald Tribune* Sunday Book supplements and for other publications.

Desiring the opportunity of deepening his spiritual life, he joined the faculty of St. Bonaventure College near Olean, New York, in 1940, teaching English literature. In the peaceful atmosphere among the woodlands of the Allegany valley, he experienced a quickening of his religious life and a stimulation of his interest in poetry and other writing, mostly of a spiritual nature. More and more he strove to compensate for the years of a worldly life and of religious indifference by prolonged periods of prayer and meditation. His supreme goal in life became the achievement of holiness: the perfect love of God and man.

He made a retreat at the Trappist monastery of Our Lady of Gethsemani in Kentucky and then spent the summer of 1941 debating various courses: the possibility of going to Europe and becoming a Carthusian; of entering Gethsemani; of joining the workers at Friendship House in Harlem, New York. After much anguished searching and prolonged prayer, he entered the Cistercian monastery in Kentucky in December 1941, and was clothed in the white habit of a Trappist novice on the first Sunday of Lent in 1942.

Here he had the great joy of seeing his only brother, from whom he had been separated so much but for whom his affection remained undiminished, embrace the faith at the end of a retreat preparatory to going overseas with the R.C.A.F. in the summer of

1942. It was the last that Thomas was ever to see of his brother; the latter lost his life when his plane was wrecked on a bombing flight over the North Sea. The poem which Thomas wrote in memory of his brother is one of such surpassing beauty and poignant sadness that few eyes can read it and remain undimmed. It is reproduced toward the end of *The Seven Storey Mountain.*

In the spring of 1949, Thomas Merton reached the goal of the priesthood and is known in religion as Father M. Louis. The quiet, contemplative Cistercian life, steeped in liturgy, wrapped in prayer, silence, and peace, and close to God and nature, has contributed powerfully to the literary formation of this young writer and has been largely instrumental in bringing his latent talents to a rich flowering in prose and poetry.

Among his volumes of poetry are *Thirty Poems, A Man in the Divided Sea,* and *Tears of the Blind Lions;* they have been widely acclaimed for their originality, insight, and beauty of expression. His outstanding success is, of course, *The Seven Storey Mountain,* which has won favor with people of all faiths. A volume of spiritual considerations, *Seeds of Contemplation,* is reaching thousands who were previously strangers to meditation. *Waters of Siloe* is a history of the Cistercian Order written with genuine insight and sympathetic appreciation, in such a way as to grip the interest of the general public. Thomas Merton has earned for himself a foremost place among the literary figures of our day —a recognition accorded to him by readers on both sides of the Atlantic.

I N THE Apocalypse, St. John puts these words upon the lips of God. "To him that overcometh, I will give the hidden manna, and will give him a white counter, and in the counter, a new name written, which no man knoweth, but he that receiveth it."[1] The "counter" in this sentence means a pebble, a token that might be given out as a lot in a game of chance. Each one in the game is identified by his lot, or his counter, or his pebble.

So it is with our lives, in the eyes of God. The supernatural destinies of the elect are hidden in the hands of God. Our vocation to the faith, and to the particular, individual part that each one of us must play in the life of the Church, is a

[1]Apocalypse 2:17.

secret gift of God. Our supernatural identity is hidden in a little white counter, a little white pebble in the hand of God. If we want it, we must reach out and take it from His hand.

If we do not accept it, we shall never know our true name. We shall never find out who we were meant to be. And we shall fall into a hopeless and everlasting void that is peopled by all the missing persons who have never found out that they really had a name and a character and an identity reserved for them in heaven, that they were destined for life instead of death, if only they had known how to reach for their pebble and make the effort to begin to live.

Each one gets his pebble from the hand of Christ. The hands of Christ are pierced by nails. He bought us our supernatural life with His own human life. The white counters that he gives to those who "overcome" are tokens of a share in His divine life. All true life flows into the souls of men from the wounds of Christ on the Cross.

St. Paul says, "We . . . are baptized in His death. We are buried together with him by baptism into death; that as Christ is risen from the dead by the glory of the Father, so we also may walk in newness of life."[2] And this new life is a divine life. "We are dead to sin but living to God in Jesus Christ our Lord."[3] It is no longer we who live, but Christ lives in us.[4]

We too often tend to think of supernatural life as a gift given to individuals for themselves alone, as if the Kingdom of Heaven were a conglomeration of strangers drawn together like a football crowd—men who have little in common except that they are all sitting in the same stadium and are all excited about the same game. It is as if we thought supernatural life were a gift dealt out to each one without any reference to the other elect—like the graded series of prizes in a lottery. Each one takes his prize and goes off by himself to enjoy it as best he can.

According to this view, we tend to think of conversions to the faith as phenomena that are completely understandable when you tell the story of how an individual got to be

[2]Romans 6:3–4.   [3]Ibid., 11.   [4]Galatians 2:20.

baptized. When he is baptized, he is "in." He has been initiated. He is a fellow Christian. Of course conversion stories do stand on their own merits. They do express their own significant lessons. Nevertheless, each conversion is only really understandable in the light of the *Parousia*—the second coming of Christ—and of the *Pleroma*—the fullness of the Mystical Christ.

We are all baptized into *one* supernatural life, into one Christ. "In one Spirit we are all baptized into one Body."[5] Our lives are thenceforth so intimately identified that "if one member suffer the others suffer with it and if one member glory the others glory with it."[6] We are all like grains of wheat ground into flour and baked into one Host and consecrated as the Body of Christ: "For we, being many, are one bread, one body, all that partake of one bread."[7]

Now this Mystical Christ, the "whole Christ," head and members, is not a static moral organization. It is a living and growing organism which is developing toward a definite end which will be the perfect manifestation of the power and the Kingship of Christ, the full and final expression of His victory over death and sin. The Mystical Body of Christ is not simply a kind of mythical clearinghouse through which individuals pass in order to enter into a reward. It is *the central reality of all creation*. This "one new man"[8] made of the union of the elect with the Incarnate Son of God is the whole reason for the existence of the universe because, as St. Paul tells us, God "chose us in Him [Jesus] before the foundation of the world . . . and predestinated us unto the adoption of children through Jesus Christ unto Himself . . . unto the praise of the glory of His grace in which He hath graced us in His beloved Son."[9] It is this "one Man" who gives God perfect glory. This Mystical Christ gathers into Himself everything in heaven and on earth, because God reveals through His Son "the mystery of His will" which is to "restore all things in Christ"—*instaurare omnia in Christo*.[10]

[5]I Corinthians 12:13.　　[6]I Corinthians 12:36.
[7]I Corinthians 10:16.　　[8]Ephesians 2:15.
[9]Ephesians 1:4–6.　　　[10]Ephesians 1:10.

[237]

There is no other purpose in the world than this: that God be perfectly glorified by the "whole Christ." The day when that perfect glory will be given has not yet arrived. But it is coming. The "whole Christ" is constantly growing and advancing toward that "day of Christ Jesus," the day of "the perfecting of the saints"[11] when the Body will be complete, when the number of the elect will be filled up, and we will all "meet into the unity of faith and of the knowledge of the Son of God, unto a perfect man, unto the measure of the age of the fullness of Christ."[12]

All the rest of creation, below man, also awaits without realizing it the "day of Christ Jesus," this day of fulfillment. For "every creature groaneth and travaileth even until now . . . waiting for the adoption of the sons of God."[13]

The final end of this development is the perfect union of all the elect with God, in one Spirit. "For by Him we have access both in one Spirit to the Father."[14] This will be the final, perfect, mystical union of the "whole Christ" with the Godhead, revealed by Jesus in the seventeenth chapter of St. John's Gospel, that stupendous unity of love and vision in which all the saints become absorbed, without losing their personal identities, in the depths of the intimate life of the Blessed Trinity. They all become one with God and one with one another as the three divine persons are one. The same divine life flows through the exultant body of the elect. They see God as He sees Himself, for they see Him and all things in His Word. They love God and one another as He loves Himself, for they are all caught up into the uncreated flame of Love which bursts forth from the Father and the Son and unites them in Love—the Holy Spirit.

It seems to me that it is extremely important for a full and normal development of the Christian life and spirit that Christians should acquire this long-range view of their baptism and their individual vocation. Everyone should see his baptism in the light of eschatology. Every Christian should

[11]Ephesians 4:12.   [12]Ephesians 4:13
[13]Romans 8:22–23.   [14]Ephesians 2:18.

regard his Christian life in relation to the *Parousia* and to the *Pleroma*—the final fulfillment of the life of the whole Christ. Jesus Himself constantly reminded His hearers that the Master who had given various talents to His servants would one day return and ask for an accounting. These parables should not merely be understood in the light of personal justification and sin. It is not merely a question of making certain that one is personally discovered at the hour of death to be in the state of grace. Supernatural life itself is a talent which is given us to be developed. The virtues of faith, hope, and charity, by which we are united to God, are talents given us to be developed. And they are given us that we may develop them not only on our own account but for everybody else in the Mystical Body.

The final perfection of the "whole Christ," the final glory that the resplendent Bride will give to God in the "day of Christ Jesus," depends in some measure upon each one of us, because it depends on the use we make of God's gifts. These gifts are given us, remember, not for ourselves alone, but for others as well.

No man enters heaven all by himself. We either bring others in with us or we are brought in by others. The sublime economy of divine love, the feast of love which is the heart's blood of the body of Christ, demands this sharing in merits and graces, because every gift that is shared with another is sweeter and more meritorious. One of the most fundamental laws of life is the need to multiply itself, and this law applies to the supernatural life as well. Good is diffusive of itself. The grace that is given to *me* must pour out into *your* heart through works of love, through prayer, through sacrifice. The more fully one enters into the Christian life, the more he feels the necessity of communicating that life to others, if not by word, then by prayer and by the deep, sweet anguish of desire, the craving for souls that burns in the depths of the heart of the priest.

Here, then, are our principles: We are baptized into the whole Christ. Baptism implies a responsibility to *develop* one's supernatural life, to nourish it by love of God, to re-

[239]

produce and spread it by love for other men. All this is ordered to the final perfection of a plan that extends far beyond our own individual salvation: a plan for God's glory which lies at the very heart of the universe. This mystery we must believe and seek to understand if we would make anything of conversion and vocation.

I might add that every baptism implies a distinct individual vocation, a peculiar function in the building up of the Mystical Body. This follows clearly from St. Paul's teaching on the functions of the different members. Each one has something to do. We are not called merely to vegetate in the Mystical Body, but to act and to grow and to help the growth of other members.

Finally, every circumstance of every individual life, every grace, every trial, every joy, every suffering, every gift, and every loss, must be seen in the light of this same universal plan. It is all part of our vocation. It is all sent to us by God as a means for working out our own salvation and perfecting the Mystical Body. There is nothing on earth which cannot be made to contribute to the good of the elect and of the "whole Christ." "And we know that to them that love God, all things work together unto good."[15]

I know from my own experience that baptism was not the end of my conversion but only the beginning. I was baptized twelve years ago. I came to the font seeking what most people seek—faith, truth, life, peace. I found all that the first day, and yet I have continued to seek and have continued, also, to find. This seeking and finding goes on more and more. The pursuit becomes more ardent and more calm. The experience of discovery is something deeper and more vital every day.

The faith, the love of God, the light of God's presence, the sense of rich and living spiritual union with my brothers in God, all this grows and broadens with the ordinary joys and sufferings of life. You do not always have the sense that you are getting somewhere, and yet, whether you feel it or not, this expansion and deepening is always going on. The

[15]Romans 8:28.

[240]

life of a Christian who does what he can to develop his Christian life is every day more serene and more profound. I say, by way of parenthesis, the life of the Christian who *does what he can*. Many Christians inhibit the growth of the life within them by their morbid depression at not being able to do what they can't. One of the great secrets of the Christian life is the kind of peaceful humility which trusts in God for results and does not get too disturbed by the constant failures of human weakness.

The story of my own conversion has been told elsewhere in considerable detail.[16] There is no need to go into it all again here, except to say that I had tried most of the typical solutions that men apply to their problems before I became a Catholic. I found that all these other solutions were inadequate. I knew something of the life of the artist and intellectual because my father was an artist and I was brought up, for better or for worse, as an intellectual.

I went through schools and colleges in America and France and England. After a year at Cambridge I came back to Columbia and then went into teaching and writing. That was what I was up to when I finally found my way into the little church of Corpus Christi on 121st Street, just off Broadway, at the edge of the Columbia campus.

Meanwhile I had tried to construct a philosophy of life on four different foundations. I had begun with plain, atheistic hedonism—which is a fancy title for a life of absolute selfishness. Believe in nothing, have a good time, and try to satisfy all your capacities for pleasure without hurting other people too much. It was what my generation believed in, when it was entering into manhood after having considered the society of its elders during the 1920s. In order to give this vague and irrational code an intellectual structure, I rebuilt its foundations with the fragments I was able to gather from a hasty and superficial reading of Freud and Jung.

The reason why one had to lead this life devoted to self-satisfaction was that mental health depended on keeping one's mind from becoming a tangle of repressions. This

[16]*The Seven Storey Mountain,* New York, 1948.

made me excessively introspective. In order to escape into the world outside myself, and also in order to take revenge for my own disgust with myself by venting it all on a "scapegoat," I became a communist sympathizer and unloaded all my sins on the back of the bourgeoisie. It made me feel good, but not for long. Campus communism at Columbia was untidy and feeble, and I did not take well to the incantation of slogans as a substitute for thought. When it became clear that the unprincipled opportunism of the party line had no other end than to promote the interests of those in power in "the party," I gave up communism in complete disgust.

Then I tried to return to the religion of my childhood—a vague Protestantism. It was too vague. I wanted a solid foundation of doctrinal truth to build on, and I could not find any. Protestantism was so highly subjective that each individual was isolated with his own personal experience, and faith had become, in practice, almost incommunicable. It was almost impossible to find out exactly what my Protestant friends really *believed*. Nevertheless, the element of personal experience in religion fascinated me, and I explored the literature of oriental mysticism without much profit except that I came away with the conviction that man could, by detachment from created things and by a profound interior transformation, enter into direct experimental contact with God.

The fact that God could exist had meanwhile been impressed upon me by Gilson's *Spirit of Medieval Philosophy*. When I began to find out more about scholastic philosophy and theology by reading Jacques Maritain and parts of St. Thomas, and when I began to understand something of the nature of the soul and its life, my conversion followed quite logically.

The intellectual basis of my conversion was simply this: I found that God existed, and that He was the source of all reality; was, in fact, Reality, Truth, Life itself. He was pure actuality. On the other hand, I found that I had an intellect made to apprehend the highest and most perfect Truth in a supernatural intuition born of love, and that I had a free will that was capable of turning all the powers of my being either toward that Truth or away from it. Finally, since I could not attain this consummation by my own unaided natural powers, I would have to enter into the economy of means and helps called "graces" won for me by Christ. Therefore I was baptized and became a Christian at least in name.

It is evident that the story of my life up to the day of my baptism is hardly the adequate story of my "conversion." My conversion is still going on. Conversion is something that is prolonged over a whole lifetime. Its progress leads it over a succession of peaks and valleys, but normally the ascent is continuous in the sense that each new valley is higher than the last one.

I have said that the problem of the Christian life is not solved by baptism alone. Sanctifying grace, which makes us "live in Christ" and nourishes us with the fruits of His Passion and endows us with a share in His risen glory, is a talent that has to be increased and developed. We must enter deeper and deeper into this life of Christ. We must give ourselves over more and more fully to the mighty and transforming power of grace. Why? Because, as I have said, the purpose of our lives is to make us more and more productive members of the Mystical Body of Christ.[17]

We increase and deepen our participation in the life of the Body by the activity of our minds and wills, illuminated and guided by the Holy Ghost. We must therefore keep growing in our knowledge and love of God and in our love for other men. The power of good operative habits must take ever greater and greater hold upon us. The Truth we believe in must work itself more and more fully into the very substance of our lives until our whole existence is nothing but vision and love.

What this means in practice is summed up by one word that most men are afraid of: *asceticism*. "We are debtors not to the flesh to live according to the flesh. For if you live ac-

[17]John 15:1, 2, 6, 8.

[243]

cording to the flesh, you shall die: but if by the spirit you mortify the deeds of the flesh, you shall live."[18] Our divine sonship and our inheritance of the joys of the divine life depend on our union with Christ who died for us on the Cross. We are only "joint-heirs with Him," "if so we suffer with him that we may be glorified with him."[19] "For they that are Christ's have crucified their flesh with its vices and concupiscences."[20]

The reason for this is not purely negative. Penance and mortification are not imposed on us merely as a vindictive punishment. We tend to forget the medicinal value of penance. We must deny our faculties the satisfactions proper to a lower form of life in order to accustom them, little by little, to the higher life of the Spirit in which God is known and loved as He is in Himself and not as He appears reflected in His creatures. Asceticism is essential to the Christian life. Without self-denial we cannot be Christ's disciples. "If any man will come after me, let him deny himself and take up his cross and come, follow me."[21]

It took me almost a year to discover that it was not possible to live a life exactly like that led by non-Christians and remain a Christian, no matter how convinced one might be of the truth of Christianity. I admit that it is possible and necessary for many Christians to live immersed in "the world" and all that it implies, but they are precisely the ones who ought to practice the most difficult asceticism. If they are to live as true members of Christ and radiate the divine influence among the men with whom they are in contact, they will be obliged to develop rich interior lives of union with God, and this union will have to be deep enough to weather the demands of hard work and constant contact with things that would defile a weaker spirit.

My own weakness convinced me that I ought to take upon myself the obligations of a higher state of life, not because I felt strong enough to live up to these obligations, but because I realized that they implied special helps and graces

[18]Romans 8:12–13.   [19]Romans 8:17.
[20]Galatians 5:24.   [21]Matthew 16:24.

from God. I became a Cistercian novice in the Trappist Abbey of Gethsemani, Kentucky. God had been exceedingly generous with me. In exchange for a half-articulate acknowledgment of my absolute helplessness, He had called me to one of the most austere orders in the Church. And a few years before, I had been quite convinced that I did not have good enough health to lead the ordinary life of men in the world.

If I began a meditation on this second great step in my conversion, I would go on for pages and fill another book, which would perhaps be tedious to everyone but myself, because the mystery of God's goodness to me is something that dazzles me more and more from day to day and I cannot exhaust its fascination.

The monastic life is nothing but a search for God, a search that has been streamlined and intensified by the rejection of every other concern. A Christian living in the world can temper his pursuit of God's Truth with other secondary interests, as long as these do not conflict with his Christian vocation. But God becomes the monk's whole reason for existing. Nothing that does not lead to God, nothing that does not give him glory, is of any account. The monk, and especially the Trappist Cistercian, is by profession a contemplative. He is immersed and swallowed up in the tide of life and vision that is poured out upon the world through the Passion of Our Divine Saviour. The monk's life is a life of ardent love for Christ, who is "the way, the truth and the life."

And yet, however great may be the grace of monastic profession, it still falls far short of the priesthood. There is no greater gift given by Christ to the members of His Church than the grace of the priesthood. Ordination impresses upon the soul an indelible character which identifies a man with Christ as priest and victim. The grace of the priesthood sinks a man into the very depths of the Christ-Life, places him at the heart of all that is real and vital, and arms him with the power which has secretly shaped all history until now and which is fast preparing the final revelation of the glory of the sons of God, in Christ Jesus. The priest holds in his hands the Judge and Saviour of men. He speaks five words and the Life of the world is present on the altar before him. He holds between his fingers the Heart that is throbbing in the deepest center of all the hearts of the saints. He holds the life of all the saints, he holds God Himself in his hands!

Is it possible to imagine a man, endowed with such power from God, not being completely transformed by his daily exercise of it?

I cannot write much here about this third and most tremendous step in my conversion. Its effects are only just beginning dimly to dawn upon me. I am just beginning to see something of the breadth of the new horizons that are opened up before me by the Christ of my daily Mass.

At four o'clock in the morning, after the choir has finished chanting the night office begun at 1:30 or 2 A.M., in the Basilica of the Abbey, the Cistercian priests file through the shadows of the transept into their sacristy. High up in the belfry the little bell tolls for Masses that are about to begin. We take off our white cowls and put on our vestments, and depart severally to our dim altars in the candlelit side chapels. And the great Sacrifice begins, as we bow at the foot of the altar of God. We go up to God with our hearts steeped in the peace of the Psalms, our minds swimming in the calm wonder of revelation. We offer the host and the chalice to God, for His blessing upon the Sacrifice.

We bow down before the thrice Holy God, and begin the Canon, drawing into the heart of our Mass the lives and souls of all those whom Christ's Heart loves in our hearts. We press them to His Heart in our hearts, as more than once during the Canon we cry out to God with a great cry that shakes our depths, the cry of those who are still divided and separated in some measure from the perfect union of the saints in Christ. We bow in silence, holding the thin white host. Everything becomes luminous and calm. With a simplicity and a peace that are more powerful than all thunder, Christ utters Himself through us and is present upon the altar. The might of His Spirit sings within us, and the Spirit cries, "Abba, Father!" and prays for us within us with a pleading too deep and too magnificent for us to understand.

It is a sweet and terrible thing to feel the fire of that wonderful pleading grow up and begin to burn in the secret depths of your being. Yet, by the mercy of God, you are not consumed, and your hand does not tremble when you lift up the body and blood of Christ and offer Him to the Father: all honor and glory! You are sustained by the expectation of the final act, the Communion that completes the Sacrifice. The wonderful calm anguish, generated within your heart by the prayer of the Spirit, is quenched in the chalice of your Communion and you sink into the clear-eyed peace of Christ, the peace which is the peace and simplicity of an Eternal Child!

Then, for an hour, perhaps more, it is this peace that prays within you with an ineffable power. You go off somewhere in the dark recesses of the church and kneel behind something, and half the time you forget where you are.

Day after day it is the same external act: but always with a new inner meaning. Morning after morning you go to the dim altar weaker and more lowly than you have ever been before, and leave it lost in a more incomprehensible greatness than you have ever known before. A few months of the Mass have emptied me more and filled me more than seven years of monastic asceticism.

I used to have what I considered a degree of prayer. It was something I thought I could refer to as "my prayer." I rested in it, and it was silent and sweet. It seemed to me to be something rich and beautiful. Now I have no prayer. I am possessed by the prayer of One who is Almighty. And His prayer in me is something more than prayer because it is an infinite Sacrifice.

Prayer used to rise out of my soul as a desire that raised me up to God. It was my desire, and I could see where it was going, and I could take complacency in it. Now prayer is an earthquake which rends the rocks on which the substance of my being is built, and I do not know where it is going or what it is doing: sometimes it raises the dead, but only to assuage my terror. And sometimes it throws me to the living, the way the early Christians were thrown to the lions.

The Mass has made an end forever of what I used to treasure as an interior solitude. It has shown me the way to a height of solitude I never dreamed of because its paradox was utterly beyond my own imagining. This is the solitude of Christ in the Blessed Sacrament. Jesus in the host is alone, not because He is remote and isolated from everybody, but because He is *given to everybody, given utterly.* And because He is given to everybody, He can belong exclusively to nobody. And yet He is so alone that He belongs entirely to each one who possesses Him.

If you are afraid of love, never become a priest, never say Mass. The Mass will draw down upon your soul a torrent of interior suffering which has only one function—to break you wide open and let everybody in the world into your heart. If you are afraid of people, never say Mass! If you want to guard your heart against invasion, never say Mass! For when you begin to say Mass, the Spirit of God awakes like a giant inside you and bursts the locks of your private sanctuary and calls all the people in the world to come into your heart. If you say Mass, you condemn your soul to the torment of a love that is so vast and so insatiable that you will never be able to bear it alone. That love is the love of the Heart of Jesus, burning within your own miserable heart, and bringing down upon you the huge weight of His pity for all the sins of the world!

Do you know what that love will do to you if you let it work on your soul, if you do not resist it? It will devour you. It will kill you. It will break your heart.

I wish I could speak intelligibly about the absolute imperiousness of Christ's love in the heart of a priest. Without actually doing violence to your heart (for Christ's love always works with a power that is smooth and delicate, even when it smashes you!), the Spirit strikes like lightning as soon as there is the slightest opening in your will, and in a flash He is upon you with His new demand. And almost every time it seems to be a sweeping demand for your whole self, everything, a holocaust.

Where is there a hiding place, where is there a high mountain or a deep forest or an unvisited desert, where a poor priest can go to escape from the voices of men that are brought to the ears of his soul by the Holy Spirit? Where can a creature without courage and without virtue, and almost without faith, hide his head and blot out the image of the faces that look at him and hands that reach out to him? Where can he go to stop his ears against the voices that cry, "Die for me! Die for me!"?

That is not all. It is not only the ones we must die for that terrify us: it is most of all the ones we must live for. They demand not only our strength and our health and our time, but if we listen to the voice of Christ in them, there will be many among them who will claim, as an imperious right, the deepest recesses of your heart and soul: because we are their Christ and we have to love them with the same love with which Christ loves them. "This is my commandment, that you love one another as I have loved you."[22] It is not enough to be a mere agent of God, transacting His business and then retiring within ourselves. We have to do the work of Him that sent us, which is to live consumed in the suffering of love.

"A woman when she is in labor hath sorrow because her hour is come: but when she hath brought forth the child she remembereth no more the anguish for joy that a man is born into the world."[23] The great work of Christ would be completed more quickly if we were more willing to bear the anguish of His love. Yet is it any wonder that we flee from a love that destroys us? Alas, we forget that it destroys us only to transform us. The things the Spirit of God demands of us in order to form the Mystical Body of the Whole Christ, in order that "a man may be born into the world," contradict our own ideals of a sanctity in which we ourselves are not sacrificed, consumed, and transformed.

[22]John 15:12.   [23]John 16:21.

We resist the exigencies of a love that seeks to fulfill us by melting us down in the crucible from which the *Pleroma* is to emerge. But it is only in Christ, in the whole Christ, that each individual personality can be completely perfected and fulfilled. For Christ is our life, and until we live perfectly in Him, and He in us, we still fall short of the man we were intended to be, because something of our life is still lacking to us.

Let us all enter into the great prayer of the Church, which centers upon the Sacrifice of Christ in the Mass, and in that prayer let us remember one another, readers and writer, priest and faithful. Let us ask God through Christ, and in the unity of His Spirit, to give us the courage not to run away from His love, not to run away from His fire, and not to run away from the divine love we find in one another.

THE OPEN DOOR

John A. O'Brien

There is a Door—and only One
Yet its sides are two
Inside and outside.
On which side are you?

IN THE preceding chapters, fourteen pilgrims have described their journey into the Catholic Church. A brief scrutiny of their testimony will throw light upon the motivation of their quest, the evidence which brought conviction, the operation of divine grace in their souls, the nature of conversion, and the resulting peace, security, and happiness which they experienced. Their testimony indicates that though they traveled by different paths, the motive underlying all the pilgrimages was fundamentally the same: the desire to find God and the fullness of divine revelation.

The soul estranged from God suffers from a spiritual distemper that allows no peace of mind or soul. Yet this is precisely what man wants most of all. But peace is the tranquillity of order; and as long as God is absent from the human soul, chaos and anarchy reign and serenity is conspicuous by its absence. Hence we witness on all sides today a mad, restless, feverish search for peace—a search that is filling the offices of physicians and psychiatrists and crowding our sanatoriums.

The quest for such peace is, however, no transient phenomenon of our day; it is as old as the race and as universal as mankind. Uttered by our first parents in the Garden of Eden, that cry has continued its reverberations in the bosom of all their progeny; and it will still be echoing in the heart of man when his little planet disappears with him and all his works into the abyss where time ends and eternity begins. In searching for such peace, man is but seeking to appease a hunger planted in his heart by God: the craving of the soul for its Creator, the yearning of man for his Maker, the cry of the orphan for his Father.

God, Christ, the fullness of divine revelation, the institution founded by Christ to transmit such a spiritual legacy to mankind in all ages: these are what the pilgrims found at the end of their Odyssey. They could demand nothing more and be content with nothing less. They wanted not mere probability, but certainty; for the possibility of being in error would open the floodgates of doubt with its torrent of disquieting fears and anxieties. These pilgrims sought, and found, not a partial truth but the whole truth.

"The difficulty of explaining 'why I am a Catholic,'" says Chesterton, "is that there are ten thousand reasons all amounting to one reason: that Catholicism is true." The truth of the Catholic faith, he points out, is like a magnet with powers of attraction and of repulsion. The repulsion arises from the vague fear that one may be caught in a baited trap, but the bait is simply the truth. "The moment men cease to pull against the Catholic Church," he continues, "they feel a tug toward it. The moment they cease to shout it down they begin to listen to it with pleasure. The moment they try to be fair to it they begin to be fond of it. But when that affection has passed a certain point it begins to take on the tragic and menacing grandeur of a great love affair."

When asked to state the "real" reason why she embraced the Catholic faith, Clare Boothe Luce replied that it was because she had found, after careful investigation, that the Catholic religion is the solid objective Truth. "And when I say the solid objective Truth," she added, "I mean just that, and not, as some imagine the convert means, 'one of the best aspects of the Truth.' If Catholic doctrine had seemed to me 'only one aspect of the Truth,' I should still be seeking the whole Truth, of which it was only the part."

[252]

Such, too, is the basic reason which prompts every convert to embrace the Catholic faith. It satisfies completely the deep and ineradicable craving of the human soul for the security and peace which flow only from the certainty of possessing the whole truth. "Without faith," the Apostle Paul declares, "it is impossible to please God."[1] What is faith? "Faith," answers St. Paul, "is the substance of things to be hoped for, the evidence of things that appear not."

Faith implies a firm and unwavering assent. Any element of hesitancy, vacillation, or doubt vitiates it and destroys that unfaltering acceptance and implicit trust which render the act so meritorious and so pleasing in the sight of God. Job gives a memorable voicing of the indestructible trust which lies at the heart of faith when he cries out, "Though he slay me, yet will I trust in him."[2]

Such firm, unwavering, and absolute trust characterizes the faith of all Catholics. Outsiders, groping in uncertainty, sense it in Catholics and marvel at it. Recall, for instance, how Lucile Hasley reports that when she was upset, her Catholic roommate, McCarthy, would remark casually, "Don't worry. I offered up my Communion for you this morning. Everything will be all right." Therein was mirrored the serene confidence which only unquestioning faith in God and in the power of prayer could inspire.

Writing some twenty years after his conversion, Cardinal Newman testifies to the fullness with which the Catholic faith satisfied the hunger of his soul. "There is a depth and power to the Catholic religion," he writes, "a fullness of satisfaction in its creed, its theology, its rites, its sacraments, its discipline, a freedom yet support also, before which the neglect or misapprehension about oneself on the part of living individual persons, however exalted, is as so much dust, when weighed in the balance. This is the true secret of the Church's strength, the principle of her indefectibility and the bond of her indissoluble unity. It is the earnest and the beginning of the repose of heaven."

Converts to Catholicism from all religious systems and of

[1]Hebrews 11:6.   [2]Job 13:15.

[253]

all nationalities are as one in testifying to the unique certainty and absolute truth which they find in their new faith. Thus Mr. Sadanand Srinivaspur, a scholarly convert from Hinduism, who had long been searching for absolute truth, writes: "I need not go in search of this or that truth, as once I used to do, since I possess Truth itself. My long quest after Truth, as typified in the age-long yearning of the soul of India, summed up in the words of the *Chandogya Upanishad,*

> Lead me from unreality to reality,
> From darkness lead me to light,
> From death to immortality,

is over, because the Catholic Church has answered it in the words of her Divine Founder: 'I am the Way, the Truth and the Life.'" Therein is mirrored the conviction of converts in all countries and in all ages that in Catholicism they have found not an aspect or a fragment of the truth, but the whole and absolute truth, vouched for by God Himself.

Such is the faith which the Master wished to instill in the disciples when, after causing the fruitless fig tree to wither away, He said to them: "Amen, I say to you, if you shall have faith, and stagger not, not only this of the fig tree shall you do, but also if you say to this mountain, Take up and cast thyself into the sea, it shall be done. And all things whatsoever you shall ask in prayer, believing, you shall receive."[3] It is precisely in this element of absolute trust and unwavering confidence that the saving, healing, justifying, strengthening, and thaumaturgic power of faith consists.

That is why miracles do not seem to Catholics the utterly strange and inexplicable phenomena which they appear to those outside the fold. They involve no intrinsic contradiction and are well within the competence of an omnipotent God. Every land has its Catholic shrines wherein miracles bear striking witness to the veracity of Christ's description of the power of faith and prayer. *The Annals of Lourdes,* containing affidavits of physicians of all faiths and of none concern-

[3]Matthew 21:21–23.

ing the incurable nature of the disease of the pilgrim and later of its complete and, in many cases, almost instantaneous cure, offer objective and demonstrative evidence to a world which, like the doubting Thomas of old, must needs see in order to believe.

As a humble pilgrim, the writer visited the shrine of Our Lady at Lourdes in France, of Our Lady of Guadalupe in Mexico, of St. Anne de Beaupré in Quebec, and of St. Joseph in Montreal. He saw great numbers of wheel chairs, crutches, plaster-of-Paris casts, and other evidences of invalidism left remaining there to bear mute witness to the miraculous cures received. Most impressive of all was the carefully documented testimony at Lourdes.

It was the objective, dispassionate character of this evidence that appealed so profoundly to the eminent medical scientist, Alexis Carrel. In his great masterpiece, *Man the Unknown,* he shows how unscientific it is to refuse to face this evidence and to draw the only conclusion possible from the premises, namely, that the effect so far transcends the forces of nature that it must be attributed to God alone.

Spending a day at the writer's home a few years before his death, he spoke at length of the phenomena at Lourdes, which he had examined with characteristic thoroughness and open-mindedness. Hence it was no surprise to the writer when he learned that this eminent scholar, honored with the Nobel prize for his scientific discoveries in medicine and crowned with honors from many other countries, turned to embrace the Catholic faith before death stilled his brilliant mind and questing heart.

He had the simplicity and the open-mindedness of a Pasteur, and history will bracket the two of them together for their world-renowned contributions to medical science as well as for their deep faith in God and in the Church which He founded. Pasteur gave a memorable expression to that faith when, at the pinnacle of his fame, with the world acclaiming him the greatest scientific genius of the age, he wrote to his children: "The more I know, the more nearly is my faith that of the Breton peasant. Could I but

[255]

know all, I would have the faith of a Breton peasant woman."

In the process of conversion, as reported by the contributors to this symposium, we can distinguish three distinct steps. The first is the investigation of the credentials of the Church. The circumstance which draws a person's attention to the Church and prompts him to begin his inquiry is as various and as manifold as there are individual inquirers.

With Daniel Sargeant, it was his study of Dante that led him to investigate Dante's faith. With Fulton Oursler, it was the spell which the Holy Land cast over him that prompted him to re-examine the life of Christ and thus led him to the Church which He founded.[4] With Jacques and Raïssa Maritain, it was their acquaintance with Léon Bloy, and later their reading of the lives of the saints, which aroused their interest in the Church. Any of a thousand circumstances can lead to the awakening of an interest in the Church and a determination to investigate her teachings.

The second step is the study of the Church, her divine establishment, her doctrines, her means of sanctification, and her credentials. To be fruitful, this examination must be made with an open mind and a willingness to confront all facts with one's reason instead of with one's prejudices. The Church invites the fullest investigation; she conceals nothing of her doctrine or of her long history; during this inquiry she makes no appeal to the emotions, but to the intellect alone. She is confident that Christ has stamped clearly and indelibly His own divine imprint upon her and that the unprejudiced mind of the honest inquirer will be able to discern it.

The marks which distinguish Christ's Church from all others are chiefly her unity, sanctity, catholicity, and apostolicity. Running as a unifying thread through all these marks is her divine origin: Christ is her Founder and her Guarantor. She has been governed by Peter and an unbroken chain of successors from the days of Christ to the

[4]*The Road to Damascus,* edited by John A. O'Brien, Doubleday & Company, 1949, New York.

present time. She presents the historic credentials of her foundation and of her divinely appointed commission to teach all mankind in the name of Christ Himself.

So overwhelming is the historical and objective cogency of her credentials that they can scarcely fail to bring conviction when examined with an open mind and a sincere desire to embrace the truths of Christ and the means provided by Him for man's sanctification and salvation. The experiences of the scholarly converts described in this book offer ample corroboration of this truth. Regardless of the point at which they started, they all arrived at the same destination. The conclusion reached at the end of this second stage, then, is simply this: The Catholic Church, founded by Christ and authorized to teach in His name, is the true Church.

This leads to the third and last step: the act of faith. The intellectual conviction that the Catholic Church is the true Church precedes the act of faith but is not to be identified with it. One may have the intellectual conviction just mentioned and yet hesitate or refuse to make the act of faith. This latter requires the "good will to believe," the disposition of the will to bend the intellect in a genuflection of faith before the throne of divine truth. The act of faith amounts essentially to this: I believe what the Church teaches because God has revealed it.

While all three steps imply the grace of God, it is the last step which requires a special grace—the gift of faith. That grace is obtained through earnest prayer. God will not deny it to the man of good will, who on his knees begs for it. He will receive the grace of a gentle submissiveness prompting him to render homage to God by freely, piously, and reverently submitting his mind to God's word; this grace enables him to give effect to his conviction by proclaiming: "I *do* believe that God has given me the Church to be my teacher. I believe it on the authority of God Himself who can neither deceive nor be deceived." Such is the essence of the act of faith.

[257]

It is to be noted that faith rests upon the authority of God revealing, and thus engenders a certainty which transcends that attainable by mere human reason. Once reason has brought the conviction that God has spoken and that it would be wrong and foolish to deny His word, it opens the door that admits him to a far higher and different kind of certainty, the certainty that rests directly and immediately upon the authority of God the revealer.

The various lines of human reasoning by which he climbs to the final summit of God's revealed word, upon which he then reposes, may be compared to the rungs of a ladder by which one climbs to a secure platform upon which he stands with no further need of the ladder. The supreme consideration prompting belief in a doctrine thenceforth is not the argument developed by this or that theologian, but simply the authority of God who has revealed it.

The intellect alone cannot coerce an ill-disposed person, even if convinced of the truth, to make an act of faith. The good will to believe is all-important. "As men may be convinced," observes Cardinal Newman, "and not act according to their conviction, so may they be convinced and not believe according to their conviction . . . The arguments for religion do not compel anyone to believe, just as arguments for good conduct do not compel anyone to obey. Obedience is the consequence of willing to obey, and faith is the consequence of *willing* to believe; we may see what is right, whether in matters of faith or obedience, but of ourselves we cannot will what is right without the grace of God."[5]

Long before Cardinal Newman, the Apostle Paul, who peered deep into the wellsprings of conduct, voiced this same truth when he declared: "To will is present with me, but to accomplish that which is good, I find not. For the good which I will, I do not."[6] Psychologists have long pointed out the important difference between velleity and volition: it is the difference between mere ineffectual wishing and actual willing—a world of difference.

[5]*Discourses to Mixed Congregations,* pp. 225 and 226.
[6]Romans 7:18–19.

[258]

We have developed this point at some length because it throws light, we think, upon how the will may be deterred from action even after the intellect has been convinced. Take, for instance, the person who has been taught from his earliest years that the pope is Antichrist and Catholicism is pagan idolatry. Later on he examines the Church and her doctrines and discovers that his previous conceptions were mere caricatures, that this is the Church actually founded by Christ to teach all mankind His truths. Nevertheless, the fear of the Church which was planted in his young mind still colors his imagination and prevents his will from following through with his present intellectual convictions.

How often circumstances of such a nature hamstring the will and delay, if they do not completely prevent, the act of faith. Hence the enormous emphasis which the Church places upon the importance of praying for the grace of faith: it emancipates the will from unreasonable fears and unworthy motives and disposes it to elicit the all-important act of trust in God and in His revealed plan for man's salvation. Indeed, it can be safely affirmed that the truth seeker comes to God most effectively on his knees in prayer; and it can be doubted if he reaches Him in any other way.

It is well here to come to grips with a common misconception of Catholic teaching: that the Church holds that only those who are visible members of her faith can be saved. The idea stems from an utterance of St. Cyprian, one of the Fathers of the early Church, who said: "Outside the Church there is no salvation." The saying has often been repeated in Catholic books, but it needs to be interpreted properly.

There is membership in the *body* of the Church: this embraces all those in visible communion, who attend her services, receive her sacraments, and acknowledge her authority. There is also membership in the *soul* of the Church: this includes all who follow the light of their conscience, who worship God according to the dictates of their reason. Obviously a just and merciful God cannot punish such individuals; in their blamelessness and good faith, they share as members of the soul of the Church in the graces and fruits of the Redemption in working out their salvation.

"God our Saviour," the Apostle Paul tells us, "will have all men to be saved and to come to the knowledge of the truth."[7] Like her divine Founder, the Church desires the salvation of all men and nourishes at her spiritual bosom all who earnestly seek the light and follow it to the best of their ability. She is the spiritual mother of all mankind and she loves every human being, regardless of race, color, or creed, with a deep, persistent, and intense love; she loves even those who calumniate and persecute her and, like her Founder, prays for their forgiveness.

The one thing which excludes a person from membership even in the soul of the Church is sinning against the light: deliberate rejection of the Church by one who knows her to be the true Church. This has the cancerous malignancy of treason, the sinister ugliness of the act of Judas Iscariot, and it cannot be condoned. Christ's words are so explicit as to preclude all doubt. "Every one therefore that shall confess me before men," He said, "I will also confess before my Father who is in heaven. But he that shall deny me before men, I will also deny him before my Father who is in heaven."[8]

The circumstances which lead a person to examine the Church are, as we have seen, as varied as the individuals. But, once that investigation is under way, do each of the converts follow a distinctive line of reasoning or do they follow a somewhat general pattern? A careful scrutiny of the narratives of the fourteen converts in this volume and of the fifteen recorded in *The Road to Damascus* shows that there are two great truths which grip most of them and lead them joyously into the fold of Christ.

They constitute the major and the minor premises in the following syllogism: Jesus Christ, the Son of God, is divine and speaks with divine authority. But Christ founded the Catholic Church and commissioned her to teach His revealed truths to all mankind in His name and with His in-

[7]Timothy 2:4.   [8]Matthew 10:32–34.

[260]

fallible authority. Therefore the Catholic Church is the true Church of which I should be a member. In other words, the divinity of Christ and the foundation of the Church by Christ constitute the double-barreled truth which dissipates all doubt and convinces the honest inquirer that the Catholic Church is the true Church of Jesus Christ. At whatever point the inquirer's line of reasoning may start, it comes almost inevitably into this final groove which can lead to but one destination.

This is precisely what we would expect an infinitely wise and loving Saviour to do. One who wished all men to be saved and to come to the knowledge of the truth: to stamp His imprint so unmistakably upon His Church that all mankind could see His image upon it. Hence it requires but ordinary intelligence and good will to find Christ's Church. The line of reasoning, stripped of nonessentials, is so simple and clear that it brings conviction equally well to the simple peasant as to the highly trained philosopher.

We have spoken of the important role which grace plays in leading an inquirer to the act of faith. While there are many phases of this subject which transcend our intelligence, since they involve the operations of the infinite intelligence of God, there are some aspects which are reasonably clear. One is that God sometimes gives this grace with startling suddenness and force.

Saul of Tarsus, traveling on the road to Damacus to persecute Christians, is stricken from his horse and blinded by a brilliant light, while he hears a voice saying, "Saul, Saul, why persecutest thou me?"

Amazed, Saul asks: "Who art thou, Lord?"

The voice replies, "I am Jesus whom thou persecutest."[9]

Here is a divine intervention wherein God's grace shoots down like lightning from the sky—vivid enough for all the world to see.

A somewhat similar case of conversion would seem to be that of the Emperor Constantine the Great. Advancing against the tyrant Maxentius at the Milvian Bridge in 312,

[9] Acts 9:4–6.

Constantine beheld in the heavens a cross bearing the inscription, "In this sign thou shalt conquer." Whereupon, with his little army of twenty thousand, he gained a complete victory over Maxentius and his army of one hundred thousand. In gratitude to the God of the Christians, Constantine immediately issued the Edict of Toleration permitting the Christian Church to emerge from the catacombs and embark upon her world-wide mission.

The first conversion gained for the Church one of her greatest Apostles. The second gained for her one of her greatest defenders, and at a time when she stood in desperate need of one.

The conversion of Augustine would seem to be another case of the sudden intervention of divine grace. Tangled in sensual habits, Augustine has been putting off his conversion for many years. While in the garden weeping over his sins, he cries out in anguish: "How long? How long? Is it to be tomorrow and tomorrow? Why not now? Why not this very hour put an end to my shame?"

Suddenly he hears the voice of a child, saying over and over again: "Take and read; take and read."

Opening the Book of Epistles, Augustine reads the first verse which meets his eye: "Not in rioting and drunkenness, not in concupiscence and impurity, not in contention and anger: but put you on the Lord Jesus Christ and provide not for the flesh in impure lusts."

As a result of his surrender to divine grace, the Church gained one of her greatest philosophers—and at a time when a mastermind was sorely needed to Christianize the culture and thought of Greece and Rome.

In the conversion of John Henry Newman, grace acted in less precipitate manner but with scarcely less force and vigor. Honored and loved by the British public, almost idolized by the students of Oxford, Newman had virtually no friends among the Catholics, who as a result of centuries of royal oppression had dwindled to a pitiful handful. In a letter to his sister on March 15, 1845, he gives an inkling of the power of that grace which could bring him to take the step he contemplated.

"I have a good name with many," he writes. "I am deliberately sacrificing it. I have a bad name with more: I am fulfilling all their worst wishes, and giving them their most coveted triumph. I am distressing all I love, unsettling all I have instructed or aided. I am going to those whom I do not know, and of whom I expect very little. I am making myself an outcast, and at my age—oh! What can it be but stern necessity which causes this."

As a result of his yielding to the insistent grace of God, the Church gained her ablest apologist in the English-speaking world—and at a time when the Church in England sorely needed such a spokesman. Newman started the Oxford movement, which brought more than nine hundred clergymen in England into the Mother Church; it has brought, and is still bringing, into the fold of Christ many thousands of people in other lands as well.

Similar to Newman's experience is that of Dr. Erik Peterson, distinguished theologian of the University of Bonn, Germany. Writing shortly after his conversion to his friend, Karl Barth, he reveals the force of the grace prompting him to run the gantlet of his old associates rather than sin against the light. "I am now forty years old," he writes. "I have renounced my family, my profession and social standing. My action was prompted by my conscience, that I might not be a castaway of God. Whosoever judges me, let him know that I shall appeal against his judgment to the judgment seat of God."

As a consequence of his yielding to the pressure of divine grace, the Church gained an able apologist in Germany— and at a time when she sorely needed one because of the rising tide of Nazi totalitarianism.

In France, the conversion of the brilliant writer, J. K. Huysmans, would seem to evidence the forceful and sudden intervention of divine grace. For years he had been wallowing in the mire of sensuality. Then slowly he began to lift himself and to experience a disgust with his past. "But at

[263]

the same time," he says, "I kicked against the articles of the Faith. The objections I raised in my own mind seemed irresistible; and lo! one fine morning when I woke they were solved—I never knew how. I prayed for the first time, and the catastrophe was over."

Not only was Huysmans converted, but with one fell stroke he cut the moorings of a sordid past and went off to enter a Trappist monastery to spend the rest of his life in silence, prayer, penance, and contemplation—making God the object of his every thought and deed. What mysterious force could have transformed this uninhibited debauchee into a soul intent only upon prayer, atonement, and the love and service of God?

It is no wonder that we find this erstwhile champion of sensuality asking: "Why, by what impulse, have I been incited to take a road at that time shrouded in darkness from my view?" Answering his own question, he says: "Providence was merciful to me and the Virgin kind. I confined myself simply to not resisting them when they gave token of their purposes; I merely obeyed; I was led by what they call 'extraordinary ways.' If any man can have the certainty of the worthless thing he would be without God's help, it is I."

Does the working of divine grace impair the freedom of the will and lead one to belief in a fatalism that is the negation of scientific psychology? Aware that such a question is implicit in the story of his experience, Huysmans frankly raises it and answers it thus: "Not so, for faith in Our Lord is not fatalism. Free will remains free. I could, if I chose, continue to yield to the temptations of the senses and stay on in Paris, instead of going to suffer tribulations at a Trappist monastery. God doubtless would not have insisted; but, while certifying that the will is intact, we must nevertheless allow that the Saviour has much to do in the matter, that He harasses the sinner, breaks him down, *shadows* him, to use a forceful phrase of the police; but I say again, one can, at one's own risk and peril, reject his offices."

To those who do not believe in God or who think of Him

as a vague impersonal force or simply Nature with a capital
N, all this talk of the working of His grace in the human
soul must sound meaningless. But to all who believe in God
as a Heavenly Father solicitous for the welfare of His children, such helpful illuminations of the right path, such tugging at our heartstrings, such gentle yet urgent whisperings
within the human soul pleading for our love are not only
possible but are precisely what would be expected. If a
human father would reach out to help his children, why
would not our Heavenly Father, whose divine Son gave His
life for our redemption, do as much and more?

Realizing that the story of his conversion will seem strange
to some ears, Huysmans, like the clear thinker and the brilliant analyst that he is, observes: "For all those who do
not believe in the grace of God, all this seems folly. For
those who have experienced its effects, no surprise is possible; or, if surprise there were, it could continue only over
the period of incubation, the period when one sees nothing
and notices nothing, the period of the clearing of the ground
and laying of the foundations of which one never had even
a suspicion."

Manifest and striking interventions of divine grace are not
peculiar to previous centuries or other lands; they are taking
place in our own land today. God's ear is ever sensitive to
the cry of His children for help. In *The Seven Storey Mountain* it is not difficult to discern the working of grace as it
gently yet insistently leads its young author to the baptismal
font and then to a life of prayer and contemplation in a
Trappist monastery. In this symposium, Thomas Merton
takes the readers behind the monastic enclosure and gives
them a glimpse into the beauty and the joy of a life spent
in loving communion with our Father and our God. He
draws aside the veil upon the meaning of membership in
the mystical body of Christ and shows how we all can share
in the divine life.

Man knows little about the real nature of electricity but
much about its operations and its effects. Indeed, much
of our material civilization is built around the instruments

for the harnessing and use of this mysterious power. So, likewise, we know little about the nature of divine grace but much about its workings and its effects. The whole spiritual life of man is built around the channels of grace: prayer, meditation, deeds of love and service, penance, the corporal and the spiritual works of mercy, and the sacraments. Conversion is especially shot through with the operations of grace; we would scarcely have scratched the surface of this subject if we did not attempt to point out the important role which grace plays in the drama of the soul's quest for God.

Without His divine aid, no one comes to Christ: such is his explicit teaching. "No man can come to me," He said, "except the Father, who hath sent me, draw him."[10] While there are many things about grace which are shrouded from our eyes, we do know this: Grace assists the earnest searcher to find God, Jesus Christ, His divine revelation, and the Church which He founded to transmit that precious legacy in its entirety to all mankind. It is helpful in awakening interest in that quest, in the actual process of investigation, and, above all, in bringing that to a successful ending in the act of faith. God will not deny that grace to the man of clean mind and pure heart who searches earnestly for the truth and on his knees humbly begs for light to see the truth and the strength to follow it.

In following that light as it leads him into Christ's Church, one surrenders himself to the divine will and, in that conformity of his will to God's will, he penetrates to the secret of all sanctity. "Not my will," said Christ in the Garden of Gethsemani, "but thine be done." There is the pattern for us to follow. "At bottom," observes Rudolph Allers, "there is only one ideal, doing one's job in life, involving self-surrender and service. In the same way there is only one virtue—humble and willing conformity to the will of God. And only one sin—defiance of God's will."

In a letter to Charles Kingsley, Thomas H. Huxley, writing as a scientist, sounds substantially the same note. "Science seems to me," he writes, "to teach in the highest

[10]John 6:44.

[266]

and strongest manner the great truth which is embodied in the Christian conception of entire surrender to the will of God. Sit down before fact as a little child, be prepared to give up every preconceived notion, follow humbly wherever and to whatever abyss nature leads, or you shall learn nothing. I have only begun to learn content and peace of mind since I have resolved at all risks to do this."

Absolute honesty in following the light is the path that leads to sanctity and to science, to holiness and to wisdom. The intelligence with which the Creator has endowed man is God's candle burning within the human soul, and it can lead only to God, the infinite source of all light and truth. "I am the light of the world," said Christ; "he that followeth me walketh not in darkness but shall have the light of life."

It is God's image in man, His candle in our soul, which constitutes the dignity of the human personality and the transcendental value of the human soul. It is the denial of this dignity to the individual which constitutes the essential heresy of all totalitarianism: communism, nazism, and fascism. Against this heresy the Church has never ceased to war. Pope Pius XI was the one great moral leader in all Europe who raised his voice in stern protest against the anti-Semitic laws of Hitler and his other invasions of human liberty.

Albert Einstein voiced the admiration of free men everywhere when he said: "The Church alone has protested against the struggle being waged by Hitler against liberty. Up to this time I had taken no interest in the Church, but today I profess a great admiration and a great attachment for the Church which alone has had the unfailing courage to battle for spiritual freedom and moral liberty."

The individual's right to liberty stems basically from his spiritual nature, his God-given freedom of the will; and it is in the common possession of a spiritual and immortal soul that the essential equality of all men consists. "The deepest moral issue of the modern world," observed Ambassador William Bullitt, "is the issue of man as a son of God with an immortal soul, an end in himself, against man as a chemical compound, the tool of an omnipotent state, an end in

[267]

itself." By keeping God's image in man clear and distinct, the Church makes it shine as a precious diamond before the whole world. Thus does she sound the death knell of totalitarianism as a way of life for free men.

In returning to the historic center of Christian unity, our separated brethren part with no doctrine or practice of historic Christianity, but simply regain possession of some parts of the divine legacy which they lost in the last few centuries and which their forefathers held as their priceless spiritual treasure for more than fifteen centuries. Samuel Johnson recognized this fact back in 1769 when he said: "A man who is converted from Protestantism to popery parts with nothing; he is only superadding to what he already had. But a convert from popery to Protestantism gives up as much of what he had held sacred as anything that he retains."[11]

All the world is hungering for spiritual and religious unity. The world conferences of our separated brethren at Stockholm, Lausanne, Edinburgh, and Amsterdam voiced that need. The final declaration, adopted at Edinburgh, mirrored the thought of all the conferences in asserting: "We humbly acknowledge our divisions are contrary to the will of Christ, and we pray for unity."

In an impressive ceremony on Christmas Eve, Pope Pius XII opened the Holy Door of St. Peter's Basilica in Rome with the words: "Open the door, for God is with us." The ceremony inaugurates the Holy Year of prayer and pardon, during which millions of pilgrims will come to the shrine of Peter, the chief of the Apostles. The ceremony symbolizes likewise that the door of the Mother Church is open to all who have strayed from the historic center of Christian unity. The Holy Father uttered an earnest and loving appeal to all believers in Christ to return to the Church which the Saviour founded.

"Oh that this Holy Year," he said, "could welcome also the great return to the one, true Church, awaited over the centuries, of so many who though believing in Jesus Christ

[11]Boswell's *Life of Samuel Johnson*, October 26, 1769.

[268]

are for various reasons separated . . . With good reason men are anxious about the effrontery with which the united front of militant atheism advances. And the old question is now voiced aloud: Why are there still separations? Why are there still schisms? When will all the forces of the spirit and of love be harmoniously united?"

Recognizing the world-wide hunger for religious unity, the pontiff, with moving warmth and affection, concluded: "If on other occasions an invitation to unity has been sent forth from this Apostolic See, on this occasion we repeat it more warmly and paternally. We feel that we are urged by the pleadings and prayers of numerous believers scattered over the whole earth who, after suffering tragic and painful events, turn their eyes toward this Apostolic See as toward an anchor of salvation for the whole world."

Thus does the Church invite all outside her world-wide family, particularly those with no religious affiliation, to investigate the credentials of her divine establishment and to examine the truths committed to her charge by Christ. Only after a person is convinced of her divinely established authority to teach all mankind does the Church invite him to membership in her fold. She makes no emotional appeal, exercises no pressure, because she knows that the objective evidence is overpowering and because faith involves the free assent of the will and must be based upon a profound and unalterable conviction of the truth of her teachings. The great restraint which the Church exercises in presenting her claims must commend itself to every serious and thoughtful person. She combines with that restraint, however, an earnest and sincere invitation to all truth seekers to examine her teachings and, when convinced of their truth, to enter her fold.

They will find that a thousand paths lead to her great open door, for she is the trysting place of all the truths in the world, the greatest moral fact of all the ages, the ever-enduring miracle of two thousand years of human history, the city of God on earth. Arnold Lunn, the brilliant British writer, closes the story of his pilgrimage to her with the words of Hilaire Belloc, which express the verdict of history: "There is a city full, as are all cities, of halt and maim, blind and evil, and the rest; but it is the city of God. There are not two such cities on earth. There is One. One thing in this world is different from all others. It has personality and a force. It is recognized, and (when recognized) most violently loved or hated. It is the Catholic Church. Within that household the human spirit has roof and hearth. Outside it is the Night."

May the stories of the fourteen pilgrims who found the path to the center of Christian unity serve as torches to light the way for all sincere seekers for God, Christ, and His truths. The path may lead over fields strewn with rocks and boulders and through new and strange lands. But, at the end, the pilgrim will find the great open door of his Father's house and, in it, the gentle and loving Christ who extends His arms to embrace him as, pressing him to His bosom, He whispers, "Welcome home, my child!"

NOTE

Readers desiring to learn more about the Catholic religion will find the following books helpful:

The Faith of Millions, Our Sunday Visitor Press, Huntington, Indiana. This is a comprehensive exposition of the credentials and doctrines of the Catholic faith, written in a non-controversial manner and in a popular style. It has been published in many foreign languages.

What's the Truth About Catholics?, Our Sunday Visitor Press, Huntington, Indiana. This is a simple popular presentation of Catholic belief and practice in conversational form.

Truths Men Live By, The Macmillan Company, New York, N.Y. This is an exposition of the basic truths which underlie the Christian religion and demonstrates their harmony with the findings of science and philosophy.

Acknowledgments

"The Outstretched Arms," from *The Next Thing*, by Katherine Burton, copyright 1949 by Longmans, Green & Co. and reproduced as condensed in *The Catholic Digest*.

"Through the Church to God," by Duane G. Hunt, originally published as "My Conversion to the Catholic Church" in *The Epistle*.

"From Communism to Christ" is condensed from *From Union Square to Rome*, by Dorothy Day, copyright 1938 by Preservation of the Faith Press, Silver Spring, Md.

"The Maritains Find God" is condensed from *Adventures in Grace* by Raïssa Maritain and translated by Julie Kernan, copyright 1945 by Longmans, Green & Co.

"Finding Christ's Church," from *Conversions to the Catholic Church*, copyright 1933 by Burns, Oates & Washbourne, Ltd.

The lines from *The Negro Singer*, by James David Corrothers, from *Century* magazine, are copyright, 1912, the Century Company; reprinted by permission of Appleton-Century-Crofts, Inc., publishers.

"House of Light," by Lucile Hasley, "Into the Light," by Dale Francis, "The White Pebble," by Thomas Merton, reprinted from *The Sign*, copyright, 1950, by The Passionist Missions, Inc.

Also By The Editor Of
WHERE I FOUND CHRIST

and an excellent companion volume to this inspiring book—

The Road To Damascus
The Spiritual Pilgrimage
Of Fifteen Converts To Catholicism

This volume contains the powerful, moving stories of fifteen
well-known people who tell, in their own words, their reasons for turning to Catholicism. They include Frances
Parkinson Keyes, Senator Wagner, Clare Boothe Luce,
Evelyn Waugh, Sheila Kaye-Smith, Fulton Oursler, and
others.

Saturday Review of Literature: ". . . highly readable . . .
In it some will find example and all will find interest."

New York *Times:* ". . . a contribution to an understanding
of a changing world."

Extension: "A literary gem and a spiritual one as well."

The Sign: ". . . the book has a deep spiritual significance."

Pittsburgh *Press:* "It deserves to be widely read."